THE LUMINOUS LIFE OF OUR PROPHET

THE LUMINOUS OUR
LIFE PROPHET
OF

REŞİT HAYLAMAZ

TUGHRA
BOOKS

New Jersey

Copyright © 2023 by Tughra Books

Originally published in Turkish as *Efendimiz'in Nurlu Hayatı* in 2013

26 25 24 23   4 5 6 7

Published by Tughra Books
335 Clifton Ave., Clifton,
NJ, 07011, USA
www.tughrabooks.com

Library of Congress Cataloging-in-Publication Data

Haylamaz, Resit.
[Efendimiz'in nurlu hayati. English]
The luminous life of our prophet / Resit Haylamaz.
pages cm
ISBN 978-1-59784-310-2 (alk. paper)
1. Muhammad, Prophet, -632--Biography--Juvenile literature. I. Title.
BP75.27.H3913 2014
297.6'3--dc23
[B]
2014036473

ISBN: 978-1-59784-310-2

CONTENTS

Preface

How Well Do We Know Our Prophet?

The pride of this entire universe, Prophet Muhammad, peace and blessings be upon him, is still living within us, fresher than the scent of daisies, despite the long centuries that have passed since his birth.

Time passes by and people grow older; some thoughts stale, fossilize, and become parts of history. However, the path that the Prince of Prophets opened centuries ago, keeps its greenness and freshness by renovating and adjusting, like a new sprout.

Today, throughout most of the world, whether it be Africa, Central Asia, or the United States of America, the revival of this path is witnessed. Real men and women of Allah continuously discuss the Prophet's conceptions, and, in doing so, with their tools for embroidery making, they knit the finest lacework and canvas embroidery on behalf of faith and virtues.

Turkish poet Mehmet Akif Ersoy once stated:

> Worldly possessions are tributes of his
> Let all and single owe that Innocent
> All humanity owes him, in fact
> O Lord, revive us with that thought only!

Our Prophet, a person, that all of humanity is indebted to, was also a human. That is not to say that he was not a distinguished human being. That much is clear to us, as it was recorded and communicated to us by the Sublime Creator.

If we were to look into the life of the Prophet, then we would clearly see that he acted according to revelations, he did not overlook even the smallest of his duties, he was so sincere, he constantly called people to Allah's unity and existence, and his intentions and objectives were open and clear.

On a different note though, if we were to observe the way he lived, then among the most notable things that we can see would be the profound truthfulness of his words and attitudes, his being the best in the matter of being a trustee, his being precise in accomplishing a taken duty, and his solving seemingly unsolvable problems in a tremendously easy manner that was accepted by everyone and his sincerity.

Because of his being the last and most universal among Prophets and his position in the sight of our Lord, all of the Prophets that were sent before him and their sacred scripts told about Prophet Muhammad, peace and blessings be upon him, informed about his coming and gave glad tidings about him. These glad tidings and messages were so obvious and detailed that some members of those religions learned all the peculiarities that belonged to him as well as the ability to recognize him. This helped in the sense that he was recognized and believed in almost instantly.

Our Prophet used to be a recipient of revelations, similar to all of the Prophets before him. As a proof of his Prophethood, clear and tremendous miracles that were easily understood and regarded by everyone were experienced. Each and every phase of his life effectuated in various ways the fact of his being selected and inaccessibility. The smallest and whitest of lies couldn't even be detected in his jokes. He was so honest.

From the very moment that he honored the face of this earth till his passing away, he showed extraordinary patience in facing problems, torture, and trouble. In the face of innumerable non-humanly attitudes of others to him as well as his kith and kin, he was able to set forth an example of forgiveness and forbearance.

With his immense compassion that embraced not only all of humanity, but even animals, he attracted attention from everyone, despite their being his friends or enemies. While he had the chance of achieving and possessing everything, he preferred leading a modest and simple life. He never expected anything for what he did. Even in times that he found himself cornered and left alone, he never showed signs of fear and despair. But when it came to worshipping Allah, he was the most advanced and profound out of everyone… In short, he was an ideal example of perfect conduct of a good temper.

The message conveyed by an ideal example of the entire humanity, Prophet Muhammad, peace and blessings be upon him, is a source of tranquility. The only way to convey this tranquility to humankind again is to introduce him and his luminous message to our people. For this reason, people will love him the more they get to know him, and because of that love, a luminous generation that embellishes our reveries, will emerge.

While in the gallows, the disbelievers asked one of the leaders of the blessed generation, Hubayb ibn Adiyy, "Would you be happy if he was sacrificed in your place?" If he had answered, "Yes," he would have been saved from being sentenced to death. As, he was (not an ordinary person but he was) a Companion of the Messenger of Allah, he gave an appropriate answer: "By Allah, I would not like that to happen. Let alone his being executed instead of me, I would not even wish that a single prickle hurt his feet." This is merely one simple example of the ecstatic love that people have for our Prophet.

Attaining that very love and care can only come from knowing him. Knowing him, above all things, is possible through reading books and listening to lectures about him. Very nice treatises and books were published concerning that topic and continue to be. A treatise that you are now holding in your hands is one of the latter, which is aimed at understanding and explaining the luminous life of our Prophet.

We sincerely hope and wish that this book is beneficial to everyone who reads it.

Life Chronology of Our Prophet

Before going into the life experiences of our Prophet, we have chronologically listed important dates throughout the Prophet's life. We hope that this list will help enliven the Prophet's life in your eyes.

571 – On the 12th night of the month of Rabi al-Awwal (April, 20), Prophet Muhammad, peace and blessings be upon him, honored this world with his birth.

575 – The foster mother of the Messenger of Allah, Halima, handed him to his mother, Amina bint Wahb.

577 – Our Prophet lost his mother in the village of Abwa, situated in between Mecca and Medina. His grandfather, Abdul Muttalib, adopted him into his family.

579 – Abdul Muttalib left this world to the Hereafter. Our Prophet started to share a home with his uncle Abu Talib ibn Abdul Muttalib.

583 – With his uncle, Abu Talib, he went to Damascus (territories of contemporary Syria and Lebanon) for trading purposes. Here, Priest Bahira discovered that the Messenger of Allah was the last expected Prophet.

590 – He joined the Alliance of the Virtuous.

591 – Started his trading business.

596 – He went to Sham again for trading purposes. Three months later he married Khadija bint Khuwaylid.

In their wedlock, they had six children, two boys and four girls. Their names were Qasim, Zaynab, Ruqayyah, Umm Kulthum, Fatima, and Abdullah.

605 – He hammered out a conflict that happened between tribes during the reconstruction of the Ka'ba.

610 – In the Cave of Hira on the Mountain of Light, he communicated his first revelation and had attained the duty of Prophethood.

613 – At Safa, he had openly communicated the message for the first time. He had arranged dining tables for his close relatives during the conveying of his message. Disbelievers started to torture Muslims.

615 – The first migration to Abyssinia, the territory of contemporary Ethiopia, took place. A group of fifteen people, four of which were women, set off to Abyssinia to protect themselves from violence and practice their religion in a much better way. The son in law of our Prophet, Uthman ibn Affan, led them. In the same year, Hamza ibn Abdul Muttalib and Umar ibn al-Khattab converted to Islam.

616 – The second migration to Abyssinia took place. This time, a group of 101 people, eighteen of which were women, moved to Abyssinia under the leadership of Jafar ibn Abu Talib. During that period, attempts of a non-believer, Amr ibn As (who converted to Islam later) to convince the Negus in the matter of not protecting Muslims ended in vain. The Negus allowed Muslim migrants to stay in his country.

617 – A group of prominent people of Quraysh, consisting of 40 people, gathered at the chieftaincy of Abu Jahl, where they decided not to have any kind of business with Muslims, not to allow their children to marry Muslims, not to

have meetings with them, and to cease all economic and social relations with them. They wrote it down in the form of a treaty and stamped it, after which appealed it on a single piece of cloth and hung it inside the Ka'ba. In doing so, they hoped that by harassing Muslims, they would make them surrender the Prophet. By taking the pledge of not doing anything against this decision, they started intolerantly applying these laws. In this manner, a social and economic boycott against Muslims took place that lasted for three long years.

619 – The Boycott ended. The son of the Prophet, Qasim, and then his other son, Abdullah, passed away. After a while, his uncle Abu Talib and Khadija died in the same year as well.

620 – The Messenger of Allah went to Ta'if, where he was treated terribly.

621 – The Night journey and Ascension took place this year. In the same year realization of Aqaba Pledge took place, where twelve Medinans Pledged to the Messenger of Allah. Six people conferred in the Hill of Aqaba with the Messenger of Allah and then converted to Islam. After the Hajj Season, they returned to Medina. By explaining everything experienced to their kith and kin, they started to spread Islam all over Medina. A year later, in the Season of Hajj, there came twelve people, ten of whom were from the tribe of Khazraj and two more—from Aws, who had already become Muslims, to confer with the noble Prophet. The Messenger of Allah appointed Mus'ab ibn Umayr to preach Islam in Medina.

622 – The Second Aqaba Pledge was committed. Muslims of Mecca and then our Prophet emigrated from Mecca to Medina. The Prophet's Mosque was constructed. The first *adhan* was recited.

623 – The Direction of the *qiblah* was changed from Al-Aqsa Mosque in Jerusalem to the Ka'ba by the command of Allah the Almighty.

624 – The Battle of Badr took place with the hypocrites of Mecca. In the same year, Muslims confronted Jews of the tribe of Banu Qaynuqa and sent them away from Medina. Fasting in the month of Ramadan was ordained. The first religious festive day prayer was performed. Paying purifying alms was ordained, too. The daughter of the Messenger of Allah, Ruqayyah, passed away. Ali ibn Abu Talib married Fatima. The first prayer of the Eid of Sacrifice was performed.

625 – Battle of Uhud took place.

627 – Battle of the Trench took place. According to the covenant, Jews of the tribe of Banu Qurayza were to protect Medina together with Muslims during the Battle of the Trench. However, they did not fulfill their duty. Moreover, they disregarded all clauses within the Aqaba Pledge, and in a very critical part of the battle, they joined hypocrites. After the battle, the Messenger of Allah drew his army towards the Banu Qurayza and eliminated them, too.

628 – The Messenger of Allah and his Companions set forth to Mecca for minor pilgrimage. Uthman ibn Affan was sent there as an emissary. As soon as news of Uthman's martyrdom reached our beloved Prophet, he took pledge from Companions to fight against them. This pledge was called the Pledge of Ridwan. When that information reached hypocrites, they set Uthman ibn Affan free. The hypocrites were very resolute in not letting Muslims visit the Ka'ba. Therefore they sent an envoy to the Messenger of Allah to negotiate a treaty. The Messenger of Allah accepted all the clauses of

The Luminous Life of Our Prophet

the treaty, which primarily seemed to not be in the Muslims favor; however, later on they turned to be in favors of Muslims. In this way, a Hudaybiya Reconciliation with the Meccan hypocrites was signed.

629 – Letters of calling into Islam were sent to rulers of that age. The Messenger of Allah sent Dihya ibn Khalifa al-Kalbi to the Byzantine emperor, Heraclius; Amr ibn Umayya ad-Damri to the Abyssinian king (the Negus) Ashama ibn al-Abjar; Abdullah ibn Hudhafah as-Sahmi to the Persian (Sassanian) king (Khosrau II) Khusraw Parviz; Hatib ibn Abu Balta'ah to Egyptian vicegerent (the Muqawqis) Juraij ibn Matta; Sulayt ibn Amr al-Amiri to the chief of Yamama, Hawdha ibn Ali; Shuja ibn Wahb to the king of Damascus, Harith ibn Abi Shamir al-Ghassan, with the purpose of inviting them to Islam. In the same year, the Battle of Khaybar took place. Victory, gained at Khaybar almost made all the Jews of Arabia surrender to Islamic government. Furthermore, Battles of Byzantine and Muta took place in the same year.

630 – Mecca was conquered. The Holy Ka'ba was purified and cleared from all idols. During the Battle of Hunayn (against tribes of Saqif and Hawazin), Muslims prevailed and won. The Expedition to Tabuk was accomplished. The Byzantine army did not dare confront the Muslim army because of their poor military preparations. Therefore, a battle did not take place.

632 – Our beloved Prophet performed the Farewell Pilgrimage. He later fell ill and passed away.

Our Beloved Prophet is from the Progeny of Prophet Abraham

After Prophet Ibrahim, peace be upon him, his son Ismail, peace be upon him, lived a settled life here, and he had twelve sons. It was clear that his son Nabit was different from the others. The same kind of particularity could be seen in his son Yashjub, and this line of distinction passed down with Yarub, Tayrah, Muqawwim, Udad and Adnan. It was clear that this line had a special nobleness and a particularity that could carry the weight of Prophethood. The same special character of the Prophet's forefathers to the twentieth degree could be well observed, after Adnan, Maad, Nizar, Mudar, Malik, Fihr, Ghalib, Luayy, Ka'b, Murra, Kilab, Qusayy (Zayd), Abdimanaf (Mughira), Hashim (Amr) and Abdul Muttalib (Shayba), and a light that was the indication of the Prince of the Universe could be seen on their foreheads.

Abdullah, the last son of Abdul Muttalib, was a monument of chastity. That's why Abdul Muttalib loved him above all his children.

One day, Abdul Muttalib went to the leader of the Zuhra tribe, Wahb ibn Abdimanaf, and told him that they were asking for the hand of Amina, who was an honorable girl of great lineage. After a short while Abdul Muttalib's son Abdullah and Wahb's daughter Amina got married, so a new family was formed.

Abdullah was a tradesman, and soon after his marriage, he went on a trade caravan. He became ill and died, and was buried in Medina. The inheritance he had left behind was five camels, some sheep and an Abyssinian slave girl by the name of Umm Ayman. When news of his death reached Mecca, the family of Abdul Muttalib was thrown into great grief. However, they had to be patient, for Amina was pregnant with the one, whose coming the whole world was eagerly awaiting.

Meanwhile, Abraha, the governor of Yemen at that time, gathered his army to destroy the Ka'ba in Mecca. However, his army was miraculously completely destroyed. Minds were blown away, and it was now clear to all that the Ka'ba built by Prophets Ibrahim and Ismail, peace be upon them, through prayer and physical efforts would never be destroyed. Now the world was getting ready to see the fruit of their prayer.

The Happy Birth

The date was 20 April 571. Around 50 days had passed after the incident with the elephants. The lunar calendar was showing the 12th of the month of Rabi al-awwal. It was a Monday. The dawn was about to break and a birth was taking place that would bring light to all darkness. With Amina were present Shifa, the mother of Abdurrahman ibn Awf, and Fatima, the mother of Uthman ibn Abi'l-As. Then the Last Prophet, peace and blessings be upon him, whose good tidings had been sung for centuries, honored the world with his coming, with a very easy birth.

Word was sent immediately to Abdul Muttalib who was praying at the Ka'ba at the time. He hurried to the house. When he held the Light that the universe had been waiting for, his beard was washed with tears. The fatherless son of the son he loved most, the son of Abdullah, had now come to life and was looking at him with meaningful eyes. The mark between his shoulder blades had caught everyone's attention; this was the mark of Prophethood of the Last Messenger as described by many religious scholars.

The Years with the Wet Nurses

It was the custom in Mecca to send children to wet nurses in the villages so that they may grow up to be strong and that they may learn a pure Arabic since Mecca had a very hot and tiring atmosphere. Some tribes who lived away from the city were able to preserve their pure culture unadulterated by the inequities witnessed in the cities at the time of the Period of Ignorance. It was common practice for children to be sent away to have a healthier upbringing, and this practice had turned into a trade. There was a market for wet nurses in Mecca, people would gather here at particular times, the wet nurses and the parents of children would meet there and then the children would go with the wet mothers to the desert.

Likewise, Harith ibn Abduluzza and his wife Halima bint Abdullah ibn Harith had come from the land of the Banu Sad with ten other women. The drought had been going on for some time, and there was nothing left at hand. The children in their entourage cried for a morsel to eat, but the mothers had no means to feed them. Because they themselves had not been able to eat for some time, their milk had dried up, and they were desperate for a little drop of anything in order to calm their children. Their only hope was for rain to fall. The way to Mecca had seemed endless. The thin donkey that Halima was riding and Harith's old camel had trouble walking, and they kept falling behind their friends. When they finally made it to Mecca, their friends had already done their trade and each of them had taken a child to look after for a while and was now getting ready for the journey back. Halima and Harith started to look for children to wet nurse too. Only Muhammad, Abdullah's fatherless son, was left in the town. Those who had knocked upon their door had decided not to take him when they learnt that his father was dead for fear that the family would not be able to pay the wet nurse's wages. Of course they were unaware that he was the person to whom everybody would turn to soon.

Halima and Harith came to the door as well, and like the others, they also went to look for another baby, in fear of not getting paid. But they found none, and they did not want to return empty handed after their long journey. Halima said to her husband: "I don't want to go back among my friends without having taken a child to breast-feed. Let's go and take that orphan and then return."

"Do so if you want to, maybe Allah will give us plenitude and good fortune through him," said Harith, and so they returned to Abdul Muttalib's door.

When Amina saw that they had returned, she first told them that the boy they wanted was no ordinary child. She then spoke about the ease she experienced during her pregnancy, her dream and what she had been told to be the meaning of this dream, for he was entrusted to Amina to keep not just for herself but for the whole of humanity till the end of time. That's why he had to be shown extra care, and not a single hair strand on his head could be injured.

The family of Harith felt great contentment when they took the child from Amina. When Halima as-Sadia took him in her arms, she wanted to breast-feed him immediately. She was surprised to see that her breasts that had dried up were now filled with milk! First the Messenger of Allah and then the son of Halima, Abdullah, suckled from the breast. Then they both went to sleep. Normally, Abdullah was a restless child who would be impossible to put to sleep.

When they came near the old camel, they saw that the camel's udders were also full of milk, for even it had benefited from this good fortune. They milked the camel and drank, and the night they spent in Mecca was the happiest ever in their lives. The next morning Harith had turned to Halima to say: "Know this well Halima, you have chosen your suckling child very wisely, from a very auspicious family."

Just like her husband, Halima had also realized the plenitude bestowed upon them. She said: "I swear by Allah, that is what I believe as well."

They finished their business in Mecca, and having found a suckling child, they set off for their homeland. Amina looked at her son affectionately as he departed for a long while, and she entrusted him to the hands of the Gracious Lord who has all the power and honor, so that nothing bad should befall him.

When Halima as-Sadia mounted her donkey with the Messenger of Allah, peace and blessings be upon him in her arms, she realized that the thin and weak animal that she had come to Mecca with had somehow changed and now was walking very briskly. Such was their pace that they had caught up with their friends who had left Mecca a day earlier, and it was clear that they would not be left behind this time. Their friends were trying to understand how it was that they did not seem to have any sign of tiredness while they themselves were exhausted from the journey. The called out to Halima: "O daughter of the Zuayb tribe, what is going on with you? Were you not the one who was always left behind? Or is this not the same donkey you rode when coming to Mecca?"

The now self-assured Halima answered with the joy of the grace she had been bestowed: "I swear it is! It is the very same donkey I came to Mecca with."

And then she added: "I have verily chosen the most auspicious suckling baby ever."

They asked: "Is that the son of Abdul Muttalib?"

Yes, there was true goodness in this event and Halima and Harith, who were always after good deeds, were now experiencing the goodness they had always hoped for.

The grace they had attained was not limited to the easing of their journey; on their return they would see that their land which was normally dry and not very fertile, would start to yield much better, and their sheep, whose stomachs would be full with the good produce of their land would produce much more milk. The owners of other herds would chastise their shepherds: "Woe to you! Go graze the sheep where Halima grazes hers so that our sheep also return with their bellies filled with milk."

Halima as-Sadia was now someone whom everyone viewed with envy due to the plenty she was experiencing.

Two years passed in this manner, with visits to Mecca every six months. The Pride of the Universe had thus grown up. He was no longer suckling; the time that had been agreed upon had come. Although they were reluctant to do it, they had to bring the little Muhammad back to his mother.

The Death of Amina

For a while, the most beloved servant of Allah lived with his mother. Amina was doing her best not to let little Muhammad feel the absence of his father. Sometimes he would go around with Abdul Muttalib, and sometimes he spent time with his uncles.

Amina loved Medina; she set off for the city both in order to visit her relatives and to pray at the grave of her late husband. She took what he left behind, their slave Umm Ayman and their only son, on this journey with her. They came all the way to Medina. Memories of the past had been awakened and it was a bitter-sweet reunion. The Messenger of Allah was praying at his father's grave whom he had never seen. He was bereft. Maybe this was the first time he felt deep inside that he had lost his father. His state affected his mother as well. Before long, Amina fell ill there. Her illness advanced very quickly. A month or so had passed since she had come to Medina and they had to return to Mecca at the first opportunity. They set off on the road despite the difficulties.

When they came near the village of Abwa, Amina's illness reached unbearable proportions. She had no more power in her knees and she could find no energy to take a single step further. They made a stop under a tree. It was clear that their time together on earth was going to end here and Amina was about to take her leave. The sad mother had locked her eyes unto her son from whom she expected great deeds in the future. Her eyes gave way to tears and her heart was gulping down grief. She was now going to leave her fatherless son a complete orphan in the middle of this desert. The tears running down her cheeks had also made Umm Ayman and the Messenger of Allah weep as well; it was as if the whole of Abwa was in mourning. There was a great and indescribable flow of emotion between mother and son. At last, she took her son's soft velvety hand into her own and after looking at her dearest son for a long while, she said the following: "May Allah give you grace. You are the son of a father who escaped death, with the help of Allah, from the King of Mannan in return for a hundred camels! If what I saw in my sleep is true, you will be the awaited Prophet who will be sent to all creation by the All Forceful and All Giving One. You will teach them the allowed and prohibited things and acts, you will consolidate what you have been bequeathed by your forefather Ibrahim who was the epitome of goodness, and with the help of Allah you will draw the people away from the idols that they have long formed an attachment to."

She seemed very sure of herself as she said these final words. She seemed to be speaking with the awareness that she was entrusting her one and only child, who now had no one, to the Owner of all things. Then she added the following: "All living things face death every minute of the day, each new thing will have to grow old, and each great thing will also fade. I die today, but my name will remain forever, for I gave birth to a pure child and I leave the best here as I leave."

Having said this, she closed her eyes never to open them again and then she breathed her last. Sadly, with his father in Medina, another trace of the Last Messenger would be left in Abwa.

Maybe Allah had taken his father and mother away to His realm so that they may not feel the obligation of being the Prophet's parents and instead, be the Prophet's "foster children" when it came to his teachings; making both of them and the noble Prophet content.

On the face of it they seemed not to have had the chance to become members of the *Ummah*; but Allah the Almighty had raised them to the level of a spiritual *Ummah* and let them thus partake in the virtue, goodness and happiness of the other *Ummah*.

It is known that the mother and father of our beloved Prophet were living a life that was in keeping with the Hanif religion of Prophet Ibrahim. They were people of the *fatrat* (interregnum) period in which revelation had not yet been revealed. As can be understood especially from the words of mother Amina, they were among the few people who had embraced this sound and pure belief and they had left the best child on earth to the world of humanity and that's how they left this world to the abode of the Hereafter.

The calendars were showing the 576th year after the birth of Jesus and the Messenger of Allah was left all alone. He only had Umm Ayman with him. From now on she would have to take on the role of mother and father for him, trying to ease the heartache and loss.

The Protection of Grandfather
and Uncle

The death of Amina and the orphaned state of our beloved Prophet had grieved Abdul Muttalib just as everybody else. He showed such great affection to his grandson that it would help him forget the absence of his mother and father. There was a divan that had been set up for Abdul Muttalib in the shade of the Ka'ba. He would meet people here, he would see to the business of Mecca at this place. Nobody else would sit on this divan except for him, including his sons, as a token of respect; they would form a circle and sit around it. There was only one young man in Mecca who did not abide by this rule, and that was the son of Abdullah, our beloved Prophet. He would sit by his grandfather; he would hold him from the back of his turban and pull him. To those who tried to prevent him from doing so, Abdul Muttalib would say: "Leave my dear grandson to his devices. I swear by Allah that his future is very bright, his situation very serious."

He would then stroke his grandson's back and then sit by him. It was clear that his grandson's actions pleased him and he was not ready to let anyone interfere with his behavior, for he expected many great things for him in the future.

By now the Pride of Humankind was a little older than eight years of age. Abdul Muttalib had grown old and was about to leave the world. One day he called his other son Abu Talib to his side. With due dignity and gravity and said: "The fame and glory of this son of mine will be great and I entrust him to you."

And before long, Abdul Muttalib who was now around eighty two years of age, breathed his last.

The Pride of Humankind who got news of his grandfather's death stood by his lifeless body, and cried over the great man who had taken care of him with deep affection.

The words spoken by Abdul Muttalib were the testament of a father to son. Abu Talib took his nephew Muhammad, peace and blessings be upon him, to his side and embraced him with the affection of a father. Now the Messenger of Allah would receive affection from Abu Talib like a father, and from Fatima, the wife of Abu Talib and mother of Ali, he would be shown much warmth.

Just like the youth of the Quraysh, Abu Talib also worked in commerce. He sometimes took his nephew with him and tried to prepare him for the future. He was twelve years old. He would go towards Ajyad and graze sheep during the time he spent in Mecca, and was thus gaining experience about all aspects of life.

One day, Abu Talib started preparations to go on a journey towards Damascus. His nephew was sad to learn about it that he requested of he could go with him. This touched Abu Talib greatly and so he said: "I swear by Allah that I will not go without taking him with me; I will never stay away from him from this day forth, nor will I allow him to stay away from me."

The Pride of Humanity, who heard his uncle's oath, was filled with joy. He was now going to leave Mecca for the first time for trade. Who knew what cities he would pass, what kind of people he would meet, and what kind of incidents he would witness throughout the journey.

The Damascus Trip and
Priest Bahira

Then it was time to leave, both uncle and nephew took their leave and joined the moving caravan. It was a long and tiring journey. Sometimes they would stop to rest and see to their needs and then continue towards Damascus. When they arrived near the town of Basra, between Jerusalem and Damascus, they had a stopover once again to rest.

Just as the caravan had started to relax, they saw a man approach them from afar in great excitement. The man had a disheveled look and seemed to have abandoned ties with the world. Thus, the people in the caravan thought he could not possibly have anything to do with them and they continued to rest. But then the man reached one of them and said: "Priest Bahira in that yonder monastery is inviting you to dinner."

Only then did the people in the caravan realize that the man indeed had them in mind, but they did not know anything about the reason for this invitation.

Bahira was a priest who had given up on the world and he was spending what was left of his life worshipping his Lord in a monastery. He was a good Christian scholar. In fact, he used to follow Judaism and then later he had chosen Christianity; but he had not stopped there and had searched deep into religion and he was one of the greatest scholars of his time.

In the church where he was, there was an ancient book that would pass from the hands of one priest to another. He was one of the few priests who could actually read and understand it. He had given up worldly life and was living the life of a holy man in the church. He had no use for those who came to trade; he had no possessions or wealth. But as it happened, his eyes had caught sight through the cloisters. It was clear that the diversion of his gaze outside was also part of what was meant to be. As per usual, a caravan was approaching town. But this caravan stood out amongst the previous ones; for a cloud was following the caravan and was protecting them from the scorching sun. He had an epiphany. Cloud... Shadows... End of time... The Last Messenger... Ahmad... The ancient book... All these struck like lightening in his mind and it increased his interest in the caravan. Was destiny coming to him on its two feet? What if that was the case! Then it made no sense to wait around where he was. The old man, who had closed his windows to the outer world, was rejuvenated and he started doing things he had not done in years. There was the happiness of having found something that had been lost to him in his eyes. Was what he now saw, coming towards him; Paraclete, who was to appear in between the Paran Mountains?

The clouds had gathered around a particular point in the caravan and were protecting the person underneath it from the sun. When the caravan stopped for a break, and the person in question had retired under a tree to rest, the cloud would follow him and settle upon that tree to shade him. Even the branches of the tree had come to life, and they had come closer together to stop the sun from filtering through in order to protect the person from the effects of the heat. In order to find out whether what he was seeing had any connection with what he had read and what he knew, he had to come closer and so Bahira approached their caravan and called out to them: "O people of Quraysh! I have prepared dinner for you today and I want you all, young and old, slave and free, to attend it."

The people in the caravan were very surprised! For they had passed through this town many times before but they had never seen a priest at the monastery, let alone Priest Bahira take any interest in them. One of them came to the fore and said: "I swear by Allah, O Bahira, there is some strangeness about you today; you never did such things before."

"You tell the truth," answered Bahira and continued: "It is just as you say; there is some strangeness today. But you are guests. I have had the desire to extend my hospitality to you. Come all together around this table and eat from it."

Of course such a sincere invitation could not be rejected. They had walked for weeks, and they had longed for such an invitation. Those who had completed their business in the caravan thus set out for the church.

In the meantime, the volunteers of the church had set into action and they were preparing a grand dinner for the caravan. Everyone had come; however the scene that he had wanted to attract to the church was still by the side of the caravan. He had not yet seen the face he had longed for among his guests. He was about to burst with curiosity, and not able to resist any longer, he asked: "O you people of Quraysh! Is there anyone among the people of the caravan who did not come with you to dinner and stayed with the caravan? Is there anyone who did not come?"

"There is no one who should have accepted your invitation but remained behind, except for a little boy. He was the youngest among us by age and we left him behind to look after our wares," they added.

"Do not do so!" Bahira said and added: "Call him as well; let him join you in this dinner."

Even though he was a little boy he was meant to come as well, and so the Pride of Humankind was invited as well. One of them had come running back to where the caravan was and invited the one that all eyes had been looking for. He was coming. As he stood up and walked towards the church, the cloud that was protecting him also set into motion and it too was coming to the place of the gathering. Now it was as it should be. Bahira's conviction grew stronger, and he was very excited thinking that he might be able to get answers to questions that had been troubling him for some time. When The Pride of Humanity arrived near Bahira with his shining, beautiful face, the priest had been cleared of all doubt, and could now see the truth. His eyes were locked on to Muhammad, peace and blessings be upon him. He looked at him for a long while. Then, an air of happiness got hold of him. There was no doubt that this was no one but Ahmad whose good tidings had already been given in ancient books.

The food had been eaten and people were starting to get up and leave. What if he also left without speaking? There had to be a way to speak to him, he had to verify what he had seen through conversing with him. At last he found an opportunity to address him: "O you young man," he said and added: "I will ask you a few questions. You will answer what I ask only in the name of Lat and Uzza."

But the Pride of Humankind had been disturbed by the names that had been spoken and said: "Do not ask me in the name of Lat and Uzza. I swear by Allah that I feel anger towards them like I feel towards no other thing."

Bahira knew that the Quraysh swore by these two idols and he wanted to gage the reaction of the Pride of Humankind concerning idol worship, and he had got what he wanted. For the priest, all signs were supporting each other and he was now sure more than before. He was aware of the uniqueness of the person he was in the presence of.

"Then promise me only in the Name of Allah and answer what I ask you," said Bahira, thus preparing the ground for his questions. The answer he received relieved Bahira further: "Ask whatever you like."

Bahira asked Muhammad, peace and blessings be upon him, about the manner of all things, from his sleep and dreams to his everyday life, and to his hopes. Bahira was asking and the Pride of Humankind was answering with ease. Everything was very clear; all was as described in the books that he read. The conversation was completed and all signs pointed to the fact that the interlocutor was him. All that remained was the mark of Prophethood. He asked to see it as well. However, the Pride of Humankind thought it unseemly to bare his shoulders without enquiring about the reason. Seeing that there was no way round, Bahira whispered in his ear. The Pride of Humanity did not keep the curious old man waiting any longer. Just as Bahira had given up hope of seeing him, he had been given the good grace of his presence so close to him, and Bahira was thanking his Lord for this good fortune. There was no room for hesitation any longer. Bahira had one more historical duty to perform and so he turned to the uncle, Abu Talib and asked: "What relation are you to this child?"

Among Arabs when there was no father, an uncle or grandfather would take the place of the father, and so Abu Talib introduced himself by saying: "I am his father."

Bahira, who had till that time found everything in keeping with his expectations, was startled by this unexpected answer from Abu Talib. He hesitated for a while and he started to shake his head from side to side in agitation. His demeanor seemed to say "No, this can't be!" For according to his knowledge, the father of this child should have died before he came to the world. Bahira said: "No, you can't be the father of this child. The father of this child cannot be living today. He must have died before he was born."

It was through being his guardian that Abu Talib had given that answer. It was thus time for Abu Talib to tell the truth: "He is my brother's son," he said in all seriousness. Although Abu Talib was becoming wary of this questioning, Bahira kept asking: "What does his father do?"

Abu Talib gave a short answer: "He died when the boy's mother was pregnant with him."

This was as it should be. For Bahira, the comparison that he was trying to make with the truncated historical knowledge continued and he said: "Now you have said the truth."

He then took Abu Talib to one side and said to him, in a very grave manner: "You and your brother's son should return to where you came from, to your own land. You should be careful about this boy when it comes to the jealous clergy around here. I swear by Allah that if they also see what I see in him, and if they recognize him through his characteristics, they will do some harm to the boy, for there will be a great event concerning your brother's son. Just take care and return where you came from with great haste."

The priest spoke with years of experience, and taking his advice, Abu Talib was also reminded about his father's testament about the boy and so decided to return home before anything happened to him. He sold the wares he had brought with him to Basra, and then taking his nephew's hand, he returned to Mecca.

Second Journey to Damascus

He had reached the age of twenty five. One day his uncle Abu Talib took him to one side and said: "O dear son of my brother, my nephew! You know that I am a man with no possessions or money. Day by day our difficulties increase along with problems that are most distressing. We have nothing left, we have no trade."

It was clear that a suggestion would follow these words since they had been chosen very carefully.

When speaking, Abu Talib had the countenance of a man who was fearful of taking a wrong step. It seemed he was on the verge of a very important decision.

"I have heard that the tribe has organized a caravan bound for Damascus. The daughter of Khuwaylid, Khadija, is looking for a trustworthy man with whom she can be partners in trade and whom she can send on this caravan. Although I do not like the idea of sending you to Damascus due to the jealous religious scholars whom we have already been warned about, and whom I fear may harm you, I am desperate. Go to her, I think she will choose you to head her business due to her trust for you and your pure and clean nature."

It was easy said than done. This wasn't to be left to chance. This is where our noble Prophet's aunt Atiqa intervened and said that someone who was the embodiment of morals and good manners should not be put in a situation where he was offering himself. Allah's Messenger's aunt Atiqa was married to Awwam ibn Khuwaylid, who was the brother of Khadija bint Khuwaylid, and father of Zubayr ibn Awwam. She was speaking as someone who knew both sides and she wanted to facilitate the business.

The reality was that the bulk of the work fell upon the shoulders of Abu Talib. But first they had to get the consent of Muhammad the Trustworthy, peace and blessings be upon him. This proved not to be too difficult, to the faces that awaited an answer, the Messenger of Allah said: "Let it be as you wish," with a very positive attitude.

When he got his nephews consent, Abu Talib went straight to Khadija. He felt he needed to speak about his nephew to Khadija himself, for Muhammad, peace and blessings be upon him, was the most trustworthy and most qualified man in Mecca. Thus, when doing business with him this had to be taken into account and his wages had to be arranged accordingly. He knew how much money Khadija gave for such a job and he was going to ask for twice the amount.

Soon, Abu Talib had a meeting with Khadija. After the usual introductions and preambles of conversation, he started talking about the caravan and spoke of the virtues of his nephew Muhammad the Trustworthy, peace and blessings be upon him. "Muhammad the Trustworthy," this name was not unfamiliar to Khadija. This was a name that was always on the lips of her cousin Waraqa ibn Nawfal. Since her childhood, his news had been whispered in her ear; when interpreting the dreams that she had, they had always looked for his trace.

What a great blessing this was, she had been looking for him and waiting for him and there he was, within reach. Khadija was really excited.

She felt that she had gained the best prize already, even before her caravan set off for Damascus. She was about to engage in the most beneficial and auspicious business deal she would ever make in her whole life. While she was lost in contemplation, she was brought back to reality with the voice of Abu Talib: "O Khadija! I heard that you will pay the price of two camels for this job; my nephew Muhammad is the most trustworthy of men, so I will ask for twice as much for him."

For a while she considered this offer. How could she bargain for such an auspicious business, especially at a moment when worldly happiness had opened their gates? What importance did camels hold? Right after Abu Talib finished his words, she said the following: "O Abu Talib! In truth you ask for a price that is easy and to my liking. Had you asked for many times more than this, I would still have accepted and would have given it to him without hesitation. I would have been ready to do this for someone whom I did not love, who was distant to me; but you ask it for someone whom I love very much and to whom I feel very close!"

Now that they had come to an agreement about the price, there were no obstacles left for the caravan to start its journey. Abu Talib, in his position as uncle, was reminding her of the words of priest Bahira whom they had met on their last trip to Damascus, expressing his worry that he did not want to lose his nephew in an attempt to maintain worldly needs.

Then the day came, the Messenger of Allah and the caravan set off from Mecca. One aspect of the journey was attracting attention. A man called Maysara was watching every step of Muhammad the Trustworthy, peace and blessings be upon him, never letting him out of his sight. This was a journey that would take three months. The travelers got to know each other throughout the process and people had had the chance to get to know the Messenger of Allah.

Priest Nastura

At last they had finished their business in Damascus and they had set off for the return journey. When the going got very tough, they decided to take a break and rest. Everyone was trying to rest and do their accounts at the same time. The Pride of Humankind was also resting in the shade of a tree. Before long, Maysara saw someone running towards them from a distance. This was none other than the Priest Nastura who had been watching them from afar. He came near Maysara and asked: "Who is that sitting in the shade of that tree?"

This was an easy question for Maysara to answer. Without hesitation he said: "He is Muhammad, the son of Abdullah. He is a young man from the people of the House."

The priest first shook his head. It was clear that he did not approve of the answer or the manner in which it was given, for he had seemed to imply something specific when he had asked who the man was. He had an attitude that seemed to say "you do not know," so he asked another question: "Is there any redness in his eyes?"

"Yes there is," answered Maysara.

The priest seemed to have verified his position, and taking an oath, he said: "I swear that under this tree none other than the Messenger has rested."

It was clear that the priest had much more to say and that he wanted to speak more: "There is no doubt that he is the Messenger that the people are waiting for and he is the last of the Prophets."

Maysara's astonishment continued. He was not able to make sense of what had happened. He listened carefully with a sense of duty he had promised his mistress Khadija; and he was trying to record truthfully all that was taking place. There was much to be learned from the priest. Similarly, it was clear that the priest now had found what he had been looking for so close to him, he wanted to gain as much knowledge about the object of his desire as possible. That's why he was asking questions to Maysara about the Pride of Humankind who was resting under the tree, and he wanted Maysara to tell him about the strange incidents that had happened on the journey. Duly, he told the priest about the oath incident during their trade. The priest's excitement grew. It was clear that he could hardly contain himself. His observation was now definite and he started to speak once more, this time very sure of himself: "I swear that he is the Messenger we have all been waiting for. Please look after him well, be a spare set of eyes and ears for him!"

He then ran to where Muhammad the Trustworthy, peace and blessings be upon him, was. First he kissed him on the forehead with due respect and then went down to the Prophet's feet to say: "I bear witness that you are the person that Allah speaks of in the Torah."

After this break they prepared once more to set off on the road to Mecca. The weather was very hot. On the way, Maysara had seen two angels in the shape of clouds and had stared in disbelief. Two clouds in this hot weather... Two clouds who followed a particular person... Two clouds that went wherever he went and stopped whenever he stopped...

He on the other hand continued on his way in peace and security as if there was nothing strange. All this had provoked such a love in Maysara that he had devoted his whole being to Muhammad the Trustworthy, peace and blessings be upon him, and he considered himself a slave to him.

When they reached Mecca it was the hottest time of the day and the sun was right above their heads. Khadija, who had received news about the caravan's imminent arrival, had climbed up a high place to watch their arrival. She too was looking at the angels that had spread their wings over Muhammad the Trustworthy her partner in trade, who they were protecting from the rays of the sun. Khadija wanted to share what she saw with her close friends. She called them to her side and wanted them to partake in the beauty of the scene. It was surely a sight to be savored. All those who saw could not hide their amazement and surprise.

Of course for Maysara this journey was very different from previous ones—he had not seen an instance of injustice and he had felt no discomfort throughout the trip. They had made good trade of the wares that they had brought to Damascus, and the wares that they had got from Damascus had been sold in Mecca with great profit. It was clear that Khadija had found the quality she had been searching for. She had made trade with other people before, but naturally, The Pride of Humankind was different. What mattered to Khadija was not the manifold profit that she had gained. She was more interested in seeing Maysara and asking him what he had witnessed throughout the journey, and when he eventually came, she started to question him hastily.

Maysara first told her what the priest had said. Then he talked about the two angels he saw on the way back. He also talked about the incident of oath taking in Damascus, about his master's reaction, and the man's response. He spoke much, telling and re-telling what he had experienced throughout the trip, and he could not praise the master's fortitude and self-confidence enough. This was exactly what Khadija was waiting to hear. She was trying to hide the intensity of what she felt inside. This emotional reaction was only natural since all roads seemed to be pointing to him.

She stood up immediately and went straight to her teacher and cousin Waraqa ibn Nawfal to share what Maysara had told her. Waraqa was also excited when he heard what Khadija had to say. He, too, was now sure that he had found what he had been looking for. He said to Khadija, who was waiting for a reply: "O Khadija, if what you tell me is true, there is no doubt that Muhammad is the Prophet of these people! I knew already that these people had an awaited Prophet. Now is his time," he said.

Waraqa was one of the few people who could read the Torah and the Gospel from their original and who could also write the script. What he had seen in the books had for some time put him in a state of waiting and he often asked "When?" to himself, waiting for the Last Messenger to come. He was composing poems about this longing and he often spoke of the sadness about the Prophet's tardiness in coming. Waraqa's observations were very important for Khadija. Everything seemed to point to the Prophet; what she had listened to till that day, Mecca bearing witness and what May-sara had said… They all pointed to the crossroads where all this met… Muhammad the Trustworthy was the right address. She had no more hesitations.

The Messenger whose good tidings had been given for so long was now so near to him. She had no thoughts of marriage, but this seemed to be the way to get closer to him.

The Road to Marriage

K hadija had already been married twice and she had by now closed all doors to such suggestions. She had reached a certain age and she no longer needed the support of anyone. She had what one could call an international business by today's standards and the people who worked for her were people from many different corners of the world. She had men working for her in Greek, Persian and Ghassanid lands, along with others in closer regions such as the Hira and Damascus. She was rich; she was a woman who took good care of her business, a mature and beautiful woman of good name whom everybody respected.

In those days there would be no man who could refuse such a woman among the Quraysh. All men in her tribe would have been happy to marry her had they had the power to do so. Many had come to her door, but she turned them all down, having decided against marrying again.

Khadija had now made up her mind about marrying the Prophet, peace and blessings be upon him; maybe it was the dream of such a perfect match that had made her turn down all previous offers till that day. She had made up her mind but she did not know how to approach the subject.

Khadija's friend Nafisa, the daughter of Munya, who took notice of her friend's thoughtful state and transformation, approached her one day and said the following with great affection: "What is with you, dear Khadija? I have been with you long enough and yet I have never seen you as thoughtful as you are now!"

Khadija hesitated before sharing her predicament with her. She first stayed silent. But it was clear that it was not possible to attain her goal without taking any steps and so she told her friend what was on her mind. She first said: "O Nafisa! There is no doubt that I see in Muhammad, the son of Abdullah, an exalted quality that I see in no other man. He is straightforward, trustworthy, he comes from a very good family, and he is the best man one can ever come across. On top of that, there are many good tidings concerning him! It is a strange situation. When I look at what Maysara has told me, when I listened to what the priest said and witnessed what happened at the marketplace, when I watched the cloud that protected him as he came back from Damascus, I thought my heart would fly out of its cage; I was sure that he was the awaited Messenger."

Nafisa was still trying to understand what was going on: "But what has this to do with you losing your color and being in this contemplative state?"

It was clear that Khadija had to be clearer about what was ailing her. She turned to her friend and said truthfully: "I hope to join my fate with his by marrying him; but I do not know how I would go about doing this."

Now the situation was clear. Nafisa understood her friend's predicament and responded in the following way: "If you'll allow me, I'll inquire as to how this situation can develop and be arranged!"

This was what Khadija was expecting and she said excitedly: "Nafisa, if you can indeed do this, do it in all haste, with no delay!"

Before long, Nafisa left that place and started to ask for directions as to where Muhammad the Trustworthy, peace and blessings be upon him, was. She quickly found him. She first saluted him and then said: "O Muhammad!"

Our noble Prophet turned his whole body towards her and was listening to her. She continued: "What stops you from marrying? Why are you not getting married?"

This was a question that the Pride of Humankind had not been expecting and he replied: "I don't have the means to get married."

It was true that the Messenger of Allah did not have the financial means to get married. In order for him to take the responsibilities of others upon himself, he first needed to have the means to see to their needs. But Nafisa told him that this need not constitute a problem; for money and possessions were things that could easily be lost, whereas nobility, honor, trust and character were values that were hard to find. Since she had come so far in the conversation, she decided to pursue it further and asked: "If this was no longer an obstacle for you, and if someone came to you with beauty, wealth, honor, someone of your own caliber, would you not accept them as a spouse?"

Her questions made it clear that there was such a candidate, and understanding her intention, the Sultan of Both Worlds asked: "So who is this person?"

"It is Khadija," answered Nafisa.

Of course he knew Khadija, the daughter of Khuwaylid; he had taken her caravan to Damascus only a few of days ago and had returned it to her with trade profits. But marriage was not as easy as trade and so he asked: "But how can his be?"

But for Nafisa the question was not a matter of "how," she was just waiting to hear his consent.

She was relieved to hear his response, for his words could be taken as consent. His response seemed to denote "This is not a problem on my side, but how can such a marriage be?"

The rest of the conversation came easier to Nafisa, so she said: "You can leave the "how" of this business to me."

Conventionally, silence meant a favorable response, and Nafisa left his side quickly and ran to our mother Khadija. She herself wanted to give her the good news. She ran and told her all that had been spoken. The news made Khadija breathe a sigh of relief. When she learnt that he looked upon the matter favorably, she sent word to the Awaited Messenger about her interest in him and the reasons why she wanted to marry him. This is how she started her statement: "O my uncle's son! Verily I am interested in marrying you because of our close family ties. Your remarkable status within your tribe, your beautiful morals and your steadfastness in protecting what is entrusted to you and in speaking the truth. Tell your uncles that they may start the marriage procedures!"

It was clear that she was trying to express her admiration for the Messenger of Allah in the sincerest and finest way possible. The Pride of Humankind did not want to take such an important step without discussing the issue with his elders. After receiving the offer, he went straight to his uncle Abu

Talib and spoke about what had taken place between himself and Nafisa.

His nephew, Muhammad the Trustworthy, peace and blessings be upon him, was very precious for Abu Talib and he did not know any other person as worthy as him. However, Khadija was no woman to be written away either. She clearly lived a life of honor and dignity. She was one of the leading people by way of nobility and honor. He understood that his nephew looked at it favorably as well and he decided he had nothing to say against the match, and so he blessed the union.

The time had come for the union that would shape their lives. Before long, the sons of Abdul Muttalib, Abu Talib, Abbas and Hamza would set off to ask for the hand of Khadija for Muhammad. Although the couple had given their consent, the usual rituals between the families had to take place, and the match had to be made known to the public through this process. First, Abu Talib took word: "Praise be to Allah who has given us the honor to be of the lineage of Ibrahim, descendants of Ismail! Verily it is He who has made our kin the server of the people, He who has honored us as protectors of His house, put us in the service of the Haram, the Prohibited Place; it is He who has made His house a place the direction to which all turn their faces, a place where all feel secure. It is He who has favored us when it comes to judging people."

This address that he chose before he started to speak of the matter made clear the earnestness of the situation. Attaining the respect of people could be acknowledged on no clearer terms. Then he said the following to the seated members of the family: "When it comes to Muhammad, the son of my brother, the son of Abdullah. Whoever should challenge him, he shall be beaten. Although he may not have much by way of money and possessions, he is above all by way of honor, nobility, courage, intellect and virtue. Money and possessions are like shadows that disappear; they last only a short while. However, there is great news about him, new and happy tidings about his future that will leave everyone in awe! He is asking for the hand of Khadija who is your sister, and as dowry, he wants to give her twelve *uqiyya* and one *nash* some of which is to be paid now and some later."

In response to the request of the groom's family, the bride's family also had words to say. After Abu Talib, Khadija's uncle Amr ibn Asad stood up and said similar laudatory words about Khadija's virtue. Khadija's father was not present; he had died in the battles of Fijar and the daughter of Khuwaylid had grown up an orphan just like the Messenger of Allah. He said the following:

"Just like you say, praise be to Allah, Who has favored us among others in the aspects that you have mentioned! There is no doubt that we are the leaders among Arabs, and so are you. No one among the Arabs can deny your virtue or honor or your right for pride. I bear witness by the same lineage that we come from and our shared honor that I, O you people of Quraysh, wed the daughter of Khuwaylid, Khadija to Muhammad, the son of Abdullah, with the dowry that has already been mentioned.

Abu Talib, who felt the responsibility of the moment over his shoulders, wanted to hear the consent of the other relatives who were also present at the occasion, so he said: "I want the other uncles to participate in this acceptance."

Upon this, another uncle who was present took word: "I call you to be witnesses, O Quraysh, that we have wed Muhammad, the son of Abdullah, to Khadija, daughter of Khuwaylid," and thus he reiterated the transaction of marriage.

The usual rituals had thus been performed, and now it was time for the wedding ceremony. Soon that too would take place. The sheep and camels were slaughtered, and people had gathered for the celebration. Thus a life of hardship but mutual understanding and peace would start for the couple, a shared life of 25 years. Abu Talib, who was going through very difficult times himself, was very happy; he was sitting on the side, thanking Allah who had opened up such a gate of happiness for him. It was of course not solely Abu Talib who was happy about this union. The Meccans had sincerely approved of this match, such that some of them would put this auspicious event in verse, reciting it to each other.

But of course on that day no one's happiness matched Khadija's. She knew so much about him already, such that she had invited the nursing mother of Muhammad the Trustworthy, Halima as-Sadia, to the wedding; she wanted to share with her the happiness of the orphan who had grown up without parents. Her happiness did not overshadow her generosity and she would not forget what she was meant to do. When Halima was leaving in the morning, she had with her the forty sheep that Khadija had given her as a gift for the sake of beloved Muhammad, to whom Halima had given her milk.

After staying with Abu Talib for a couple of days, they moved to their own house that they purchased from Hakim ibn Hizam the nephew of our mother Khadija, and thus began their exemplary life that would continue for fifteen years till the first revelation.

From then on, Muhammad the Trustworthy, peace and blessings be upon him, was a model family man. When circumstances called for it, he would help his wife with the housework, he would see to his own daily needs himself and he thus constructed a relationship with his wife on the basis of mutual respect and love. Although she had every means to leave the house work and the service of her husband to the servants, Khadija enjoyed being of service to her husband and preferred to do much of the work herself, performing her chores with joy akin to prayer. She had devoted herself to his contentment to the extent that she could not bear to see a single hair strand of his be injured in any way, she took great pains so that there was nothing to disturb him.

Allah's Messenger and Khadija had joined their lives to set up a new household, but they were not alone in this new life that they had started. They would not focus only on themselves; they would hold the hands of others and would prepare these people for life as well. Had their parents been alive, they too would have partaken in the peace of this house; they too would have had the joy of loving their grandchildren with their own children.

First of all, Umm Ayman, entrusted to the Pride of Humankind by his father, moved into this new house with them. She was trying to see to the needs of the orphaned son of her master Abdullah, the son who had lost his mother as well.

The Messenger of Allah was equally a man who never forgot the good that had been done to him. After marrying our mother Khadija and setting up a new house, he had gone to his uncle Abbas and speaking about the dire situation that his uncle Abu Talib was in, he suggested that they should jointly take on the expenses of his house. Thus, Abbas took under his care one of Abu Talib's son, and the other son Ali, would come under the care of the Messenger of Allah. This can be described as the third phase of protection in the Prophet's life; now Muhammad the Trustworthy, peace and blessings be upon him, was a father to Ali and Khadija was an affectionate mother to him. On the one hand, Ali was being educated by the most honorable member of humanity and on the other hand, he was the recipient of the affection and love coming forth from the noble Khadija.

There was another young man living in this house and his name was Zayd ibn Haritha. Although he had been the son of a free family, the house they had gone to with their mother had been raided and they had been taken as slaves and sold at the slave market. In the fair of Ukaz, the nephew of our mother Khadija, Hakim ibn Hizam, had bought him and then brought him to his aunt. Till the day of the wedding, Zayd had served Khadija and had become a member of this new household. However, soon a change would occur in his status—he had been given in service to the Cause of Pride for the Universe and he in turn had given Zayd his freedom.

Another young man in the house was Hind, the son of Khadija from her former husband Abu Halah. The little Zubayr, too, joined this household for a while when his father Awwam passed away, and he too had the good fortune of growing up in this house.

It was in such a house that peace could be established. The Pride of Humanity himself was the source of peace. His whole mission was to bring peace to those who could not even imagine peace in their dreams, to shower such people with complete peace and serenity. The affectionate behavior of our mother Khadija was a great source that fed this peace as well. She was assured in the righteousness of all the actions of the noble Prophet from the beginning and always hastened to do as he bid. Whenever something disturbed him outside, he would run to the home that was kept stable by our mother Khadija, and this is where he would find his peace. Just as there was this understanding between the two of them, there was also a sincere relationship of trust between them, so sincere that everyone looked upon them with envy.

One day, when Muhammad the Trustworthy, peace and blessings be upon him, asked leave from his uncle Abu Talib to go to Khadija, Abu Talib told his slave girl Naba to follow him to report back on their relations. When she returned, Naba told the following to Abu Talib: "What I saw was very interesting indeed. When she saw him coming, Khadija came to the door, held his hand and said to him: 'May my mother and father be sacrificed for you! In truth I would not do this for anyone but you, but I know that you are the Prophet of the future. When you reach that state please do not forget me, and my position near you! Please, pray for me, too, to Allah who has sent you!' Muhammad the Trustworthy, who heard this praise from his wife and supporter in all things, said: 'I swear by Allah that if indeed I am he, you have sacrificed many things for me, and I will never forget your sacrifice.'" And indeed he would never forget it.

Soon this household started to bear fruit. First Qasim was born. He was the child that gave our noble Prophet his name Abu'l-Qasim, the father of Qasim. But he did not stay long in this mortal world. When he was only a toddler, he left this world for Paradise.

Two years passed after Qasim's death and our beloved Prophet's daughter Zaynab came to the world. Zaynab was his first female child. A year later Ruqayyah, and three years later Umm Kulthum was born. Our mother Fatima honored the world with her presence the year that the revelations started. The last child that our mother Khadija brought to the world was Abdullah. It had been two years that the spiritual meeting in Mount Hira had taken place. Because he had been born into what was now an Islamic world, Abdullah was also called Tayyib and Tahir to signal his purity. However, Abdullah did not live long either and three months later, he too left the world. It seemed that Allah the Almighty wanted to protect them from the possible complications that would arise later.

Repairing of the Ka'ba
and the Judge

Another ten years passed and the Pride of Humankind had reached the age of thirty five. In those days, the most discussed topic was repairs to be done to the Ka'ba. A thief had got in through the walls that had fallen apart and had stolen certain precious things from it. A woman had set fire near it and the flames had inflamed the cover of the Ka'ba and burnt it. The Quraysh took all this into consideration and decided to repair the Ka'ba. A ship had recently run aground on the shores of Jeddah and news had come that this ship was full of the material needed for the repairs. Moreover there were workmen in the ship who could carry out the repairs. Without much ado, a delegation headed by Walid ibn Mughira went and bought the material that was needed, and they took the master workman Bakum of Greek origin with them and then returned to Mecca.

When it came to distribution of the work, there was immediately some tension, for all tribes wanted to gain credit for such an honorable job as repairing the Ka'ba. At the end, each wall was designated to a certain tribe for repair.

But before rebuilding, they had to tear down the walls and no one had the courage to do that. They feared that some curse would befall them. It was Walid ibn Mughira who first mustered the courage to hit the first blow with the lever. He said: "O Lord! We mean nothing but good when doing this."

He kept hitting with the lever with utmost care. No one else had the courage that day to participate in tearing down the wall. They wanted to wait a few days to see whether any bad things would happen to them; for if nothing happened, they would take this as a sign that the Lord was content with what they were doing. If something bad happened, they would give up the work and never think of it again. The next day had come and everybody had woken up just like the previous days. It was clear that the Lord was content with the work and so all the tribes took up the work that had already been designated to them, and the task of demolition was completed.

They had now reached all the way down to the foundations laid down by Prophet Ibrahim, peace be upon him. When they touched the foundations, they saw that the whole of Mecca started to shake, and fearing what would happen, they decided to build the new building on top of these foundations.

The Ka'ba was rising stone by stone and when it came to the most important pillar of the building, there was yet another disagreement between the tribes. Each tribe wanted to place the Black Stone, the Hajar al-Aswad, which they deemed to be holy, themselves. There was no way to resolve the dispute, such that they were looking for ways to attack each other. This was a fearful situation because the wounds of the Fijar battles were only just beginning to heal and such a conflict could bring the tribes near another battle that could last hundreds of years.

It was at this moment that the oldest man of the Quraysh, Abu Umayya, stood up and spoke to the Meccans who were waiting for the smallest provocation to attack each other: "O people of Quraysh! You should appoint a judge among you and thus end this dispute! Let the first man that enters the doors of the Ka'ba be that judge and let him judge among you and do as he says!"

First they debated this suggestion and then decided that it was fair. They did not want to create animosity among the tribes for a task they had set out to do in the name of good works. They had all accepted this suggestion and now they had to wait for that first person to enter through the doors. It was a Monday. After a long and silent wait, everyone had become all ears, and they tried to guess to whom the footsteps belonged to. The first face that the Quraysh saw entering the doors was the Pride of Humankind, Prophet Muhammad, peace and blessings be upon him. When they saw him they all said: "Look! The *Amin*, the Trustworthy, is coming! We will be content with his judgment."

Muhammad the Trustworthy, peace and blessings be upon him, enquired after why they were all looking at him and why they had started to cry out after seeing him; he was told of all that had happened. He then asked them to bring a big piece of cloth. Soon after they brought it to him and were watching him with great curiosity.

First the Messenger of Allah laid the cloth on the ground, and then carrying the Black Stone with his own hands, placed it on the cloth. He could see that people were watching his every move, and so he said:

"Each tribe should hold a side of the cloth and lift the stone."

It was a clever solution, and no one could say anything against it. Thus, every tribe would participate in placing the stone and lift it up all together. When the stone came to where it was to be placed, he approached it, took it into his exalted hands and put it in its place.

In the Cave of Hira

The first building on earth, the Ka'ba, built to inspire inner peace, was now causing gloom. That is why the Pride of Humanity was trying to get away from it, and while each of his steps physically took him away from it, emotionally, he was leaving his heart with it, and found it very difficult to leave.

When he left the Ka'ba, he preferred to go to a place where he could watch it from afar. This was the summit of Mount Nur. There was a cave called Hira at the summit that had a good view of the Ka'ba. This was where the Messenger of Allah would come when he left the Ka'ba; he stayed there for months on end, and devoted his time entirely to worship. Maybe this was a fate that was meant to prepare him for carrying the weight of a message whose decrees would continue till the end of time.

The blessed moment of reunion fell on a Monday. The year was 610, the month was Ramadan, and the place was Mount Nur. At this time and place, lights had united and an inseparable link was forged between the heavens and the earth. It was here that Archangel Gabriel descended and told Muhammad, the Pride of Humankind, his duty as a Messenger of Allah.

On this mountain, two sureties had come together and a new custody was going to be given to humankind. Now was the season when light would meet light, a period of reflection was about to resonate on earth. The heavenly was going to embrace the earthly and would order him to "Read!" This was the placing of a burden on the shoulders of humanity, a responsibility that had been too heavy for mountains and rocks to carry. The burden felt in the face of the majesty of such a mission was unbearable. What was it that he was meant to read? He did not know how to read or write! He had not received any education thus far. There had been no authority other than his Lord to fill his horizon.

"I do not know how to read," the Messenger of Allah responded.

Gabriel came closer and embraced him once again. He squeezed Muhammad, peace and blessings be upon him, with all his might, and then setting him loose, he said again: "Read!"

The beloved Messenger would repeat the same words: "I do not know how to read!"

It was clear that there was more to this statement than what it seemed to be on the surface. Gabriel approached him once again, and seizing him by his waist, he squeezed him again. Then releasing him, he repeated: "Read!"

"But I do not know how to read! What am I to read?" repeated the Pride of Humankind.

This time, it seemed that now they would get somewhere. Gabriel finally said to the Beloved of Allah as he let him out of his grasp:

Read in and with the Name of your Lord, Who has created—created human from a clot clinging (to the wall of the womb). Read and your Lord is the All-Munificent, Who has taught (human) by the pen—taught human what he did not know. (al-Alaq 96:1-5)

Things were clearer now; for when it was in the name of the Gracious Lord, everything could be read. It was not yet made evident what was to be read. But everything that one could see or hear was created to be read. Each thing that stood in front of man was a sign confirming its creator, and man as a creature of comprehension had to read creation in the right way in order to decipher this code of significance.

This order also called for an assessment of what the beloved Messenger had gathered by way of information till that day and to continue in the same manner in the future. The Qur'an would be revealed piece by piece and this emphasized the need to go back to the beginning every time a verse would be revealed, and read it as part of this whole, for this book was not of mettle to be left aside, nor was it to be preserved in precious material and hung in the highest of places as a show of respect. It had to be a message that would resonate with the believer is all its aspects.

For this to happen, it had to be read properly with precision and turned towards with sincere intentions of understanding. This book would open its doors to the extent of one's sincere direction towards it and would offer its pearls to those who want it to the same extent.

This order by Allah via Gabriel also spoke of a new beginning for the duty that lay ahead for the Messenger of Allah. He was going to go to the people with this mission and invite them to the true way of life. When accomplishing this task, the Messenger of Allah was called upon to read human nature correctly in his dealings with people. He was reminded that he had to know his addressee well, that he had to decipher the codes of his soul because only then would he be able to speak in a language that they would understand.

Having completed his first duty in Mount Hira, Gabriel disappeared immediately. What he had just experienced was upon Muhammad the Trustworthy with all its majesty. After a while, he realized that what he was mumbling to himself was nothing other than what Gabriel had brought him just now, for what he had brought had taken root in his heart letter by letter and he found himself repeating them. Things were clearer now; he had been given the duty of guiding people to the right path, the people he had seen to be in grave error till that day. His duty was upon him; he was to go down from the mountain and amongst the people, and starting from his first interlocutors in Mecca, he would introduce people with a way of life that was willed by his Lord. This was a duty that was like those given to those before him, but different in the way that this message was now sent to encompass the whole of humanity; the mission of Prophethood had been given to him and now he was going to Mecca to carry out this noble task.

Turning Towards Mecca

The two lights that met on Mount Nur had left one another having promised to meet often, and the Messenger of Allah had directed himself towards Mecca with the news he had been given. He was bent in two with the heavy mission he had taken on and was excited to the point of rapture with the union he had experienced in Hira. His whole body was taken over by the weight of revelation. He then heard a voice echo in the heavens: "O Muhammad! You are the Messenger of Allah, and I am Gabriel!"

When he lifted his gracious head up at the sky he could see Gabriel in all his majesty and he was repeating the same thing: "O Muhammad! You are the Messenger of Allah, and I am Gabriel!"

It seemed as if the Messenger of Allah was nailed down to where he was; he could neither put a step forward, nor could he return. After waiting for a while in that position, he started to move his head. What did he see? Wherever he turned he saw the same thing! Gabriel had enveloped the whole sky.

In the meantime, Khadija was worried because his return was delayed and she had sent his men after him to bring her his news. Because they knew that he went to Mount Hira, that's where they went, but they could not find him there.

Then the long hours of surprise and worry came to an end and the Messenger of Allah turned towards Mecca. As he walked, he heard voices on the way saying: "Let the peace of Allah be upon you O Messenger of Allah."

He turned to where these voices were coming from but he could not see anyone. Before long, he understood that the trees and the rocks that he came upon were saluting him and bearing witness to his Prophethood.

He returned home in excitement and said: "Cover me, cover me!" asking his devoted wife to cover him.

He then put his blessed head on the knees of our mother Khadija. She was watching the events unfold and she said affectionately:

"O Abu'l-Qasim (O Father of Qasim)! Where were you? I swear I sent my men after you, they did not leave a stone unturned in Mecca, but they could not return with news of you!" thus making her affection known to him. The Pride of Humankind said: "I am afraid of myself Khadija! I am afraid of harm," and his wife once again took word to soothe him: "Never fear or despair! Allah will not abandon you, He will keep you," she said first, and then added: "For you always care about your relatives, hold the hand of the afflicted and clothe those in need. You always have guests at your house, with all your actions you are always after Truth and you are someone who has devoted himself completely to the path of good."

How could He leave alone someone who was doing His job of filling the moral vacuum that might appear in a society! With this attitude, Khadija was presenting a stance that can be a model for all Muslim women; she was presenting a model that put good deeds above everything else. How could

He leave alone those who had persevered themselves in difficult days?

Before long, the Messenger of Allah told her what had happened first. Khadija, a woman of experience, resoluteness and patience would confer all her worries and deeds to Allah and so she was very calm. She knew that a trustworthy person such as her husband, whom everyone sought advice from, was not himself without a protector. She presented the resoluteness that was expected of her and supported the Great Stature with whom the universe is proud, by saying: "Rejoice, O son of my uncle! Be resolute and steadfast where you are! I swear by He who holds Khadija's life in His hand that you are the Messenger that this people wait for."

For her, this was the expected conclusion, and so with faith she bore witness to the truth of what he had come with right there! Then she covered the Messenger of Allah and left him alone in their house with the Gracious Lord, to go knock on another wise door.

The Guidance of Waraqa

There was someone else in Mecca who would be happy to hear this news. Khadija ran to her uncle's son Waraqa ibn Nawfal with haste. She related to him word for word what her gracious husband had told her. Each new sentence that came out of Khadija's mouth created great excitement within Waraqa, and at one moment, he couldn't contain himself and started shouting: "Quddus! Quddus," and then added: "I swear by Him who holds Waraqa's life in His hand that if what you tell me is true Khadija, this is the Great Honor that has also come to Moses and Jesus. There is no doubt that he is the Messenger of this people. Go and tell him this, tell him to be steadfast."

The seed from under the soil had cracked and now the new green seedling was coming out. The awaited moment had come and the unlucky fate of humanity was about to change. He wanted to have a first-hand account of this event which would change the course of humanity, and with Khadija's guidance, they met in the courtyard of the Ka'ba. The fact that he was many years older did not stop him from obedience, and Waraqa kissed the forehead of the Messenger of Allah.

"O son of my brother! Tell me what you have heard and saw," he asked, as if he was asking for mercy.

The last Messenger of Allah started to tell him what had happened, without excluding any details. Each word he heard was causing him even greater excitement, causing eruptions in his spiritual world and Waraqa was pushed from one inner state to another. The Good News that he had been reading about in books for years and the Glad Tidings that he lived with the hope of witnessing was the very person that was standing next to him.

When the Messenger of Allah finished his words, it was time for Waraqa to speak. With a quavering voice and the excitement of a heart that had found what it was looking for, he said the following historical words: "I swear by Him in whose hands my life is, you are the Messenger of this people. The same Honor that came to Moses has come to you. Do not forget that because of what you bring, you will be accused of lying, you will be subjected to hardships and torture, you will face enmity like you never have experienced before. I wish I were young on that day, living on that day, I wish I could reach the day that they will drive you out of your home so that I could be of some support to you."

What he heard at this door that he had sought for solace was very interesting indeed. The future seemed to hold some hope but this hope seemed to come with its own baggage, a heavy load full of days of hardship, ordeal and misery. The noble Messenger was surprised. It was clear that this old man knew many things. He asked with a curious tone of voice: "Will my people drive me out?"

The answer that came not only answered the question, but with more general terms, it was listing what would befall him and was explaining the causes of the holy exiles that those who will be with him will have to suffer through: "Yes, they will drive you out. There is no person who comes with the truth that you are coming and not be driven out of his home, and not have to leave his homeland!"

Khadija was the first to believe in Allah and His Messenger, and then Ali ibn Abu Talib, who was only a child. Zayd ibn Haritha and Abu Bakr followed them. Then Bilal al-Habashi, Arqam ibn Abi'l-Arqam, Asma and Aisha, the two daughters of Abu Bakr, Habbab ibn Arat, and Abdullah ibn Jahsh joined the first circle.

The Growing Circle of "Communication"

Three long years had passed and the circle of faith could grow only so much. Many people were aware of the change in Mecca, whether it was those who had witnessed a friend or a relative accepting Islam, or those who themselves had been invited to Islam, or those who had witnessed the hatred welling up inside the hearts of the Quraysh. The issue was being discussed everywhere.

Meanwhile, with every passing day, new revelation were coming and feeding the believers by way of faith, strengthening their resistance. Before long, a revelation had arrived that stated: "*So from now on, proclaim what you are commanded to convey openly and in an emphatic manner, and do not care (whatever) those who associate partners with Allah (say and do)*" (al-Hijr 15:94). It seemed that the provision was more general this time and it targeted Mecca in the first place and then the whole of humanity. How could one not carry out such an order?

The Beloved of Allah went to the top of Safa hill and called out to the whole of Mecca: "*Ya sabaha! Ya sabaha!*"

This was a kind of address that normally served to warn the people of the threat of a great enemy. When such a call was heard, normally everyone would take their own precautions and would wait ready for the enemy. That day, the Messenger of Allah was trying this call to wake the Meccans to an awareness of what was awaiting them tomorrow. No one could stay indifferent to such a call. Those who could come were coming and those who could not were sending people to report back as to what Prophet Muhammad, peace and blessings be upon him, had to say. There was a great crowd at Safa now, and the Messenger of Allah called the attention of the tribes present one by one: "O sons of Fihr! O sons of Adiyy! O sons of Abdimanaf; and O sons of Abdul Muttalib!"

Everyone was paying great attention and waiting for the news that was to come. In the meanwhile, there were also those who were asking who this man was who had called people here. The answer they received was: "Muhammad!"

Abu Lahab was among those who had come. The Messenger of Allah first asked the following question to those who were waiting eagerly to hear what he had to say: "If I should tell you that there is an army coming towards you from behind this mountain, would you say that I was lying to you?"

"No, we swear we have never seen you lie; we have never heard anything but the truth from you," they said.

This was the answer he was expecting. He was going to build his argument on it: "O people of Quraysh!" he called out to them once again. "I am a clear cautioner for you concerning a grave grief that is drawing near. Come and save yourselves from the fire of Hell! If you don't, I can do nothing for you in the eyes of Allah. You and I are like the man who comes to his tribe with the warning of an army approaching his town. He has seen that the enemy will come and harm his tribe and that's why he has warned his kin. He has gone to the top of a hill and shouted: *Ya sabaha! Ya sabaha.*'"

What more could he do? He was trying every possible way to help them but he was not able to get the result he wanted. But this wasn't the crucial point. When doing all this, he was not concerned about the end result, but rather, he concentrated on whether he was following Allah's will and orders. The underlying principle of the persistence of our noble Prophet, the Messenger of the Most Generous, was the awareness of doing his duty to the best of his capacity. He could not bear the idea of seeing people make their way towards Hell. Even though he was faced with insults and slander from his listeners, he believed that one day their hearts would soften.

Even if not these people themselves, their offspring might one day understand the value of Islam. On the Day of Judgment, Allah the Almighty would ask everyone what they had done in life and the excuse of "We had not been told" was no longer valid now. This is why the Illustrious Beloved of Allah started to say the following to his relatives who had gathered in this crowd: "O people of Quraysh! Do not leave your soul in bondage but buy your soul from Allah, and protect it from Hell; for tomorrow I will not be able to help or harm you in any way. Tomorrow I will not be able to help you when you are in the presence of Allah!"

He then started to address the crowd more specifically, calling out to them by their names:

"O sons of Ka'b ibn Luayy! O sons of Murra ibn Ka'b! O sons of Qusayy! O sons of Abdimanaf! O sons of Abdishams! O sons of Hashim! O sons of Abdul Muttalib! Take care to protect yourselves from the fires of Hell! Or else I will not be able to procure any help or harm for you; I will not be able to help you! Benefit now from what I come to you with, ask me anything and I will give it to you, but tomorrow in the presence of Allah, I will not be able to help you at all!

O Abbas ibn Abdul Muttalib! I will not be able to do anything for you either in the presence of Allah.

O aunt of the Messenger of Allah, Safiyya bint Abdul Muttalib! I will not be able to help you either!

O daughter of the Messenger of Allah, Fatima bint Muhammad, if you want something from what I have at hand now, ask for it now! You protect your self from the fire of Hell as well! Or else I will not be able to do you any good or harm on that day, in the presence of Allah. All I can do today is to speak nicely to you with respect to our blood ties!"

All these were true and no one said anything against these words. The Messenger of Allah had done his duty; he had put himself forward for the sake of his relatives. Having listened to his advice, they were now returning to their homes, without having given any response. A familiar face from among them came forward and approached the Messenger of Allah. It was clear that he was enraged and was not at all happy that the fate of the coming days had thus been revealed to him: "Woe unto you! Is this what you called us here for; let your hands dry up!" He was saying and scolding his nephew.

Not long after this, Gabriel had come to the Prophet's rescue and he was calming the Illustrious Beloved of Allah with the following words:

> May both hands of Abu Lahab be ruined, and are ruined are they! His wealth has not availed him, nor his gains. He will enter a flaming Fire to roast; and (with him) his wife, carrier of firewood (and of evil tales and slander), around her neck will be a halter of strongly twisted rope. (al-Masad 111:1–5)

This was at the same time a warning that even if he should be close to the Prophet by way of family, he would not be able to find salvation if he did not respond to the invitation from the Messenger of Allah.

Now Mecca would get to know about these verses and be truly shaken. The address that the Abu Lahab family was heading for was thus made public. Although they did not seem to care at first, inside they were full of doubt: What if what was said was true? What if there was a Hell? And what about Muhammad, what if he really was the Messenger people were waiting for?

But because he had already once said no, he would stay by his word, and when his day came, he would die like the Qur'an and the Messenger of Allah had foretold, consolidating the judgment passed on him.

The wife of Abu Lahab, the enemy to Allah, was Umm Jamil and she was in no way behind her husband when it came to enmity to the Messenger of Allah. He would spread pins and needles on the path where the Messenger was likely to pass, and she would pour rubbish on his doorstep. She had a nasty tongue and she would incite others against him; she was organizing people against the Messenger of Allah and was trying to turn enmity towards him into a popular cause. That's why when speaking of her, the Qur'an would use the term "carrier of wood," making clear her sorry state in Hell as an example to those that would come after her.

The Messenger of Allah, who paid such great attention to the sons of Abdul Muttalib, was slowly widening his circle of communication. He was now going to the Ka'ba to pray openly; he was inviting people to religion and reading them the Qur'an.

The Efforts to Prevent People
from Encountering Islam

M eanwhile the pilgrimage season had arrived, and there was a new commotion among the Quraysh. What they feared most was that the pilgrims coming from the outside would speak to the Messenger of Allah and that he would start sharing the verses with them.

They had to prevent this at all costs. Muhammad, peace and blessings be upon him, had to be prevented from talking to the pilgrims, and even if he should talk, there had to be enough propaganda against him to discredit him. In order to find a solution they came together at the house of Walid ibn Mughira. Their aim was to keep the Messenger of Allah away from going amongst the people to spread the word, to communicate the new messages; they wanted to prevent these messages so they would find new places of abode in the hearts of others.

Now the general policy had been decided and there was a consensus as to the method of how they would alienate the Messenger of Allah from society. From now on they would all speak the same thing, and they could converge on their lie and try their best to slander the Messenger of Allah. In today's terms, it can be likened to a false news item that is distributed throughout the media and its various platforms.

When the time came and pilgrims flocked to Mecca, the Quraysh were welcoming their guests and speaking of the

Pride of Humankind telling the pilgrims—even though they didn't believe the truth of it—that he was a magician. Thus, they thought they could prevent people from going to his side, and that they could prevent the heavenly message to reach these people.

On the other hand, the heaviness of revelation was upon the Messenger of Allah and the truthful Gabriel was descending with a new message again. In the revelations that came, the Lord was informing his beloved of this insidious plan. He spoke of the inner worlds of the people who were trying to set traps for the Messenger of Allah. Concerning the mind set of Walid ibn Mughira, the Lord of the worlds was saying the following:

True, there was always tomorrow to be considered. But there were steps to be taken today. Everyone was striving for their goal, and it had to be the ones who took their steps in the Name of Allah who would see their perseverance to the end. That is why when the season of pilgrimage came and people started to pour into Mecca, the Messenger of Allah continued to go around to the fairs of Ukaz, Majanna and Zilmajaz and said to all present: "O people! Come and say 'There is no deity but Allah' and be saved," trying thus to make his Lord's name be heard.

Despite all the efforts of the Quraysh, Abu Lahab's close persecution, and the destruction of anything that the noble Prophet was trying to build, the season of pilgrimage would come and go, and in the minds of the pilgrims, only the messages that the Messenger of Allah had relayed to them would remain. This was the only novelty that they had seen and witnessed in Mecca, and this novelty was of a scale that could change not only Mecca, but the entire world.

The Pressures on the Sons in Law

The Quraysh was increasingly acting in a very sinister way; apart from the Messenger of Allah, peace and blessing be upon him, they did all they could to injure Khadija as well. They were putting pressure on the husbands of the three daughters of the Messenger of Allah who had married before revelations had started. They were saying that if they divorced the daughters of the Prophet, peace and blessing be upon him, they would marry them to girls of their own choice.

The daughters of our noble Prophet, Ruqayyah and Umm Kulthum, were married to the two sons of Abu Lahab, Utba and Utayba. Utba and Utayba were not of a nature that could withstand such pressure, and when they got the guarantee that they would be married to any girl they wanted to, they left Ruqayyah and Umm Kulthum. The families that had thus been destroyed were another source of grief for the Messenger of Allah and his loving wife Khadija.

Under normal circumstances, the separation of one of their children would have been enough sadness for parents, but in this case the Messenger of Allah and his wife Khadija were grieved by the destroyed families of both their daughters, and this had happened without any sound reason. The only reason was that they were both the daughters of the Messenger of Allah.

Only Abu'l-As, the husband of our mother Zaynab, had not bowed down to the pressures. He was living a life of honor, enough not to let other people meddle in his domestic affairs. If there was a decision to be made, he would make it according to his own judgment. If there was peace within a home, then no outside force should try to destroy that. He had a peaceful home, and the fact that his wife had a different outlook on life did not disturb this peace; on the contrary, her views were helping to maintain the home as a peaceful place. That's why he had closed his ears to all pressures, and was doing only what he had to do.

It was a twist of fate that the worst enemies of the Messenger of Allah were his close neighbors. The house of Abu Lahab was right next to his. Other neighbors whose houses were next to his were no better than Abu Lahab; Hakam ibn Abi'l-As, Uqba ibn Abi Muayt, Adiyy ibn Khamra and Ibnu'l-Asda al-Huzali—they all felt an enmity towards the Messenger of Allah and just like Abu Lahab, they were trying to seize every opportunity to hurt him.

One day, one of them had thrown sheep droppings on our noble Prophet as he was praying; another had put droppings in the water that Allah's Messenger would use for his ablutions. After a while, in order to protect himself from their evil behavior, our noble Prophet had built a wall separating his own space from theirs. However they insisted on their behavior and he would pick the dirt that they threw to his house with the end of a stick, and showing it to them he would say: "O sons of Abdimanaf! What kind of neighborly behavior is this?"

Uqba ibn Abi Muayt would take things further and at a time when Abu Jahl was with him they decided on a course of action to further hurt Muhammad the Trustworthy, peace and blessings be upon him. Speaking among themselves they would point to the Messenger of Allah and say: "Which one of you would have the bravery to put the rumen of a camel with its contents on Muhammad as he prostrates in the Prayer?"

The most criminal minded of them stood up. This was none other than Uqba. He had a rumen brought to him and then started to wait. When the Messenger of Allah was approaching prostration, he went to him and placed the rumen in between his shoulder blades.

The Beloved of Allah was thus being harassed by his neighbors at a point when he was closest to Allah. On the other hand Uqba and his guests were enjoying what they had just done, scratching their bellies and laughing. They had laughed so much that they were leaning on each other not to fall down. For a long time the Messenger of Allah did not lift his head from prostration. After a while, his daughter Fatima had seen the scene and had come running to her father. On the one hand she was berating those who had done this and on the other she was trying to clear the dirt from her father's shoulders. He was the most beloved servant of Allah, had He wanted He could have destroyed them there and then, and then they would have gone straight to Hell. But our noble Prophet was always expectant of people's repentance; he was hoping that if not today, they would embrace the faith in the future. But this incident had hurt him very deeply and he supplicated to his Lord: "My Lord! I leave the Quraysh unto You!"

Such that he repeated this supplication three times. After that he called them out name by name.

"My Lord! I leave Abu Jahl, Utba ibn Abi Rabia, Shayba ibn Abi Rabia, Walid ibn Utba, Umayya ibn Khalaf, Uqba ibn Abi Muayt, all of them unto You! You are the One who will give them what they deserve!"

His words were so sincere that the way he had left his business to Allah had frightened those present. They knew that prayers made in this holy place would be accepted, and that something would indeed befall them, and especially when it was the most beloved servant of Allah who was articulating this prayer!

Scenes of Violence

They had tried everything till that day and yet had had no success. It was clear that in this war, it was not enough to respond to the Word with words in order to defeat the Muslims. They had to resort to other means. Brute force was something that those who were defeated by way of argument would only resort to, and this was what the Meccans of that time had to resort to as well.

There had been separate incidents in which brute force had already been used by the Meccans; Uthman had been locked in a cellar wrapped in straws by his uncle, Sa'd ibn Abi Waqqas had been emotionally blackmailed by his mother to recant his faith, Mus'ab ibn Umayr had been locked up and beaten by his mother, left without food and water for days and then banished from his home and from his inheritance, and then there was of course the torture that Umayya ibn Khalaf and Abu Jahl had subjected Bilal al-Habashi to.

Now Mecca was coming unto the Muslims in a more planned way. They were firstly targeting the weak, people who could not resist them because they had no one to back them up. They had made their plan. The head of each tribe would locate such people in their own tribe, and would subject them to torture till they would recant their belief. Especially when Abu Jahl heard someone say "There is no deity but Allah" he would run there and especially if this was a person with no family or friends, he would torture him or her in order to make him or her recant. As a result of Abu Jahl's vigilance and tortures, Suhayb ibn Sinan had lost his memory and had started speaking nonsense.

They had tied iron shackles to Abu Fuqayha's feet, they would bring him out to the desert during the hottest hours and would place rocks on him, and he would groan under this load till the evening. He too had lost his memory and reason due to these tortures.

There were burn marks on the body of Habbab ibn Arat, his master was torturing him so that he may recant, and whenever he approached him he was pressing hot metals unto Habbab's body. One day they got hold of Habbab from his hair and then squeezing his throat, they placed him on the fire of the shop; they were thinking they were "teaching him a lesson." It was an unbearable sight; they were holding him there for so long that the fluid from his body would quench some of the fire and so he found some respite.

A female slave named Zinnirah who faced the same tortures lost one eye, the female slave of the sons of Zuhra Umm Ubays would groan with pain under the lashes of Aswad ibn Abi Yaghus.

The female slave of Umar, who had not yet become Muslim, had her share of the torture, and she would be beaten till her master got tired. When he paused in his torment he would say: "Had I not got tired, I would have shown you!"

"Tomorrow, your Lord will do the same to you," she would say to the son of Al-Khattab, but her words would be of no avail on that day.

The Luminous Life of Our Prophet

Two slaves, mother and daughter, serving the sons of Abduddar had both been tortured; the mother had lost consciousness to the degree that she did not know what she was speaking. In this difficult time it was again Abu Bakr, may Allah be pleased with him, who ran to the rescue of the weak; he would buy these slaves from their masters and give them their freedom. Father Abu Quhafa who witnessed his attitude said: "I see that you are buying the weak and the unfortunate and giving them their freedom. Why don't you choose the stronger ones among the slaves, at least then they can help and support you." But he would say: "My only aim is to win the pleasure of Allah." Thus bolting the doors against a sense of worldly benefit to himself.

The verses, which came not long after, verified how right Abu Bakr was in his choice, and pointed to him as the example of the way in which one could reach the horizon of Allah's contentment.

Ammar ibn Yasir who became Muslim with his mother and father was the slave of Bai Mahzum. The leading men of the tribe, headed by Abu Jahl, would take him out to the field on the hottest hours of the day and they would torture him till they themselves were tired out. One day the Messenger of Allah saw this scene and said: "A little more patience, O family of Yasir, undoubtedly Paradise will be your resting place."

Indeed, the old father Yasir had walked to Paradise during these tortures. The old and weak mother Sumayya had resisted and not denied her Lord, and not said a word against the Messenger of Allah and had become the target of Abu Jahl's spear and become a martyr, the first in Islam.

The worst thing of the matter was that all this was happening right in front of Ammar. The hot stones were being placed on and off from her body. Ammar had been subjected to such great physical and mental oppression that he too lost consciousness.

"Unless you blaspheme against Muhammad, and speak good graces about Lat and Uzza, we will not let you go," he was warned.

He was let go when he pronounced the names of Lat and Uzza.

It was true that Ammar had been set free, but he was feeling the greatest remorse of his life, for he had pronounced the names of false gods instead of Allah and His Messenger whom he loved and held dear above everything else. He was exhausted. He came to the presence of the Prophet having been defeated. He was too ashamed to look at the Pride of Humanity in the face. Before long one could see the traces of the coming revelation on the Messenger of Allah. The Truthful Gabriel had come with the verse:

> Whoever disbelieves in Allah after having believed—not him who is under duress, while his heart is firm in and content with faith, but the one who willingly opens up his heart to unbelief— upon them falls Allah's anger (His condemnation of them), and for them is a mighty punishment. (an-Nahl 16:106)

This meant that those who were subjected to violence were not to be held responsible for the things their tongues had said but which that their hearts had not approved. Ammar breathed a sigh of relief; he had found peace in the presence of the Messenger and had almost forgotten all his pains and loss.

At the Home of Ibn Arqam

The polytheists came when Muslims prayed and always mocked them, always harassed them in the Prayers. That's why the Messenger of Allah and his Companions chose peaceful and remote places in order to be able to pray in peace, reading the Qur'an in silence. But the polytheists soon found out that this was the Muslims way of worship now and so they wanted to continue to harass them wherever they were.

It had been two years since revelations had started. The Companions had gathered once again at a remote place outside Mecca and they were performing their Prayers. A group of Meccans came and they started to tease them with words concerning their prayer. They were clearly trying to provoke the Muslims. They took it so far that what had started with mere words turned into physical confrontation. Sa'd ibn Abi Waqqas had given into his emotions for one moment and had started a fight with one of the polytheists; he had damaged the man in the head and the polytheist was covered in blood. The polytheists had been looking for an excuse, and this event gave them the opportunity they had been looking for.

The way things were developing did not look good for the Muslims. The Messenger of Allah who heard of what had happened was looking for a solution to the matter. He had been looking for a place where Muslims could pray comfortably and where the revelations that came would be shared in peace and the loyalty and bond to the Prophet could be established without harassment. One needed time so that the new buds and eggs could flourish and hatch, and one needed a peaceful place for this development. He did not want Muslims to waste time and energy confronting the polytheists, always being at their firing range.

Arqam ibn Abi'l-Arqam now had the opportunity to use his means for truth. He had a house on the hill of Safa and he had invited the noble Messenger and his Companions there. They could pray there peacefully, they could read the Qur'an and share the revelations that came. This was a very reasonable offer and so our noble Prophet accepted his invitation. A new process was thus beginning and the Messenger of Allah accepted the offer of Ibn Arqam, and moved to the house on the hill of Safa. This meant a new lease on a peaceful life that would last three years.

They were leaving bad neighbors behind, and with these new surroundings, a new color had come to Islamic development, there was a new momentum. Muslims were coming here secretly and were sharing the verses that had been revealed to the noble Prophet. They were engaging in deep conversation about faith and piety and they were burning with the need to help and hold the hands of others.

Utba's Plan

There was a new development every moment in Mecca; on the one hand the verses Truthful Gabriel was bringing were seeping through the town like ripples, on the other hand the Quraysh were confronting the believers with new traps. They had tried all the tricks in the book but had not been able to succeed, and now they were experiencing the defeat of having lost someone like Hamza to the believers. They could see that while the Muslims were getting stronger by way of numbers and by the ways in which they were putting Islam into practice; on the deniers kept losing blood.

Utba, who acted as their chief and ideologue, stood up one day and made a suggestion to his friends. At the time the Messenger of Allah was sitting in the Ka'ba, worshipping his Lord. Utba pointed to our noble Prophet and said: "O Quraysh, what do you say? Shall I go over and speak to Muhammad? Let me make some offers to him, who knows, maybe he'll accept some of them."

"Of course, O father of Walid! Go and speak to him!" his friends supported.

Utba had thus consulted with his tribe and then stood up and went straight to the Messenger of Allah. He approached our noble Prophet with great calm and peace; he seemed to be a different man from the Utba who had previously been foaming at the mouth with rage! He said to Allah's Messenger: "O son of my brother!"

There was no trace on him of a man who was going to enter faith, so why was it that he was approaching the Messenger so softly? He continued: "You know that your station among us and your tribe is very distinguished. But you have come with such suggestions to your tribe that you have made them go against each other, you have accused your elders of being in error, and you have been censuring their understanding of religion and their gods. In short, you have gone against everything that has been left by your forefathers. Now listen to me, I will have some propositions for you! Maybe you will accept them and then we can meet halfway."

The Messenger of Allah was listening to him very carefully; he was curious to see what kind of a proposition Utba would put forward—what could it be that it would end the enmity between them, making way for peace?

"Speak, O father of Walid," he said, "I am listening to you."

"O son of my brother, if you mean to make financial gains with the belief system you have been offering us, let us gather as much wealth among us as we can, and make you the richest among us. If with what you bring you mean to raise your honor and status in the society, let us make you our leader, and let us not take any steps without asking you. If what you are hoping to get is the throne, let us make you our king. But if all this is the working of the jinn or some kind of a dream you do not seem to be able to do away with, let us put our resources together and save you from it, for if not treated, a man will stay under the influence of the jinn."

The new plan of the Quraysh was clear. Our noble Prophet was at peace, but what were these men after! Utba took another step towards him and said: "Tell me O Muhammad, are you or your father Abdullah the better man?"

Our noble Prophet did not answer this question; he gave the best possible answer by staying silent. Utba, who had not received the answer he had wanted, continued to say the diabolical words: "If you should say that he was a better man than you, well, he worshipped the gods you so denigrate today. If you consider yourself to be the better man, then speak so that I can hear what you have to say."

Now it was the Prophet's turn to speak. The Messenger of Allah who had stayed silent till that point, asked: "Have you said your piece, O father of Walid?"

What else could he say?

"Yes," he said quietly, and then the Sultan of Speech took the word: "Then you listen to me now."

"Alright," Utba said.

With great respect he went down on his knees and said:

Ha. Mim. (This is) the Book being sent down in parts from the All-Merciful (Who embraces all beings with His Mercy), the All-Compassionate (Who has special mercy for the believers). A Book whose communications have been spelled out distinctly and made clear, and whose verses are in ordered sequence, a Qur'an (Recitation) in Arabic for a people who have knowledge (and so can appreciate excellence in the use of the language); (Being sent) as a bearer of glad tidings (of the recompense for faith and righteousness), and a warner (against the consequences of misguidance). Yet most of them (the Meccan people) turn away, and they do not give ear to it (being inwardly averse, and deaf to its excellence). They say: "Our hearts are wrapped in coverings against what you call us to, and in our ears is heaviness, and between us and you is a veil. So take action (such as is in your power), as we are taking action (such as we wish to take). (Fussilat 41:1–6)

The Messenger of Allah was reading and Utba was listening. When he came to the thirteenth verse, Utba could not take it anymore. He was shaking as if he had got the shingles. He brought his fingers to the munificent lips of the Messenger of Allah and said: "Stop, O Muhammad. Please stop for the love of Allah you believe in."

Our noble Prophet said: "So here it is Utba! You have heard what you have heard; it is now up to you to do as you like."

Utba was experiencing a great shock, what he had just heard had touched him to the bone. He was now embarrassed to have gone to the Prophet with petty propositions in the face of such a sturdy stance. Having received a great blow, he stood up and slowly walked to where his friends were.

Those who watched him coming defeated started to speak among themselves. Abu Jahl could not contain himself and said: "I swear that the father of Walid is coming with a face much different than the one he went away with!" pointing to the change in him.

Utba had reached them by then and they said: "Tell us, O father of Walid, what happened?" Upon him was still the shock he had just experienced. His eyes were fixed to a point and he managed to say: "I swear I have heard such words that I had never heard the like before. I swear it is neither poetry, nor magic nor soothsaying! O people of Quraysh! Come listen to what I say, let us lift the barriers between this man and what he wants to do! Leave him to his work! I swear by Allah that in the words I heard from him there is great news! If the Arabs win over him, people other than you will have decided the matter, but if the day comes when he wins over the Arabs, then his wealth will be your wealth, his honor will be your honor and then you will be the happiest of men."

The faces of those listening had turned sour, it was clear that they had not liked what they had heard. They could hardly contain themselves listening to such nonsense: "O father of Walid! He has bewitched you too, with his tongue," they said interpreting the matter. As they turned to leave, Utba called out: "This is my view of him; you can do as you please."

Then Utba went straight home. It was clear that he wanted to be left alone; for the verses that he listened to had struck him like lightening.

Later, Abu Jahl, the man who taught tricks even to the Satan, came to his door. He feared that Utba may start to believe and so he meant to pursue the matter. He knew very well Utba's weakness, he would use his pride as a weapon. He said: "O Utba! I heard that Muhammad was very nice and welcoming to you. I have heard that he has given you much to eat and drink, and that you were won over by this treatment. This is what people are talking about!"

Utba was angry. It seemed that Abu Jahl had hit the target once again. He stood up and said: "You all know that I do not need his food. I am the richest among you. But I have to say that what Muhammad has said had shaken me, for what he said was not poetry. Neither was it like soothsayers' words. I do not know what to say. He is a man who only speaks the truth. When I was listening to him I feared that what had befallen the tribes of Ad and Thamud would befall us as well."

Utba's plan had not worked. Before long the leading men of Mecca came together at the Ka'ba for a consultation regarding the new developments to devise new strategies, for the followers of Muhammad were increasing in number. The flood of faith had surged out of control, and it threatened to take hold of them as well, such that they would not be able to find a branch to hold onto.

The evil masterminds were all there—Utba, Shayba, Abu Sufyan, Nadr ibn Harith, Abu'l-Bakhtari, Aswad ibnu'l-Muttalib, Zam'a ibnu'l-Asad, Walid ibn Mughira, Abu Jahl, Abdullah ibn Abi Umayya, As ibn Wail, and Umayya ibn Khalaf. They had come together with the setting of the sun and were assessing the situation at the Ka'ba. One of them said: "Send word to Muhammad and speak to him! Speak all that is on your mind so that he may not have an excuse afterwards." Upon that they sent word: "The leading men of your tribe have got together and they are calling you, come at once," they said.

The Messenger of Allah hoped that this may be a sign that they wanted to accept the faith, so he came to the Ka'ba at once. He wanted them to believe so much! He was tired of their stubbornness. He was hoping that with this invitation he may open a new door. He came and sat next to them. They said: "O Muhammad! We have called you to sit down so we could have a good talk. Verily we have never seen a man who caused such strife and difference of opinion among the Arabs, someone who speaks so ill of his ancestors, who disparages the religious beliefs and gods of his forefathers. All these negative developments have happened after you appeared."

The attitude they assumed even when they started the conversation showed that his hopes were left to yet another spring. On top of these words, they repeated their usual slanders. They had accused the Messenger of Allah with their very own ills and then had left it at that—as if they were innocent! Then they brought the word to Utba's proposition and said similar things. They said: "If with this word you want to gain wealth among us, let us come together and collect wealth for you! If you want to be a man of high standing among us, let us appoint you our leader! If what you want is your own rule, then let us make you our King. If it is the jinn that are harassing you, and what you experience is some sort of bad dream you can't get rid of, then let us have you treated, you may or may not be saved from it, but we will have done our duty."

This was just too much! This was a scene that showed the difference between the two worlds. Those who ran after the world and worldly goods thought that they could stop the opening towards the afterlife; but they had failed once again. The Messenger of Allah who had listened to what was said with patience, said: "I suffer from none of the things you describe! My intention is neither to take your possessions, nor to rule over you! Allah sent me as Prophet to you and gave me a book from Him and then He told me to warn you of the future. I am fulfilling my duty of communicating this message to you and I advise you. If you accept what I offer you, this will be your greatest gain in this world and the next. If you do not accept it and close your ears to it, then I will do what Allah has told me to do and wait for him with patience to judge what has been between you and me."

There could not be a clearer statement than this. This basically meant "I leave your world to you; I am trying to save your afterlife." They tried to divert the subject to another dimension. One of them came to the fore and said: "O Muhammad! If you'll just allow us to speak to you about something, you know there is no one here that is poorer than us, more in need and less in possession. I mean to say no one that is more deserving of financial help. Supplicate with your Lord who sends you these revelations that He may flatten these mountains and that water may spring like the rivers of Damascus and Iraq! Also, pray that he may resurrect our ancestors that have gone before us like Qusayy ibn Kilab so that we may ask him whether what you say is true, for we know that he is a man who speaks the truth. If he approves and does what you say, we will accept you as well; we will have understood your standing with Allah, then we will accept that He has sent you as a Prophet."

The men were clearly making fun of the Messenger of Allah. This was nothing but arrogance and disrespect towards the Pride of Humankind. With the manner in which they were making fun of, they were not only making fun of the Messenger of Allah but Allah as well. Which of these statements could one possibly respond to? Even if he had, who was there to understand the response that our noble Prophet would give? These men did not even possess a single ounce of intellect! The best answer was surely silence.

The atmosphere froze. Despite everything, the noble Prophet was hoping that they may believe and so he wasn't closing the door entirely, for in such situations one had to show patience in the face of the madness of the times, to the severity of the addressees and the oppression of the environment. At least people could thus see the attitudes of both sides and judge for themselves and then one day could take the side of those who were with the Truth. Even if they should not come and submit themselves, there could be people in the families of these people who may one day come and become Muslims. The great had to show their stature. The Messenger of Allah spoke once again: "Allah did not send me to you to do these," and then added: "I have brought you what I am meant to bring to you and I have fulfilled the duty of communicating Allah's message. If you accept it, this will mean happiness for you in this world and the next. If you do not accept but reject, then I will wait with patience till Allah the Almighty judges among us."

It was clear that the pure soul of the Messenger of Allah had been thoroughly discomfited. How could he hide his discomfort at such a scene! He was trying to be brief in order to escape the feeling of suffocation that these people were giving him.

But the men wanted to hold him longer in conversation; they were having fun in their own way. One of them came to the fore again and started to say the following in the same manner: "If you are not going to do these for us; then ask your Lord to give you these things! He can send down an angel that verifies these things that you have been talking about, and that angel can give us information about you! Ask of Him to give you gardens and orchards like Paradise, palaces and mansions of gold and silver and put you in the class of the rich! You walk in the market like us, and you try to earn a living just like we do! If you were to become rich we would understand your worth for Allah, and if you are His Prophet like you claim to be, then we will have seen your standing with Him."

It was clear that the men had no shame any more. They were just having fun. The atmosphere was like that of a village green. People were thrusting themselves forward and saying whatever that came to their mouths. The Prophet of Mercy was keeping silent in patience. Even if he had an emotional response, his reason had the upper hand and he had to show patience. That is why he said: "*Subhanallah*! Allah is above and removed from all you say! I am only a Prophet! It would not be fitting for someone like me to ask something like that from his Lord! I was not sent to you for this! I was sent as a warner and a Messenger of good news. If you accept, you will gain both this world and the next. If you do not accept, then I will be patient till Allah the Almighty judges among you."

This time, like little children, everyone started asking something: "Put the skies under our feet so that we may believe you."

"O Muhammad! Does your Lord know that we are now sitting with you and that we are asking these from you? Come, let Him tell you of all these and teach us the truth of the matter."

"We have heard that a man called Rahman in Yamamah is teaching you all these. You also know that we will never believe Rahman."

"O Muhammad! You will have to bear with us because we will no let you be till you finish us, or we become victorious over you!"

"We worship the angels and they are the daughters of Allah."

"We will not believe you till you have brought Allah and the angels in front of our very eyes and show them to us."

A great commotion had ensued and everyone was speaking in disharmony on top of each other. This was no longer a meeting where people conversed; it was just a rowdy gathering. The Messenger of Allah stood up to leave. With him, Abdullah ibn Abi Umayya also stood up and said the following to the most beloved of Allah's servants: "O Muhammad! Your tribe has suggested certain things to you, but you did not accept any of them. They then requested things from you so that they may learn your standing with Allah and then follow you and accept you, but you did not answer their call either. They had propositions that could help you consolidate your standing but you didn't say yes to those either! They even told you to bring about the torment that you have been warning them about, but you didn't do it either! I swear that unless you climb a ladder up to the skies, and then bring things from there so that I may see them with my eyes, and then bring four angels to bear witness, I will never believe you. In fact I think I will not believe you even if you manage to do all this!"

The person saying these was our noble Prophet's cousin, the son of his aunt Atiqa. From his closest, he was hearing things that he wouldn't expect to hear even from those who were distant to him. The beloved Messenger stood up and then left for his peaceful home. He had come with such high hopes and with what sadness was he returning! He was left all alone. There was no one to defend him except for his

Lord. The Truthful Gabriel came to his aid at last. Allah the All-Mighty was saying the following in the verses that came:

> They say: "We will not believe in you (O Messenger), until you cause a spring to gush forth for us from this land (which is short of water); or you have a garden of date-palms and grapes, and cause rivers to gush forth in their midst abundantly; or you cause the heaven to fall upon us in pieces, as you have claimed (could happen), or bring Allah and the angels as a warrant (before our eyes proving the truth of your message); or you have a house of gold, or you ascend to the heaven. But we will even then not believe in your ascension until you bring down upon us (from heaven) a book that we can read." Say, (O Messenger): "All-Glorified is my Lord (in that He is absolutely above what you conceive of Him)! Am I anything but a mortal sent as a Messenger?" (al-Isra 17:90–93)

Thus as the Qur'an constructed a new society, it was right in the middle of all that was happening and at the aid of the Illustrious Beloved of Allah with Divine Will. The Messenger of Allah had experienced much discomfort, but now Gabriel had come and was declaring the sturdy ground on which he was standing, and teaching him the attitude he should adopt towards people.

In fact, even his enemies who tried to kill him knew that the Prophet was the Messenger of the time close to the Judgment Day; they knew that he was the awaited Messenger. But above and beyond this knowledge was their pharaoh-like pride, pitch-dark prejudice and stubbornness which prevented them from going and submitting themselves to Islam.

At a time when he was feeling somewhat conscientious, Mughira ibn Shuba recounted the following: "We were sitting with Abu Jahl. Muhammad the Trustworthy came where we were and communicated the message of Allah. Abu Jahl said arrogantly: 'O Muhammad! If you are doing all this to get witnesses for the afterlife to say that you have communicated these messages, do not tire yourself out, I will bear witness, now don't disturb me anymore.'

Saddened, Muhammad left our side once again. I asked Abu Jahl: 'Do you really believe him?'

He replied: 'I know that he is a Prophet. But there has always been a rivalry between us and the Hashimis. They keep bragging about their duty of serving the pilgrims, taking care of the Ka'ba's cover, offering Zamzam to the visitors. If now they also say 'The Prophet has come from among us' I don't think I can take it.'"

Another Proposition

One day the Messenger of Allah had come to the Ka'ba and was circumambulating the house of Allah. There he encountered with the leading figures of the Quraysh such as Aswad ibnu'l-Muttalib, Walid ibn Mughira, Umayya ibn Khalaf and As ibn Wail. It seemed they had made certain plans again and wanted to make new suggestions to our noble Prophet. They said: "O Muhammad! Come, we shall worship your God; but then you shall worship ours as well. Thus we will have come to an agreement! If the God you worship is munificent then we will have benefited, but if our gods are munificent, then you will have benefited as well."

What was it that they were trying to achieve with this? Had the Messenger of Allah accepted such a thing, would they have really worshipped Allah? Worship, being an obedient servant to Allah, required continuity; how could one explain the logic of turning one's face towards one direction and then another after a year or two? The Truthful Gabriel once again came to the rescue in order to silence all the deniers on this issue. The verses he brought said the following:

> Say: "O you unbelievers (who obstinately reject faith)! I do not worship that which you worship. Nor are you worshipping what I worship. Nor will I ever worship that which you worship, and nor will you ever worship what I worship. You have your religion (with whatever it will bring you), and I have my religion (with whatever it will bring me)." (al-Kafirun 109:1–6)

Umar Accepts Islam

It was a Wednesday evening. The Messenger of Allah had raised his hands for prayer in the house of Ibn Arqam in supplication to his Lord. He was so sincere and insistent that it drew the attention of those that were near him. He held up his hands high and wide at the sky, his eyes fixed to the heavens. This is what he was asking for: "O Allah! Whichever is dearer to you, let your religion be exalted with him; Umar ibn al-Khattab or Amr ibn Hisham (Abu Jahl)!"

Umar ibn al-Khattab was the more aggressive of the two men; he was very courageous and he feared no one. It was these attitudes that he had inherited from his father. That is why his brother in law and sister had kept away from him after they had become Muslims. They were performing the Prayers and reading the Qur'an without letting anyone know, and they were secretly communicating the message of the Qur'an.

Umar was watching the developments from afar, and even though he did not become Muslim by throwing off the weight of social pressure, he at least thought that the people who chose this religion were people of virtue. One evening, he had come to the Ka'ba to spend the night there. Meanwhile, the Messenger of Allah came there and started to read the Qur'an. He was reading Surah al-Haqqa.

Umar was hearing it for the first time and he was attracted by the beauty of the words. He had to find fault with it somehow in order to shake off its effect, and like the Quraysh, he said: "He's a poet." But the voice continued: *"And not a poet's speech (composed in a poet's mind). How little is what you believe!"* (al-Haqqa 69:41).

This was strange indeed! What he had thought of had immediately been answered. This time he thought, "He's a soothsayer." But the voice continued: *"Nor is it a soothsayer's speech (pretending to foretell events). How little it is that you reflect and be mindful! (It is so limited by the poverty of your minds)"* (al-Haqqa 69:42).

The Messenger of Allah had thus read the chapter to the end and Umar had listened to it in great astonishment and curiosity. He thought long and hard. There was great calm and flow in his mind. But these weren't enough to put Umar into action and to make him change sides. The next morning he was with his old friends again, back to his old habits.

Amr ibn Hisham (Abu Jahl) was a man who took pleasure in opposing the Messenger of Allah at every opportunity and preventing each development that would be in favor of religion. Our noble Prophet had tried hard to invite him to Islam; he had gone to his door many times but had always been met with insults, and at times, a spat on the face. Still, the Messenger of Allah continued to try to communicate Allah's message to Abu Jahl, kept him in his prayers so that Allah may place faith in his heart.

But these prayers would be answered for Umar and Abu Jahl would be the one to lose out. The day following our noble Prophet's prayer, Umar had turned towards the hill of Safa.

He was going in the direction of Ibn Arqam's house with his sword hanging by his waist, with the intention of doing some harm to the believers gathered there. On the way he met another Companion, Nuaym ibn Abdullah who was hiding the fact that he had become Muslim. The scene he saw worried Nuaym; Umar was so enraged that one could almost see him breathing out steam through his nose. He had to be stopped and the Muslims had to be protected from his malice.

He asked: "Where are you going, O Umar?"

"I am going to kill the *sabi* Muhammad who puts the Quraysh against each other, who slanders and censures their ancestors and gods."

Nuaym had been right about his worries; Umar had bad intentions and he had set off to put these intentions into practice, heading towards the house of Ibn Arqam. He had to do everything he can to convince him to turn away. The first argument that came to his mind was that his sister and brother in law had embraced Islam: "You have deceived yourself Umar! You are leaving the sons of Abdimanaf to themselves and are on your way to kill Muhammad? First go to your own house and handle that business."

Umar was shocked. This could not be! No member from his household could have become a Muslim without his knowing! He asked immediately: "What is there in my own home? Do you mean...?"

Yes, there were those in his family who had visited this sweet water spring and had drank from it till their hearts desired. But Umar had been unaware of this and was now pressuring Nuaym to reveal who it was. At last Nuaym chose the lesser of the two evils and gave the names of his relatives in order to change Umar's direction and buy some time.

"Your brother in law and cousin Said ibn Zayd and your sister Fatima bint al-Khattab... I swear that they too have become Muslims and are following Muhammad. They entered his religion. You should first see to your own business," he said to Umar.

A bolt of lightning struck in Umar's head. How could it be that people from his own home had gone and been swept by this tide? He had to do something about it immediately and so he changed direction. He went with flying speed. But this time his target was not the Messenger of Allah but his sister and brother in law.

He was just about to knock on the door when he heard a deep voice resonating from the inside. This was a voice that was reminiscent of the night he had spent at the Ka'ba. Although the owner of the voice was different, it was obvious that it came from the same source. This was the voice of Habbab ibn Arat: "*Ta-Ha. We did not send down this Qur'an to you so that you may have hardship...*" (Ta-Ha 20:1–2), the voice continued.

Even though he was not aware of it yet, the great Umar's heart had already started to melt.

But it didn't look like he would submit so easily. He gathered himself and started to pound the mallet of the door. He was also shouting at the top of his lungs, telling the people inside to open the door. The household was seized with worry when they heard Umar's voice at the door. It was clear why he had come. They hid Habbab, who was teaching them the Qur'an at the time, somewhere in the house. Umar's sister

The Luminous Life of Our Prophet

Fatima hid the verses of the Qur'an under her knees. When it was fit for Umar to see the house, they opened the door, their hair standing on end.

Umar was a very clever man; he had already become suspicious when the door opened late. He asked at once: "What was that voice I heard a minute ago?" They tried to convince him that he had heard nothing.

"No, I did," he said and then came towards them in rage.

He was mumbling in anger and he said: "I heard that you entered the religion of Muhammad and that you are now his followers," and not able to contain his rage, he pounced on his brother in law Said ibn Zayd and hit him. When his sister Fatima tried to stop him, he also hit her. It was difficult to stand the blows of someone like Umar; she was covered in blood. But this was the start of another attempt for her. There was nothing she felt she could lose anymore. Now her brother knew everything anyway. Fatima was made of the same mettle as his brother as member of the Khattab family. There was no sense in hiding it anymore so she stood up to her brother and exclaimed: "Yes, we have become Muslim! What is there in that? We have submitted in faith to Allah and His Messenger. Now you can do as you like." This was the third blow for Umar. It would have been unthinkable that someone should talk back to him like that under normal circumstances. Least of all a woman! How could his sister talk back to him like that and show such attitude? There was an aggressive silence. Umar looked long and hard at his sister; although she was covered in blood, there was nobility in her stance. She looked like an injured lioness and yet she was still after her honor. There was a dare in her stare: "What if you kill us? We have found true peace with Muhammad." This dare seemed to have worked on Umar. For Umar to understand, it seemed that his brother in law and sister had to be subjected to violence by him. It was fate's work that Umar would start to melt at the house of his sister after having opposed Islam till that day. He sincerely regretted what he had done. The change in Umar surfaced when he called out to his sister: "Give me the pages that you were reading as I was coming here, let me look at what it is that Muhammad has come with." They were surprised. They hesitated as to whether or not to give them to him, for Umar could take the verses and rip them, start slandering the Qur'an and say unseemly things about the beloved Prophet. That is why Fatima said: "We fear that you will do some evil."

"Do not fear," said Umar, and then he assured her that he would give the pages back without damaging it in any way.

His sister, who had been beaten till blood was drawn, was overjoyed and she could sense that his brother was slowly coming towards Islam. She knew him well... Umar was beginning to unravel. That is why she took another step: "O my brother! You are still in the dirt of *shirk,* the unclean cannot touch the Qur'an."

Fatima told him about the *ghusl* (the major ablution), for what he was about to hold was the Word of Allah and it had be held in a way that would be pleasing to Allah.

This was a great test for Umar. But after this blow, he had already caved in and made his last decision. He went and took ablution like his sister described. The gloom of a while ago had left its place to the peace of Paradise, one could see the happiness on their faces.

Meanwhile, Fatima had given Umar the pages on which chapter Ta-Ha was written, and he started reading. At one point he could not contain himself and said: "What beautiful words! What sweet expressions!"

Habbab ibn Arat who could hear Umar reading the Qur'an and observe his response to it from where he was hidden could hardly stop himself from crying out the *takbir*, the proclamation of the greatness of Allah. The prayer that had been made only last night from Ibn Arqam's house was fresh in their memories. How amazing that a prayer should be answered so quickly! Here was one of the Umar's already at the presence of the Qur'an! This was what Habbab was observing from where he was hiding. Before long, he could not stop himself from coming out from where he was hiding. He walked up to Umar and said: "O Umar, I believe you have been the recipient of the prayer of the Messenger of Allah! Only yesterday I heard him say 'O Allah! Please validate your religion with one of the two Umars. Umar ibn al-Khattab or Amr ibn Hisham.' I swear by Allah you are him, O Umar."

Umar was experiencing two surprises at the same time. First of all, what was Habbab doing here? And secondly, where had he been till now? Why had he hidden and why was he coming now to say these things? The second surprise was the greatness of the Messenger of Allah whom he had come armed just hours ago to kill. There could be no greater difference in the outcome. He had come with the intention to kill him, and he was, unbeknownst to him, praying for his deliverance to his Lord, that he may come into the faith. What magnificence is this!

The great Umar was now humbled. He turned to Habbab and said: "O Habbab! Can you tell me where Muhammad is? I want to go to him right now."

"He is with his friends in a house on Safa hill right now," Habbab said.

Now the destination of Umar was clear. In fact it was the same destination as the one he had set out that morning, but amazingly now, the intention was different.

Before long, Umar was knocking on the door of Ibn Arqam. The Companions of the Prophet looked through the keyhole and when they saw that it was Umar they ran to the noble Prophet in excitement and fear:

"O Messenger of Allah! Umar is at the door and he is armed."

Hamza came forward:

"Let him come in, O Messenger of Allah! If he means well, then we will embrace him, but if he has bad intentions we will take his sword and kill him with it!"

The Messenger of Allah was not thinking otherwise. It was him who had said that prayer was the greatest weapon, and it was him who had prayed for Umar. Naturally Allah the Almighty would not leave His Beloved alone in such dire circumstances and would answer his call. Our noble Prophet was feeling deep gratitude for the acceptance of his prayer and said to them: "Let him come in."

He then stood up from where he was sitting. He wanted to welcome Umar standing. The door opened and the heavily built Umar came in. The Messenger of Allah welcomed him with affection. Such warmth and love could only be found in Paradise. The Pride of Humankind first embraced Umar and then said: "Where have you been until now, O son of Al-Khattab! I swear by Allah that I had started to think that you were not going to come until some trouble would touch you."

"Here I am, O Messenger of Allah! I am here to submit in faith to Allah, His Messenger and what comes from Him."

From the house of Ibn Arqam on Safa hill, a *takbir* started echoing towards Mecca, and these words proclaiming Allah's greatness continued to resonate through the night. The Companions who had witnessed the supplication of the Messenger of Allah the night before, including the Messenger himself could not contain themselves and they were also calling out the *takbir*, proclaiming the greatness of Allah in unison. This was a fitting way to welcome the great Umar into the faith! The coming of Umar signified the start of a new period. The Companions of the Messenger of Allah who now had another force like Hamza beside them, were leaving the house of Ibn Arqam with their *takbir* into Mecca from Safa hill. The coming of Umar had given extra zeal to the Companions, with him a Muslim by their side they would now be walking with more pride; they would now be performing their Prayers more easily and they would not worry about being heard as they used to when they were reading the Qur'an. Just like ibn Mas'ud had said, Umar's coming to Islam meant a conquest for religion.

Umar had indeed become Muslim, but it seemed he did not feel comfortable unless he let everyone know the change he had just gone through. That is why he turned to the Pride of Humankind and said: "O Messenger of Allah! Why are we hiding our faith even though we are in the right? They are in error and they have no qualms about making it public."

Our noble Prophet was a man of patience and caution. Just as he had cautioned Abu Bakr, he also said to Umar: "O Umar, you see what we already have to put up with. We do not have enough numbers to be able to do as you suggest yet."

"I swear by Allah who sent you in Truth that I will go to all the circles I used to attend before and will declare my faith to them," and thus he left the house of Ibn Arqam. The first place he went to was the Ka'ba. First he circumambulated it to show the error in the way people had been worshipping in the Ka'ba. Then he went to the Quraysh. It was clear that they had expected him to come. Abu Jahl came forward: "So you have become *sabi*," he said mockingly

Umar roared: "I swear there is no deity but Allah and that Muhammad is His servant and Messenger."

They could not stand to hear these words, even if it did come from someone whom they had called friend only yesterday, and they all pounced on him.

But Umar was a force to be reckoned with. Utba was the first to attack him and he took him down in no time. He had put his finger in Utba's eye, and Utba was crying out of pain, his cry echoing throughout Mecca. It was clear they would not be able to beat him easily; it seemed that Umar was even more powerful than before. The crowd around him dispersed at once. Umar was now walking in the streets of Mecca, representing the pride of Islam and no one was able to challenge him.

He visited all the circles he used to visit in order to keep the promise he had made in the presence of the Messenger of Allah and he even let the deaf know about the beauties of Islam. Still, the Messenger of Allah was worried. When he saw him come, he asked delicately what had happened. Umar started to speak with the satisfaction of someone who had carried out his duty: "May my mother and father be sacrificed for you, O Messenger of Allah! There is nothing to be worried about! I swear by Allah that I visited all the circles I used to frequent before I was honored with Islam and I declared my faith without fear for anyone."

The Migration to Abyssinia

F ive years had passed since the coming of the first revelation. It was the month of Rajab. The house of Ibn Arqam as a temporary sanctuary had met their needs to a certain degree, for there was now a place where believers could speak about issues concerning their faith in a peaceful environment. But this environment was limited to the one house only; people who left the house were being followed and especially those who were weak and had no protection were being subjected to increasing violence. With each passing day the Meccans were becoming even more merciless and they were giving no space to the Muslims to live according to their belief. Hence, there was need for a more fundamental solution. In the meanwhile, Allah the Almighty had shown a way to the believers through the Truthful Gabriel:

> O My servants who believe: Keep from disobedience to your Lord in reverence for Him and piety. For those devoted to doing good in this world, aware that Allah is seeing them, there is good (by way of recompense), and Allah's earth is vast (enabling worship). Those who are patient (persevering in adversity, worshipping Allah, and refraining from sins) will surely be given their reward without measure. (az-Zumar 39:10)

The verse was not giving a clear order of migration to everyone, but spoke of the ease and comfort such a journey may

The Luminous Life of Our Prophet

afford for living a religious life. Since the world was a vast place; then one had to take advantage of such vastness. Accordingly, the Messenger of Allah would offer the following suggestion: "I wish you could go to Abyssinia, for that is a safe place; and there is a king there under whom no one is oppressed!"

Abyssinia was a known place for Mecca as there was quite a lot of traffic between the two places due to trade. There was a general knowledge about Abyssinia in Mecca due to these visits. That is why the believers were encouraged to go to this land, the land of Najashi (the Negus).

A mere gesture of our noble Prophet would set masses into motion. He was now saying that it was safer to go and live in Abyssinia, and he was encouraging the believers to go in that direction. That is why preparations were now underway and fifteen people, including four women, set for the road in order to escape being the target of violence in Mecca and to be able to live their religion more freely. Among them was the son in law of the Messenger of Allah, Uthman. Naturally, this journey would be made without the knowledge of the Quraysh. In the darkness of the night they set out away from Mecca towards a new world. This was the first migration. It was not clear what would happen but such concerns were hardly important. When it was Him Who led, what could they possibly worry about! They came to the shores of the peninsula, some on animals, and some on foot. It was Divine will that had decreed that they should go on this journey. They met two ships that were waiting at the shore, and with the price of half a dinar, they bought their passage into Abyssinia.

On the other hand in Mecca, the absence of leading believers who left for Abyssinia, such as Uthman and his wife

Ruqayyah, Mus'ab ibn Umayr, Abdurrahman ibn Awf, Abu Salama and his wife Umm Salama and Uthman ibn Maz'un, was greatly being felt. The Quraysh sent men after them to seek and find them. But they were too late, for when they reached the shore, the ships had already set off and the believers had already set sail for a peaceful land.

At last they reached Abyssinia, a place where neither the judgments of Abu Jahl and Abu Lahab, nor the insults of Utba and Shayba, nor the harassment of Uqba and Umayya could follow them! At once all the obstructions that they had faced to live their belief when they were in Mecca had disappeared; they could now pray in peace and read the Qur'an in rapture.

The Messenger of Allah had for a long time not been able to receive any news of those who had gone to Abyssinia, and he was wondering what had become of them. At last a woman who came from those parts said that he had seen Uthman and Ruqayyah. The news brought joy to the Illustrious Beloved of Allah, peace and blessings be upon him, and he said: "Verily Uthman and his wife are the third household to have migrated after the household of Ibrahim and Lot."

This first journey happened in the month of Rajab. Two more months passed. On a day in Ramadan, the Messenger of Allah came to the Ka'ba again and he was worshipping his Lord. A crowd gathered around him once again to observe what he was doing. The Messenger of Allah then started to read the Qur'an wholeheartedly. He was reading Surah an-Najm. These eloquent words that came to the ears attracted the attention of those present and they were listening to him in pure concentration. Till that day, there had always been someone who made noise as the verses of the Qur'an were being read, always someone who would divert people's attention.

This was probably the first time people could listen to it uninterrupted to appreciate its beauty and wonder. Everyone had forgotten their original intentions and was completely enraptured by the sweet melody of the Qur'an. This Divine articulation was cleaning away the dirt and the rust in minds, and it was transforming them into new people. When the Messenger of Allah read the verse of *sajda*, in which the prostration was mentioned, he went down to prostrate. Amazingly, all those listening to him also went to prostrate with the Messenger of Allah without questioning what they were doing! It was as though it had not been them who had declared war on this word and to the Messenger of Allah who was delivering it to them. It looked as if the Lord of the Ka'ba had shown a scene from what was to come to the Meccans.

Of course there were others who were watching this scene from afar, and because they had not been close enough, they could not interpret the meaning of what they were seeing and were censuring the Meccans who had prostrated themselves with the Messenger of Allah. This was a censure that called the people to the status of *kufr*, disbelief that they had been in, and before long many of them would say that they had been bewitched and they turned back. But news of this scene had reached Abyssinia in a very different manner and out of context, only as what had appeared to the onlookers. According to the news that spread, the Meccans had now all become Muslim! Then what reason was there to be away from the Messenger of Allah, peace and blessings be upon him! If the

Meccans had become Muslim, that meant the town no longer held any dangers or oppression for them.

Yes, they were very happy indeed, but they marveled at the news. How could the hatred and rancor that they had encountered change so drastically within the space of two months? How could these cold, hard hearts have softened and gone down in prostration in the presence of their Lord? But they reasoned that when Allah willed, everything was possible and so they decided to return to Mecca at once.

They once again boarded the ship and reached the opposite side of the shore. Unlike before, now they were walking with the excitement and the prospect of reuniting with our noble Prophet, with Mecca, the Ka'ba, their brethren in belief, their families and their homes. But when they came within an hour's journey to Mecca they finally understood how things really were in Mecca! They had been the victims of a huge misunderstanding! This was a difficult situation indeed! They wavered for a while between going back to Abyssinia and going to Mecca for a little while. Then some of them decided to go back to Abyssinia and some decided to push on towards Mecca.

Yes, those who chose to return to Abyssinia had been saved once again, but they had not been able to see the Messenger of Allah to whom they had come so close! They had not been reunited with their friends in the Ka'ba to converse with them. But at least they had been spared the wrath of the Meccans, and before long, they were back to a land where they could perform their Prayers in peace. Some of those who came to Mecca had found refuge with people who could give them protection for a while. But the others had returned to

The Luminous Life of Our Prophet

days of hardship that were even worse than before. The Meccans knew that they had tried to escape and now they were trying to inflict even more injury, verbally and physically, wherever they saw them.

When he heard that the Meccans were migrating to Abyssinia, Mus'ab ibn Umayr had also found a way to escape his imprisonment and joined those who had migrated. He was thus among the first who had migrated in the way of Allah, and was now free of the aggression of his mother and the censure of his father. But now the period of peace he had experienced in Abyssinia was over and he had returned to Mecca.

This was a great opportunity for his mother who tried to lock him up again when he came home. But they were both very adamant, and they were both shedding tears. His mother was crying because she felt she was losing her son for what she considered was an empty cause, and he was upset about his mother who had closed her heart to the Truth and who was insistent on making life very difficult for him. This strife between a young man of faith and his enraged mother was the struggle between dead set denial and steadfastness in faith.

The situation would continue till she expelled her son from the house. Hunas ibn Malik was a woman who could not consider someone who did not listen to her word as her son. One day she had totally become enraged. She had once again insisted, but Mus'ab had not prostrated in front of the various idols, and he had not denied Allah. Her rage overshadowed her feelings as a mother and she said: "Do as you please. I am no longer your mother."

She deprived Mus'ab of everything. As she expelled her son from her home and bolted the doors, she also bolted her heart against faith. Just as it was difficult for a mother to be separated from her son, it was equally unbearable that a son should leave his mother alone to her devices on this "eternal journey." Mus'ab was not going to forsake his own mission for worldly cares. What did wealth and possessions mean to him? He had no concerns for worldly goods or his future. His one and only care had become the faith of people; that people should believe, starting from his own mother. He pleaded with his mother: "Dear mother! Please listen to me once! Come and believe that there is no deity but Allah and that Muhammad is His servant and Messenger."

The invitation was sweet and soft, but the response to it was equally hard and without compromise: "I swear by the stars, never! I have lost neither my mind nor my conscience that I should enter your religion."

His efforts were yielding no results, and so he bid his farewell and left his mother's home. He had been expelled from what was before his warm hearth, but now he was going to set up camp in the warmest of hearts! He came to the presence of the Messenger of Allah submitted himself and never left again.

From now on Mus'ab was like the other Companions; he dressed in rough clothes that he could find, sometimes with a full stomach, but too often suffering from hunger. He had now entered the ranks of the poor and slaves like the Habbabs and Bilals. His skin, which he was used to adorn with beautiful scents and lotions, had now become crinkly and was peeling off in places.

One day he was coming to the gathering from afar. The Messenger of Allah was watching him approach with some of the other Companions. Mus'ab's worn-out but peaceful state had brought tears to the eyes, heads were bowed down, and everyone was sad together! For Mus'ab was in old and worn-out clothes. This was a heart-rending sight to see for those who knew his state before Islam. Bilal had always been poor. Habbab and Ammar had never been rich; they were used to poverty! But Mus'ab was never like that. The Messenger of Allah was deeply moved by what he saw and started to say the following: "I used to see Mus'ab before as well. There was no man more powerful than him in Mecca when he was with his mother and father. He left all that for Allah and His Messenger and came here."

Mus'ab did not care the slightest bit about all that had befallen him since he had embraced Islam, for clothes could not give man peace. If there was no faith in a heart, what enveloped the body was continued torment. He had one goal, to hold firm onto a medium that reached out beyond the skies in the name of faith. He was getting deeper in this understanding day by day, he was continually making progress. He was memorizing the verses that came day by day, he was learning the fine aspects of his religion from the Perfect Guide, peace and blessings be upon him, and he was trying to live according to the principles he was learning.

Second Hijra to Abyssinia

The troubles that the Muslims faced grew with each passing day and at last the noble Messenger said that the solution might be in migrating to Abyssinia once again. He had received news about how those who had gone before were treated and that is why the Messenger of Allah was encouraging his followers to go to Abyssinia to experience a peace that had not yet been instated in Mecca. But those leaving wanted to see the Messenger among them. That is why Uthman said the following: "O Messenger of Allah! We went with the first group and here we are going to Najashi once again! We wish you were coming with us!"

"You thus migrate to both Allah and me, thus you'll get the reward of two hijras."

"This suffices for us, O Messenger of Allah."

Now it was time to set off. But this was a road that the polytheists also knew, and they had taken their precautions this time to be careful to not let them escape. This time, a bigger group was planning to go, so they had to be extra careful in order for people to not learn about their plan and they had to move very cautiously without leaving things to chance.

Then one evening they set on the road again and the journey towards the shore started. This time there were a hundred people, eighteen of them women.

Despite all the precaution, the Quraysh were worried to hear that the Muslims had left. They knew the result of Muslims' migration last time and the way Najashi had treated them. This time the number of people going was much greater. The Quraysh were thus facing a big problem, for an issue they had not been able to solve by themselves had now taken on an international dimension, becoming harder to solve! The whole thing was spiraling out of their control. Their backs had already broken by having lost both Hamza and Umar, for the two of them had given much strength to the other front. Now the issue was also developing on grounds that were totally removed from them. They gathered together to discuss the issue in a way to find a permanent solution. They agreed that it was essential that they should convince Najashi to turn the Muslims over to them. They chose two men from among themselves to see to this business. These were Amr ibnu'l-As and Abdullah ibn Abi Rabia. Both of them were men who knew how to speak in front of kings and who knew Najashi well. The Quraysh did not want to leave things to chance so they kept explaining to the two men about how they should behave. They were also preparing very special gifts for Najashi and the influential people around him. They were even making plans as to how these gifts should be offered. They suggested that first gifts should be given to the king's men, they should be won over and then Najashi's gift should be given so that he may be persuaded to turn over the Muslims to them.

According to the plan, first the circles around the king, the viziers and clerics would be persuaded and then these men would support the plea of the men of Quraysh. Then Najashi would agree with the general sentiment and hand the Muslims over to them.

Meanwhile, the Messenger of Allah sent a letter to Najashi with Amr ibn Umayya and requested him to provide protection for Jafar ibn Abi Talib and his friends who had gone to seek refuge in Abyssinia. This meant that the relations between the Muslims and Abyssinia were not only superficial, but that there was correspondence based on knowledge between the two parties. There was continuous flow of information, and the Messenger of Allah was trying to prevent any risks that the migrating Muslims may face. The letter read:

"In the Name of Allah, the All-Merciful, the All-Compassionate.

From Muhammad, Messenger of Allah, to Najashi of Asham.

May Allah's peace be upon you! This letter occasions me to give thanks to Allah who is Mu'min, The Supreme Author of safety and security Who bestows faith and removes doubt, and Muhaymin, the All-Watchful Guardian. I bear witness that Jesus, son of Mary is a soul and word from Allah that He has given to Pure and virtuous Mary. He the Almighty created Jesus who Mary was pregnant with, from His own soul and breath, just as He created Adam with the power of His own Hand, and exalted breath. I invite you to Allah and the friendship of Allah Who is One, and has no likeness; I invite you to follow me and believe in what I bring from Truth, for I am the Messenger of Allah. I send you my cousin Jafar ibn Abi Talib and a group of Muslims with him. When they come to you, show them your hospitality and let them stay in your land, do not make things harder for them. Verily I invite you and your army to Allah. I have done my duty and have communicated the Word of Allah to you, given you my advice; accept this from me!"

After he took and read the letter of the Messenger of Allah Najashi wrote a letter back expressing his feelings and sent it to Mecca. The letter contained the following:

"To Muhammad, the Messenger of Allah, from Najashi of Ashama ibn al-Abjar.

May Allah's peace, bounty and grace be upon you, O Messenger of Allah! There is no deity but He, and He has shown me the right way with Islam! Your letter and what you say about Jesus has reached me O Messenger of Allah! I swear by the Lord of the heaven and earth that Jesus did not say anything other than what you yourself say. We have benefited much from what you have sent us and what your cousin and those in his company have told us. I bear witness that you are the Messenger of Allah, truthful and consolidating what has come before you. I am now your follower; I have submitted to the Lord of the universes in the presence of your cousin. I send you my son Ariha ibn Asham ibn al-Abjar. I am king of myself only; and if you decree that I should come to you, I will do that, too, O Messenger of Allah! I know that all that you say is true."

As can be understood from Najashi's letter, he had responded to the call of the Messenger of Allah saying that he would offer protection to the Muslims that came to his land, and what's more was that he was saying he was ready to leave his throne if the Messenger decreed it so. This correspondence alone, as a multifaceted strategy, is precedent for people who want to walk along the same path.

Sending the two men was a propaganda campaign on the part of the Quraysh in order to create an atmosphere that would be favorable to their claims. It seemed probable that their campaign would yield results. When he heard this campaign of the Quraysh, the heart of a loving uncle, Abu Talib, was moved again. But this time he was going to act not only for the sake of his nephew Muhammad, peace and blessings be upon him, but also those who were in Abyssinia who had put faith in him, including his own son Jafar. Using the power of poetry, the following is the poem that Abu Talib wrote to Najashi in Abyssinia expressing his concerns:

"I wish I'd known.

Why does Amr act in enmity towards my son Jafar although they are relatives?

Will Najashi receive Jafar and his friends with goodness?

Or will his hospitality be prevented by something that encourages evil?

I wish I'd known.

But I know, O King!

I know that you are a man wary of evil, an honorable and generous man.

I know those who seek refuge with you always find peace in your presence.

I know that Allah has given you great worldly and spiritual wealth; you are also the possessor of all the routes of goodness.

And I know that you are a generous man who likes to give.

So don't let these aggressive relatives of ours take advantage of your virtue and do evil against you!"

The Luminous Life of Our Prophet

As can be seen, it wasn't only his nephew Muhammad, peace and blessings be upon him, or his son Jafar that Abu Talib was trying to protect; he was also thinking of those who had put faith in him, and he was hoping to reach beyond the seas with his voice. While the Meccans were trying to make those who had migrated come back, Abu Talib was thinking that his son would be safer in Abyssinia, and leaving aside a father's longing for his son, he wanted him to stay there. He was letting his wishes be known through poetry, the most effective means of communication at the time, trying to influence Najashi before he would make his decision.

At last the Muslims had arrived in Abyssinia once again and they had started to perform their Prayers in peace, reading their Qur'an to their heart's content. Before long the two envoys of the Quraysh arrived with their hands full of gifts. First they started to give presents to the clerics and influential people in the palace, just like the elders of Mecca had advised them to. To everyone they spoke to, they asked them to support them with their cause in persuading the king to send the Muslims back to their country. This is what they were saying: "Certain runaway youths from our country are now in the country of the king; these are people who have abandoned their religion and yet not adopted your religion either, they have a new religion neither you, nor I, know of. We will go to the king and ask him to hand them over to us. What we ask of you is that when we bring up the subject you should support us, and to let him hand these people over to us without letting them speak. The whole of Mecca is waiting to see how this business will develop."

They were approaching the matter rather stealthily, making themselves appear innocent. They were also provoking the listeners against Muslims by saying things like: "These are people who have caused chaos in their homeland and have set people against each other; now they have come here to cause anarchy in your land. They will deceive your children and will degenerate your religion, they will shake your authority," posing as concerned people who had come to warn them. That is why all the people they spoke to said: "Alright, we will help you."

They had thus visited every important personage in the kingdom and now it was time to go to Najashi, give him his presents and approach the subject. The necessary appointments had been made and Najashi accepted the representatives of Mecca for a hearing.

After salutations and the usual well-wishes, Amr ibnu'l-As and Abdullah ibn Abi Rabia came to the point. They were saying: "O King! We heard that some runaway youths from our land have left the religion of their tribe and come and sought refuge in your country. The truth is they have not accepted your religion either; they follow a religion neither you, nor I, know of! In due respect for our grandfathers and glorious forefathers, we ask you to hand them over to us, for the eyes of our ancestors are upon these youths; they know what these youths are doing; they see where this business is going."

As they said these to Najashi, the eyes of Amr and Abdullah were searching for the faces of those who were present to see their expressions and how their preplanned pitch was going. They did not like what they saw on Najashi's face; they could see that he was not listening to them wholeheartedly, as if he viewed the matter differently. But since they had taken the matter so far, they did not want to return empty handed. That is why they were making eye contact with the clerics and the viziers and trying to gain their support before the king said a final "No." They were also planning to provide the king with certain information about the Muslims to prejudice the king against them before the possibility of the King summoning them to his presence. They said that the Muslims did not greet people like others, that they would not recognize the authority of the king and would not prostrate before him. This was when one of their supporters, a priest, came to their aid, and said: "O King! They tell the truth! The eyes and ears of their tribe are upon these people; it would be best if we hand these people to them so that they settle their own accounts."

Najashi, who had been silent till that point, was now angry. Matters of state required seriousness. It would not be in keeping with the principles of justice to judge according to the claims of a couple of people without giving those accused to speak for themselves. If he had not cared for the principles of justice, his land would not have become one where innocent people sought refuge in. With these in mind, he started to say the following: "No, it cannot be! I swear I will never hand them over to you. These are people who have chosen to come to this country among others, and they have preferred my justice so I cannot hand them over to these two men listening solely to what they have said. I have to listen to them; if the situation is as these two men say, then I will hand them over. But if the situation is different, then I will not hand them over, instead, I will provide them with more opportunities to stay in my land and help them live their according to their belief."

Dead silence ensued. This was much different from what the representatives of Mecca had hoped for. They had played so many tricks in order to put pressure on Najashi and yet none of them had worked, for the king was acting only as it pleased him. But they were not going to give up so easily.

Meanwhile, Najashi had summoned the Muslims living in his land to his presence as he wanted to hear them speak their piece as well. When the invitation from Najashi came to them, the believers who were informed about the situation started to talk among themselves: "What will we say to this man when we go to his presence?"

"I swear by Allah that we will say what we know; we will say what the Messenger of Allah has told us beforehand having already seen what will come to pass!"

At last they came to the court of the king and started to wait. There was a difference even in their entrance and this had not escaped the attention of those present; they were saluting people, but unlike others, they were not prostrating themselves in front of the king! Najashi turned to them and started to ask the following: "Tell me, O people, why have you come here, what is your situation and why have you chosen me? You are not men of trade, and you do not bring a petition either in the name of your country or for yourselves. Who is this Messenger of yours who has appeared, and what is the truth of this matter? Why have you not saluted me like other people? What is your view of Jesus, son of Mary? What is this religion of yours for whose sake you have abandoned the religion of your tribe and not entered mine or any other religion that you may have encountered here?"

Jafar ibn Abi Talib Takes Word

Meanwhile Najashi had called his clergy near him and had made them lay basic texts of religion open before him. It was clear that he was going to compare the novelties that Islam was bringing in the name of religion with what his own understanding was, and then reach a conclusion. That is why a very appropriate reply had to be given to him to cover all his questions and hesitations. After a brief pause, Jafar ibn Abi Talib stepped forward and said: "O King! We saluted you with the salutation of the Messenger of Allah. This is the salutation of the inhabitants of heaven; with it we find new life in our inner worlds. We only go down to *sajda* in prostration before Allah, we seek refuge in Him from having to prostrate to others," thus clarifying two of the points Najashi had raised.

Then he changed the direction of the conversation and said to the King: "I beseech you to ask these men of Quraysh the following three questions."

"Ask," said Najashi.

"Are we slaves who have fled their masters that they are here to hand us back to our masters?"

This was an unexpected question indeed and Najashi turned to the Qurayshis: "Were these slaves, O Amr?" he asked.

Although they wanted to kill the Muslims, there and then, they had no choice but to tell the truth. Unwillingly and rather forcefully, they said: "No, in fact they are generous people."

The first round was over. Jafar asked the second question: "Will you ask them, O King, whether we are people who have shed blood unlawfully and then fled, and whether by asking you to hand us over, they are seeking the implementation of justice?"

It was clear that Jafar was now engaged in a real fight with words. Spoken word had a magical power and he wanted to make use of that. Words were transforming into effective weapons and the castles that the men of Quraysh were trying to build in the name of *kufr*, disbelief, were collapsing one by one. Najashi once again turned to the envoys and asked: "Have they killed unlawfully?"

"No they have not shed a single drop of blood," answered Amr.

Wasn't real virtue the virtue even your enemies would have to acknowledge? Now it was time for the last question.

"Can you ask them, O king, whether we stole people's goods and that it is for that reason they come to interrogate us, to ask for the goods we've stolen?"

The king turned to the envoys once again. They had not killed anyone, they had not degraded the honor of anyone, and they had not rebelled against their masters—what could anyone possibly want from these people? That is why Najashi changed his attitude as he was asking the last question: "If these people owe you money, then you can collect it from me."

The meeting was spiraling out of control for the Qurayshi envoys from the very beginning: "They do not owe us anything," they replied.

Now it was the King's turn to ask the questions: "Then what is it that you want from these people?"

This was a question that made the silence even more aggressive. There was only one thing they could say: "We used to believe in the same religion and would be united around the same belief, but these people have left that unity and we have come looking for them."

Now they had come to the point. The king turned to Jafar and asked: "What was the understanding of religion that you used to subscribe to, and what religion are you following now?"

"O King! We used to be a community that was ignorant and a plaything in the hands of the Satan, we used to worship idols and eat the flesh of the dead! We used to engage in all kinds of debauchery, we did not care about family ties or neighborly rights. Whoever was strong among us would oppress the weak. Then Allah sent a Prophet from among us whose family we all knew very well, and whose truthfulness and trustworthiness was already praised among us. He invited us to know Allah as the Unique One of Absolute Unity, not to worship anyone but Him, and to leave our ancestral habit of worshipping idols that we had made with our own hands from stones and clay. He also invited us to speak the truth, to keep our promises, to strengthen the ties between relatives by visiting each other, to have good and warm relations with our neighbors. Equally he warned us against all things *haram*, or prohibited, against shedding blood, debauchery, gossip and lies, against exploiting the rights and assets of the orphans and against slandering women who live virtuously. He also invited us to worship Allah, who is the Unique One of Absolute Unity, and not to worship any other god beside Him, to perform the Prayers, to give *zakah*, the prescribed purifying alms, and we have accepted what he said and we have submitted to him in faith. We have devoted ourselves to doing what he has brought to us from Allah, to worship Allah who is One, and not to hold anything equal to Him. Now we consider what he says *haram* as unlawful and what he has allowed *halal* as permitted. But our tribe started to become hostile to us, and they subjected us to all sorts of torture. They tried to make us recant our faith, to prevent us from turning our faces towards Allah and pushed us to engage in all the said debauchery. They did everything in their power so we should go after these hand-made idols once again, and they thought it fair to resort to any means in their efforts. When their torture became too much to bear and they tried to get between us and our religion, we sought refuge in your land. We preferred your country among others, we hoped we would not be subjected to any oppression under your rule, O King," said Jafar elaborately.

Right after this eloquent speech, Najashi said: "Do you have anything with you from what Allah has sent?"

It looked like the words of Jafar had been effective and Najashi had given the first sign.

Jafar stepped forward and said: "Yes, we do."

When he asked: "Will you read it to me?"

Jafar started to read from the beginning of chapter Maryam, Mary.

This was a Divine voice that delved deep into the bone… Such that before long, tears started to come down from Najashi's cheeks… People started to look at each other; even the clergy were shedding tears along with Najashi. Beards had been watered with the tears, and blessed drops from the wells in the eyes were now falling onto the pages of the books that had been opened in front of them. When Jafar reached a certain point, Najashi intervened: "I swear that these are part of the same light that came to Jesus, it is clear they come from the same lamp. What you say is all true, you are right, your Messenger is Trustworthy." He then turned to the two envoys of Quraysh and said: "You can now go back to where you came from; I will never hand these men over to you."

The envoys were experiencing a great shock, so were the clerics and viziers who were present. The Qurayshis left the court with their heads held down. But they were not ready to give up, and it did not prove difficult to find other discontent people who would support them. Amr ibnu'l-As assessed the situation and turned to his friend and said: "I swear tomorrow I will bring forth such things that I will give them a run for their money."

Abdullah ibn Abi Rabia, however, was more cautious.

"There is no need! Do not do such a thing! Even though they may have acted in opposition to us, they are our relatives," he urged.

They spoke for a while more and then decided to go to the king again the next day. The same ritual salutations started the next day and the two envoys were now in the presence of the king. Amr ibnu'l-As came forward: "O King! Undoubtedly they say many things about Jesus, the son of Mary."

Jesus was everything to them and these words of Amr brought to mind many questions. What were these things that the Muslims were saying? Now the people present had to know what it was that the Muslims were saying. So Najashi sent word to the Muslims and summoned them to his presence. When they came, he asked immediately: "What is it that you say about Jesus, the son of Mary?"

This was again a job for Jafar ibn Abi Talib, he came forward and said: "We say what the Messenger of Allah told us; verily Jesus is the servant of Allah, and a Messenger that He has sent to the people. He is a part from His own soul, a word of His that He sent to Mary, possessor of good morals and virtue."

This was the reply that Najashi was expecting. He stood up in excitement, took a staff into his hand, drew a line on the ground, and then said: "I swear that the difference between what you say about Jesus, the son of Mary, and what we know about him is even less than this line that I have drawn here."

Some of the clergy that heard these words started to mumble and tried to voice their discontent. As if he could not hear the mumbling around him, Najashi turned to Jafar and said: "I swear that you can stay in my land safe from those who plot against you and mean you harm. Those who try to harm you will find me in front of them! I swear that I would refuse mountains of gold should it cost anyone of you even a headache!"

After saying these inspirational and touching words, Najashi turned to his viziers. His looks seemed to say "While these envoys are here, they impose on me and I cannot judge fairly" and then said: "Give back the gifts that these men brought, I don't need them! When Allah gave me my power, he did not ask for ransom, so how can I accept the ransom that these men offer?"

This was a great defeat for the Quraysh. As the defeated were leaving the courtroom, their frustration could be read from their demeanor—it was as though their backs had been broken by this treatment. What had they expected, and what had they found! From then on Abyssinia would be a land where Muslims could perform the Prayers in peace, where they could read the Qur'an out loud, where the new messages of Islam could be shared with ease. Soon after however, Najashi's country would be attacked and the Muslims would be worried. In that period, the Muslims would lift their hands up to the skies for Najashi, providing him with spiritual support so that Najashi would come victorious over his enemies and the peaceful environment of the country would continue. When the Muslim migrants found out that Najashi had beaten his enemies, there was great joy among them and they would thank Allah who had given them the opportunity of a peaceful life once again.

The Miracle of Splitting the Moon

Meanwhile in Mecca, the Quraysh were doing everything they can to put the Messenger of Allah in difficult situations. One day the leading men of Mecca had come together in Mina and they had asked for a miracle from the Messenger of Allah who was there with his Companions. They had even described the miracle they wanted to see, and that they would enter Islam if he would be able to do as they said. The Messenger of Allah who wanted them to enter Islam had his hopes high with this request and had got word from the Meccans that they would submit to belief if he would be able to split the moon into two: "Yes, if you are able to cut the moon into two then we will believe you," they said.

Our noble Prophet lifted his hand up to the sky and with his index finger made a movement pointing to the moon. Those who were around him were looking at where he was pointing.

Then all of a sudden, the moon split into two. It was so clear and obvious that one half of the moon went over the mountain of Abu Qubays and the other half had gone over another mountain called Quayqian.

Upon such an incredible miracle illustrating the power and greatness of Allah, the Messenger of Allah turned to those near him and said: "Bear witness!"

The polytheists now regretted what had they asked for and they were greatly surprised. How could it be that someone standing right next to them should point to the moon and it should split in two and then make it come together again? They had made a promise, but they had no intention to become Muslim, how were they going to get out of this one? There were men among them who could trick even the Satan and one of them stepped forward to say: "This is nothing but the magic of ibn Abi Kabsha! He has painted your eyes over with this magic. Ask the people who come from around; have they seen it as well? If they have seen it as well, then Muhammad is telling the truth. But if others haven't seen what has happened, then this means that Muhammad has bewitched you."

This was surely a way out for them. Then they sent word around and found people who were not present with Muhammad there at that time and they asked them about this miracle. The answers they got did not please the polytheists at all because everyone they spoke to said that they had experienced a strange event, that they had seen the moon split into two and go over two different mountains and then come back together again. The only way out that they had been counting on was proving to be a dead-end. They could not deny what they had seen with their own eyes because other people had witnessed it too. There was only one alternative left; they were going to hold onto their old slanders, and continue to be the victim of their own stubbornness: "This is nothing but the magic of Ibn Abi Kabsha!

But you can't paint over the sun with clay! Those who chose to close their eyes would only make night descend upon themselves. Before long, the Truthful Gabriel descended and brought the verses that registered forever the truth that the polytheists tried to distort because they could not deny it: "The Last Hour has drawn near, and the moon has split. Whenever they see a miracle, they turn from it in aversion and say: *This is sorcery like many others, one after the other*" (al-Qamar 54:1–2).

General Boycott

First, the fact that both Hamza and Umar had become a Muslim meant two great defeats for the Quraysh. Second, the envoys they had sent to Abyssinia with great gifts had returned empty handed. Naturally, the Meccans had become enraged and the men were already sharpening their swords. On top of all this, they were receiving news of people who were migrating to Abyssinia and this was dispiriting them. It seemed that before long, things were going to get completely out of their hands and carried to another untouchable platform. On the one hand there was the protection of the families of Hisham and Abdul Muttalib and so they could not do anything permanent concerning the Messenger of Allah, for people had united to protect Muhammad the Trustworthy, peace and blessings be upon him, with their lives. On the other hand each day someone from the deniers' side was crossing over to them and Mecca was experiencing dissolution of its front. They had to find an immediate and effective solution to this problem.

One night they met at a pre-arranged place and made a decision that was worse than death. They decided that they would sever all ties with the families of Hashim and Abdul Muttalib and banish them from Mecca until they handed Muhammad, peace and blessings be upon him, to them. They would cut all their routes, they would not marry their children with them, and they would dry up all their sources for food and drink. Since Muhammad, peace and blessings be upon him, did not seem to give up, the innocent would be punished along with the culprits. This decision meant that the Quraysh was going to starve the people whose only crime was to have submitted in faith to Allah. They were going to leave these people to die in the difficult conditions of the desert, thus solving the problem without having given cause to blood feuds that could possibly continue for centuries. This was similar to what one imagines concentration camps to be like today... Ultimately, this was a boycott in which the Meccans would wait for them to perish in the open field, in the silence of the mornings and loneliness of the nights, under the scorching sun and the suffocation of the desert. They also wanted their act to be sanctified so they wrote their decision item by item on a page and hung it on the wall of the Ka'ba in mutual agreement. The man who wrote these articles on paper was a man named Mansur ibn Iqrima.

What Waraqa had warned the people about was now coming to pass. Seven years after the coming of the first revelation, on a night in the month of Muharram, the Muslims left Mecca and the Meccans despite the deprivation this would cause them!

Abu Talib was again there to help. They set up tent outside Mecca, in the place of Shi'b-i Abi Talib, with meager means. Tents were made up of patchwork fabric hanging tentatively on sticks. Abu Talib's efforts were a sight to see even though he wasn't a Muslim. In order to prevent something bad happening to his nephew, he was devising ingenious ways to protect him, sometimes even making his own sons sleep in his bed instead.

Shi'b-i Abi Talib was a piece of bare land outside Mecca. This state of exclusion continued for three years. The troubles kept multiplying and each day saw the cries of someone in some tent. The encampment was hit by disease and the wailings from the camp were echoing into Mecca.

These were hard times indeed. The person who felt the brunt of these troubles was the most beloved of Allah's servants, the Messenger of Allah. But whatever the circumstances, he had to continue his mission of *tabligh* and he had to feed the people with Divine messages. Such a whirlwind of troubles could only be overcome with a strong faith and this faith had become the banner of the community that had gathered around our noble Prophet. The traces of this faith could even be seen in those who had not accepted Islam but yet had chosen to be on his side. His followers were also showing great steadfastness in the face of all the hardship.

The *tabligh* had to reach other people as well. The Messenger of Allah was trying to meet people from the outside as much as possible, and was trying to communicate the Word of Allah to those he came in contact with, especially during the *haram* months, the months of prohibition. The same effort went for the Muslims who carried the excitement of faith in their hearts and they were putting their faith into action without cease.

Three long years of fighting hunger, aridity and disease!

What oppression was this that it knew of no respite even when it came to women, the elderly, the children, and the sick! The cries of the hungry children were echoing in the mountains of Paran...

When the Messenger of Allah performed his Prayer in the company of his Lord, he would always hear the cries of the children and the sighs of the mothers, and this pierced his heart. The enmity and rancor of the Quraysh had reached such proportions that even the Muslims' presence seemed an affront to them, they did not want to live in the same city with them. Mecca was oppressing them with all its might and they did not give the believers the space to even breathe. The mastermind behind this oppression was again, the Pharaoh of his community, Abu Jahl. They were now only allowed to go down to Mecca in the prohibited months and they could only buy a few provisions with their meager means. The Quraysh was meeting the caravans that came to Mecca before they came into town, trying to persuade them not to sell their wares to the Muslims. Sometimes, although they did not need it all, the Quraysh would buy everything that came with caravans, leaving no options to the people in need outside Mecca. The Muslim camp had nothing left. They had endured such hardship that they were making use of anything and everything. For example, Sa'd ibn Abi Waqqas who had gone to a remote place to see to his needs noticed a piece of leather. He had taken it, washed it and then cooked it on the fire to eat it. This aliment had enabled him to walk without having to bend over double from hunger for three days, and he had thanked his Lord for this easing of the pain. Such was the dedication of the followers of the Messenger of Allah. Many of them were trying to stay alive by eating leaves and tree bark and their excrement had become like that of sheep.

The Luminous Life of Our Prophet

In this difficult period, Khadija was one of the people who gave people a degree a comfort. She wasn't of a nature to watch what was happening and do nothing. The means she had were dwindling fast, but she knew about the market and by using her nephew Hakim ibn Hizam as middle man, she was having him send what she had secretly to Shi'b-i Abi Talib, providing some respite for the hungry. On such a day, Hakim had set out in the dark of the night and was bringing a handful of grain to his aunt. This did not escape the attention of Abu Jahl and he stopped him. How could an individual stand up against the machinated authority of ignorance? Even though he was his brother, Abu Jahl had no tolerance for different voices. He first displayed a very tough attitude: "Bringing food to the sons of Hashim are we?! I swear that you will not be able to escape me and I will not allow you to bring them food. You will see; I will shame you in front of the whole of Mecca."

Upon them came Abu'l Bakhtari. He was from the family of Hashim. He had not submitted in faith but he had a heart. He first wanted to learn the cause of the quarrel: "What is happening between you two?" he asked. Abu Jahl answered: "He was attempting to take food to the sons of Hashim."

"And so you're trying to prevent him to take food to his aunt?" reacted Abu'l Bakhtari.

"Get away from the path of this man," he continued, trying to put an end to Abu Jahl's oppression, but a fight between him and Abu Jahl ensued. It came to a point where Abu'l Bakhtari was about to break Abu Jahl's head with a jaw bone he had found on the ground.

Meanwhile, Hamza was watching this scene from afar. This act of Abu'l Bakhtari would hearten people who thought like him, and prepare the ground for the process that ended up with the lifting of the page of articles that hung on the wall of the Ka'ba and the ending of the boycott.

In the meantime, the Messenger of Allah went to his uncle Abu Talib and said: "O uncle! It is true that my Lord Allah the Almighty has sent a little worm to the page of articles they hung on the wall of the Ka'ba, and the little worm has eaten up all the oppression, boycott and slander inscribed there except for His own Exalted Name."

Abu Talib was surprised to hear this. He knew that his nephew would not have been able to go to the Ka'ba and see this page, for he would not be allowed anywhere near that page. There was only one explanation: "Has your Lord given you this news?" Abu Talib asked.

"Yes," said the Messenger of Allah.

He had not seen or heard his nephew lie even once. Hearing him say it was enough to believe it. But he had a different plan now. He went and informed his brothers at once. A period of oppression was about to end. This excitement could not stay within the bounds of Shibi Abi Talib, and before long they made their way to the Ka'ba. Everyone who saw them coming could see that Mecca was pregnant with a new development and people were eagerly watching the events unfold.

Abu Talib called out to the Meccans and said, based on his trust of what his nephew had told him and the trust that he had for the news that the Gracious Lord had given, the following:

"The son of my brother Muhammad says that your paper has been eaten up by a worm sent by Allah, and he never lies. He says that everything to do with oppression, extremism, cutting family ties and transgression has been cleansed and that only the Name of Allah remains. Here's your opportunity; if what my nephew says turns out to be true, then you will change this bad attitude of yours; and if it turns out to be false then I will hand my nephew over to you and you can choose to kill him or let him live."

The Quraysh were unaware of the real dimensions of the matter and so they were overjoyed. Abu Talib was offering his nephew just at a time when they had thought he had gone completely out of control. So there was nothing to be worried about. They said: "Alright, you have done what mercy complies one to do."

And then they went to the wall of the Ka'ba in order to see the situation. When they opened the case in which they had placed the paper, a case they had sealed threefold, they saw that it was just as Abu Talib had described. They froze in astonishment. With the droop of their heads the case they were holding fell to the ground along with the eaten up piece of paper. They were experiencing yet another great defeat. Now it was Abu Talib's turn to speak: "Since everything has been revealed, there is no point in this imprisonment and siege," and lifting the cover of the Ka'ba, he entered it, and this is how he started to pray: "O Allah, help us against those who oppress us, who forbid us to meet with people, who attack us with no right and who do injustice to us."

Then they all left and went to the place where they had experienced the greatest hardship for three years. But nothing would be the same from now on, for the prayers spoken at the Ka'ba had been accepted and had set people with conscience into action. This had been the last drop and it seemed the journey would be rough until the conclusion was reached.

On the other hand, Hisham, our noble Prophet's, peace and blessings be upon him, cousin, was saying the following to Zuhayr: "O Zuhayr! Although you have heard what situation your uncles are in, you are eating and drinking here in peace. You are having a good time with your family and kids, dressed in the best clothes. How can your heart be content with this? They, on the other hand, can neither buy anything, nor have a moment's peace with their family. I swear that had they been the uncles of Abul Hakam, and had I called him for that, he would have listened to me and have run to the help of his uncles."

Zuhayr had understood what was meant by these words but still asked: "O Hisham! What do you mean to say? What can I do as a man on his own? Had there been another man with me, I swear I would go and rip that text apart."

"But you are not alone! You have another man with you," said Hisham.

"And who is that?" asked Zuhayr.

"Me," answered Hisham.

"Then come, let us find a third man," said Zuhayr.

Without losing any time they went to Mut'im ibn Adiyy and said similar words to him. They were growing fast like an avalanche. They looked for the fourth man. Abu'l-Bakhtari was waiting for them. Before long, Zam'a ibn Aswad joined them as the fifth man. Then these five donned their weapons against the hatred and rancor of years and made for the Ka'ba with the men from the families of Hashim and Abdul Muttalib following them, with a view to ending the issue. There was not much the Quraysh, who saw them coming, could do.

As soon as they came to the Ka'ba, they circumambulated it seven times and as planned, Zuhayr spoke: "O people of Mecca! We cannot allow the sons of Hashim perish without a chance to buy anything, all their ties to the external world cut while we eat in peace and strut about in good clothes. I swear that I will not leave without tearing that piece of paper upon which the conditions of the boycott is written."

Abu Jahl was watching what was happening from the side with great attention. He shouted out: "You lie! I swear you will not be able to do anything to this paper."

In response to his reaction, Zam'a said: "It is you who lies! We weren't happy with it in the first place. You had it written."

And then the Ka'ba witnessed the support of Abu'l-Bakhtari: "Zam'a tells the truth, we cannot stay silent anymore in the face of what is happening."

Mut'im ibn Adiyy and Hisham were supporting their friends: "Of course, they are telling the truth; you are the liar! We seek refuge from Allah from what has been written here and the treatment they have caused!"

All of a sudden the Ka'ba had seen the Meccans' much longed-for reaction and was now overwhelmed in joy with this long-overdue act.

This was a moment when denial was experiencing one of its defeats. Abu Jahl was enraged: "This is a conspiracy that was planned during the night."

Abu Talib and his friends had now come back to the Ka'ba and were watching what was taking place with great curiosity. For them, what the crowd would witness at the end was not going to come as a surprise. But they wanted to see their astonishment with their own eyes.

The defenses of denial were falling one by one! Then Mut'im ibn Adiyy, made for the case in order to put an end to this inhumane treatment that had lasted for three years. But what did he find? Only a little slip of paper with the words "In the Name of Allah" had remained and beside it was a little worm whose work this seemed.

Thus a period of oppression that had lasted three years was ending, and with the destroyed paper, the boycott itself was lifted.

The Year of Sadness

Although this period of inhumane treatment and the boycott had ended, there was still more sadness to be experienced. Maybe Allah the Almighty was turning His beloved servants' eyes completely towards the Hereafter, directing their attention to their real "homeland" with various troubles that the believers had to face. The fact that now after the lifting of the boycott they could enter Mecca did not mean that the oppression and torture would end. The Meccan polytheists who had lost the battle of the front yesterday were opening new fronts everywhere today, thereby looking to recuperate their losses. The Muslims had left their three years of exile behind, but these years had left a great impact on them; the cries of the hungry children were now haunting the parents in their sleep. Disease was rife and was decimating the community. Two important pillars such as Abu Talib and Khadija had had their share of the disease. It was not so easy to start in Mecca anew, and Mecca was bent on living in its previous state of debauchery.

The exhaustion of all his years was now upon Abu Talib, he had come to a point where he found it difficult to even walk. He had one foot in the grave, so to speak. He had carried the burden of his whole tribe, not only his own. He had stood up for his nephew even though everyone had opposed him. It was clear that he was no longer in a state where he could carry such weight. It was the month of Ramadan. Abu Talib was ill and it looked like he would pass away to eternity from this disease. The news of his illness spread through Mecca, and the numbers of people who came to visit him increased day by day.

On the other hand the front of denial was not sitting idle. They knew of his situation and around twenty five people from the leading men of Quraysh came together, including Utba and Shayba, Ibn Rabia, Abu Jahl, Umayya ibn Khalaf and Abu Sufyan. They came to speak to Abu Talib one last time. They discussed their situation before they went to Abu Talib: "Hamza and Umar have become Muslim; we lost them. The cause of Muhammad is spreading among the tribes. Come, let us go to Abu Talib, and let us ask him to hand the son of his brother to us! It seems we will not be able to overcome this difficulty otherwise," said one of them.

"Truth be told, I fear this old man as well; I fear as he dies he will say what Muhammad says and then we will never be able to stop the chattering mouths of the Arabs!" explained another.

"Best is if you wait now; tomorrow when his uncle dies you can finish him!" told the other.

They were forwarding such ideas, but the prevailing sentiment was that they should go visit Abu Talib in his death bed. They went to him with the following offer: "O Abu Talib! No doubt you know our situation and what has befallen us! What we fear is clear! What we experienced with your nephew is no secret; it's all out in the open! Tell him to stay away from us, and we shall stay away from him! Tell him to leave us to our religion and understanding so that we may leave him in peace."

For Abu Talib the issue seemed to have softened.

If everyone lived according to their own understanding, then nobody would be hurt and his nephew would be safe from harm. He called to his side the Messenger of Allah with such thoughts in mind: "O son of my brother! Look, these are leading men of your tribe. They have come here and they assure you that they will not harass you anymore," he said.

"I want just one word from them; with it, they will be sovereign over all the Arabs and with this word the Persians will also come to live like them."

Abu Jahl misconstrued the words of Muhammad to mean that he had accepted their offer and came to the fore: "One word? Of course, you will get your word; I swear by the memory of your father that we will give you not one, but ten words."

Things had to be made clearer and so the Messenger of Allah said: "You will say 'There is no deity but Allah' and you will leave aside everything you worship except Him."

This was what he had demanded from them at every opportunity, so naturally, it displeased them. They started to clap in protest and then said with sour faces: "You mean to say that you want to make one God out of all the gods?"

Another one of them came to the fore and said: "I swear that this man will not give you anything you want! You should continue what you want to do and do not leave your ancestors' religion till this issue between you and him is resolved."

Soon, the traces of revelation were upon him and the Truthful Gabriel was bringing a new message:

They deem it strange that a warner from among them has come to them, and the unbelievers say: 'This man is but a sorcerer, a fraud (who makes fabrications in attribution to Allah). What! Has he made all the deities into One Allah. This is a very strange thing, indeed!' (Sad 38:4–5)

This clearly showed that each of their steps was being watched. Everything they thought they hid in their inner worlds was being revealed to them out in the open, right before their eyes. The rest of the verse stated:

The leaders among them went about inciting one another: "Move on, and remain constant to your deities. Surely that (to which this man calls) is the very thing that is certainly intended (deliberately plotted by him and those who follow him). We have not heard of this in recent ways of faith. This is surely nothing but a concoction. From among all of us has the Reminder been sent down on him?" No! Rather, (on account of their self-glory) they are lost in doubts concerning My Reminder. No indeed! They have not yet tasted My punishment (so that they might abandon their arrogance and recognize the truth). (Sad 38:6–8)

Everyone would taste it, everything had its moment. The old and dying Abu Talib turned to the representatives of the Quraysh and said the following:

"O people of Quraysh! You are among the chosen ones from Allah's creation, and you hold a most central place among the Arabs. The masters that are to be obeyed, valiant people who care nothing for danger and generous men have always come from among you. You should know that you have been preferred among the Arabs and have been brought to a special position. When it comes to your honor; you live by it! Then it falls upon you to share with others these gifts you have, and people will have to seek different ways to partake in this bounty.

Now people are against you and there is a war between you. I would advise you to respect this constitution, for in it is the contentment of your Lord, ease of sustenance and consolidation of your position! Look after your relatives and never stop visiting them, for visiting relatives eases the sadness of your bereavement and it also means strength in numbers, and you will have someone there for you.

Stay away from excess and rebellion, for in both these you will find the causes of the perishing of centuries, and you know the histories of those before you.

Help those who seek help from you and never send away anyone who comes to you with an opened hand, for in these two you will find the honor of life and death.

Speak the truth and keep safe what is entrusted to you, for in both these there is a special kind of love and greatness.

Lastly I advise being graceful towards Muhammad, for he is the most trustworthy person in Quraysh, the most upright man among all Arabs, the most virtuous man that embodies all that I have just enumerated. He has come to you with such a thing that although the heart recognizes it, the tongue denies it for fear of being censured! I swear, I almost see the Arabs come running, I see good people from around coming, and following him and their hearts thus finding solace.

If things continue this way, while these strangers will benefit from him, leaders of Quraysh will be left behind, their stars will wane. The weak of today will become the mighty of tomorrow; the proudest of you will become the most needy, and those who are distant to him today will be closest to him in the future! Look, the Arabs have already opened their arms to him, they have run to his help; they have opened their hearts to him and have made him the crown over their heads.

O Quraysh! Take care to recognize this value that has risen from among you! Be his helpers and protectors of his cause! I swear by Allah that whoever follows his path he will reach maturity, and whoever takes what he had brought as his guide, becomes the happiest of men! I wish my life were a little longer, and my death was a little delayed, I wish I could help him fight the difficulties he faces!"

This advice that everyone needed to heed would have made sense only to those who were ready to receive them. It was clear that the polytheists had not liked what he had said at all. No doubt they too had other plans in order to further their stance in denial, and they would put these plans into action, digging a bigger whole for themselves. Once again they complained, lifted their heads in arrogance, and left Abu Talib's presence.

When the leading men of Quraysh left Abu Talib's side, he turned to his nephew and said with the experience of his years: "I swear, O son of my brother, you have not asked them to do an impossible thing."

This was a statement that heartened the Messenger of Allah. At last his uncle was showing signs of accepting Islam, for he had set his door ajar for faith. The affectionate Messenger who wanted to make use of every opportunity turned towards him with great hope; he just couldn't accept his beloved and protective uncle leaving him without having taken any steps towards faith: "O uncle! Then you say that word so that with it I may be able to vouch for you on the Day of Judgment."

This was a great opportunity for a soul who had devoted himself to saving other people's faiths; he wanted his uncle to believe so much! But faith was a matter of destiny, for even if one was a Prophet, no one was able to hold another fast to the right path as long as Allah did not will it, he could not make this route easier to get on to for people he wanted. Revelations said the same thing: *"You cannot guide to truth whomever you like but Allah guides whomever He wills. He knows best who are guided (and amenable to guidance)"* (al-Qasas 28:56).

The Messenger's strife was the result of his love for his uncle, but it did not yield any results. This last push had been a new and last hope. When he saw that his nephew had such high hopes, Abu Talib said: "O son of my brother," even this address had the tone that said "Do not have such high hopes." Then after a pause he continued: "Had I not feared that people after me may attribute senility to the son of their forefathers, or the Quraysh saying that I said these words because I feared death, I would have said those words. But I can say them to make you happy."

Our noble Prophet would still try to make something of each moment and would try to make his uncle give him a definite response.

The leading men of denial once again came to the side of his uncle. The Messenger of Allah started to walk towards his uncle Abu Talib in his sick bed. Another uncle made for the bed as well and sat where the Messenger of Allah had meant to sit. His aim was to prevent the Messenger of Allah from influencing Abu Talib in his last moments and from inviting him to Islam. Even at a moment when Abu Talib was in his death throes, denial kept up its stern front; it did not want to allow any steps that might lead to belief. They couldn't even tolerate the Messenger looking at his uncle's eyes with affection. On top of that, the Messenger of Allah was trying to invite him to faith at every opportunity. Even in these last moments, the struggle between faith and denial was being played out to the full. Abu Talib was asked: "O Abu Talib! Are you now giving up the religion of Abdul Muttalib?"

"No. I am staying on the religion of Abdul Muttalib," he answered.

He was now closer to death. Sitting closer to him was his brother Abbas. He was trying to see the movement of his lips, and then the greatest patron of our noble Prophet closed his eyes to life.

However, the Messenger of Allah would not stop praying and seeking forgiveness for Abu Talib who had been prevented by the pressure of denial to come to the path of faith: "And me, I will continue to ask forgiveness from Allah for you as long as I am not prohibited to do so."

This statement of the noble Prophet was going to be validated by the good news brought by Gabriel. The verse that came first spoke of the situation which made the scene eternal. Then it gave an example from his ancestors thereby showing the correct attitude to be taken under such circumstances:

> It is not for the Prophet and those who believe to ask Allah for the forgiveness of those who associate partners with Allah even though they be near of kin, after it has become clear to them that they (died polytheists and therefore) are condemned to the Blazing Flame. The prayer of Abraham for the forgiveness of his father was only because of a

The Luminous Life of Our Prophet

promise which he had made to him. But when it became clear to him that he was an enemy of Allah, he (Abraham) dissociated himself from him. Abraham was most tender-hearted, most clement. (at-Tawbah 9:113–114)

After the burial, Abbas ibn Abdul Muttalib approached the Messenger of Allah and said to his bereaved nephew: "O son of my brother! I swear by Allah that Abu Talib said the word you wanted him to say at his last moment."

The Messenger of Allah wasn't thinking the same way.

"I didn't hear it," he said. Upon that Abbas approached his nephew and said that he needed to be softer and more balanced towards his uncle. He was a man of balance anyway; he was the representative of the straight path, and everyone needed to take him as an example. That is why he said to his uncle: "I hope that my vouching for him on the Judgment Day will help him, and that his torment in Hell will ease and that the whole process will be made lighter for him."

Farewell to Khadija

Only three days had passed since the death of Abu Talib. The Messenger of Allah had tried very hard for him to leave a sign, an address, as he left this world but he did not hear words to that effect from the lips of his uncle. The Quraysh who considered Abu Talib's absence as an opportunity was now putting even greater pressure on the Muslims. The beloved of Allah, peace and blessings be upon him, was very sad. His greatest supporter and protector had left this world and he had not heard anything from him that would give him hope that he would win eternal peace in the afterlife as corollary to the warmth he had extended to him in this life.

This was one of the darkest moments. He was also extremely worried about the state of his beloved wife whom he had left in her sick bed. He returned quickly towards his tent, for Khadija, another one of his great supporters, was suffering from a grave illness. The Messenger of Allah was now going to visit his wife who was writhing with fever in her bed, in the throes of her last journey. He feared that he was going to be bereft of another support like Abu Talib, his closest and most loyal friend. He approached and slowly lifted the veil covering the entrance of the tent. To see Khadija in that state saddened him immensely, her sighs of pain were hiding tears of farewell... Once the richest woman of Mecca, today Khadija was in hunger and pain, bent in two, suffering from the effects of the life of exile she had endured.

Her sadness was deepened by the anxiety that she would be leaving the Messenger of Allah alone with their daughters. Her soul was leaving but her heart was still captive to the Pride of Humankind, peace and blessings be upon him, who was now being left friendless, and captive to her children whom she was entrusting to the Sultan of Prophets, peace and blessings be upon him, and the Gracious Lord. She was born too early, and yet had been awakened to the Truth early as well, and now she was going to be reunited with her two children who had gone before her. There was a sweet smile on her face before she left; it was clear that she was already having the visions of Paradise that Gabriel had brought good tidings of. However even this sweet smile had turned into a deep grief when she saw the beloved Prophet who lifted the veils of the tent with affection and mercy. Both of them were grieving for the state that the other was in.

This was a scene that would hurt the Sultan of Affection and Mercy, peace and blessings be upon him, most deeply! Tears had started to flow from his glorious face and wet his noble beard. He was crying his beautiful heart out for his wife, best friend and kindred spirit.

The Messenger of Allah approached her with feelings of gratitude and at a moment when words just couldn't express their feelings, he started to say the following: "This is because of me, O Khadija! You had to endure these hardships because of me and you were deprived of a life that was deserving of your standing."

He meant to say, "You were not a woman who deserved this. Instead of being reciprocated with generosity for your generosity, you have been reciprocated with hardship and torment," and added: "But do not forget that behind every difficulty Allah has meant abundant good."

And now after Abu Talib, the second most important support figure in the life of our Beloved Prophet was no longer alive. Khadija was around sixty-five years old when she said farewell to the world and all worldly strife, to relocate to her eternal resting place decked with pearls, a place where there would be no chaos or hardship. Her spiritual life that commenced on the holy Night of Power alongside the sun that rose in Hira also ended on the holy Night of Power. The Messenger of Allah himself went down into her grave and placed her there in her space in the Hajun graveyard, and he was the one to cover her with earth.

Difficulties one after another had rained down on the noble Messenger like hail. He no longer had a place of refuge where he could retire to when faced with difficulties, no support that held troubles at bay with the safeguard she provided with her years of experience. After his uncle who had been a loving father and a kind-hearted trustworthy protector, now he was losing his beloved spouse and her affectionate support. This encouraged the Quraysh and they started coming on to the Messenger of Allah with greater force. One day, a debauched member of Quraysh had thrown dirt on the Messenger of Allah and he had returned home, head bowed, in this state. One of his daughters was very sad when she saw her father in this state and she was crying as she cleaned the dirt off her father. With affectionate eyes that inspected the future, he said: "Do not cry my dear daughter! Allah will not abandon your father."

This year in which he would experience sadness after sadness would later be called the years of *huzn*, or sadness, for during this period the false stance of the polytheists and their reaction towards the Prophet had reached unbearable proportions and at the same time, two supports that had always been on the side of our noble Prophet had taken their leave from this world. These were developments that threw the sad Messenger into deep grief, such grief that it would give its name to these years.

Journey to Ta'if

Despite the extraordinary efforts of the Messenger of Allah and his Companions, nothing seemed to be progressing in Mecca and the Meccans had closed their doors to new openings. *Tabligh*, on the other hand was a duty to communicate, one that had to be carried out continuously to people elsewhere in the world who needed Islam as well.

The Meccans were filled with hatred against Islam, one that grew day by day, and they gave the Muslims no space to take any further steps. One could hear the grating of the teeth of those who wanted to get rid of the physical presence of the Messenger of Allah now that the protection of Abu Talib was no longer present. Allah had made a promise that one day this cause would cover the whole of the earth, and there was no doubt about that. But this did not seem very probable in the Mecca of that day. There was need for a new opening and to make that opening possible, on a day in the month of Shawwal, our noble Prophet took his Companion Zayd ibn Haritha and made his way for Ta'if.

Ta'if was a place well-known for its orchards, gardens and greenery. It was about ninety kilometers to Mecca and here lived some relatives of the Messenger of Allah from his mother's side. At the same time this was a place close to the region where Halima as-Sadia, our noble Prophet's nursing mother, was from and the region where Allah's Messenger had spent his first formative years.

The Messenger first went to the people of Saqif on the way to Ta'if; a road he had set off on to meet new faces who would accept the messages sent by Allah, to meet warm faces that he could not find in Mecca so that he may be able to walk towards the future with sturdier steps, with believers who wanted to take Allah's cause further. The people of Saqif were known to be the leading tribe of Ta'if and they were well-respected.

The first people they met were the three sons of Amr ibn Umayr; Abdiyalayl, Mas'ud and Habib. One of them was married to a woman from the Quraysh. The Messenger of Allah approached them, saluted them and then started to speak with all his sincerity. He was inviting them to know Allah as One and to further his cause; he was asking them to help him in his mission of Prophethood. But Ta'if seemed just as difficult as Mecca. The first of the three brothers whom the Messenger of Allah had met with affection took word and said rather rudely: "If Allah has sent you as Prophet, I will take the veil of the Ka'ba and throw it on the floor."

The most beloved servant of Allah had come to him to save his world and afterlife but he was intent on making fun of him. A man of great bashfulness, the Messenger of Allah preferred to stay silent once again in the face of such arrogance and insolence. But such ill-mannered behavior was not going to stop there. The other brother came to the fore and remarked: "Could Allah not find another man to send as Prophet?"

It looked like things were going to get more complicated. The third brother, who also wanted his share in arrogance, said: "I swear I will not speak to you any more! I am sure you will make me regret what I said to you! But if you are lying in the face of Allah, then it is not proper for me to speak to you anyway."

These degenerate people were mocking the Pride of Humanity, peace and blessings be upon him, and having a good time.

The Messenger of Allah was extremely upset. He had come all that way hoping that they may understand something, for he just wanted to set open the doors of Paradise for them. But now he didn't even feel the urge to answer their questions. Had he really sought to "respond" to their mockery, a Divine response would have been given on his behalf and they would have been finished, but he was the Prophet of mercy and his bosom was big enough to embrace all, even his enemies. He was hoping that they too may one day come and join the true cause. Even if not them, he believed there would be there someone from their progeny who would join to cause, and so today, one needed to be patient for that bright future.

The Messenger of Allah had only one thing to ask: "It may be that you have made your choice; but let what has passed between us stay between us."

He did not want this news to reach Mecca, for it would encourage the Meccans and this would set into motion even those who had not acted against them, making Mecca a place even harder to live for Muslims.

His sadness was reflected in his walk. On the face of it, it seemed that he was returning empty handed, however, he knew that one was not meant to do one's duty with the expectation of seeing an immediate result. He had done what it was upon him to do, he had communicated his duty of *tabligh*, and it was up to Allah to create the result. Our noble Prophet was the most careful in not meddling with actions that was up to Allah to carry to fullness, just as he was foremost in executing his duty without flaw.

However, these people who were not aware that they had turned away good fortune that had come to their very door would not be content with what they had already done and getting some street children to their dirty work, they would shower this auspicious guest with stones.

The Messenger of Allah stayed in Ta'if for ten days. During this period he wanted to meet with many people but most of them did not have the heart that could accept him, and they preferred to stay away from him and his ideas due to their fears, and they quite unashamedly said: "O Muhammad! Leave our land, you may go wherever you like!"

Zayd had made himself a shield and was trying to protect the Messenger of Allah from the stones that were raining down on him. The hovering stones did not seem to stop. This was a behavior that could cause Divine stones to be showered on the offenders themselves and extinguish them for eternity. The Messenger and Zayd were pursued thus for about three kilometers. Blood was dripping from the feet of the Beloved of Allah, the noble Messenger. Zayd's head and eyes had been wounded, and he was also covered in blood.

The Refuge in Ta'if and
a Manifestation

They had at last gone far away from this troublesome place and they had taken some time to rest under a tree. First, the Messenger of Allah started to perform his Prayers. It was these Prayers which he called the "light of my eye," and so he prayed two units under the tree. It was clear that in such situations when everyone had turned their backs on him, he had to turn towards the real holder of power with all sincerity. In order to be cleansed from worldly weaknesses and to clothe oneself in graceful aspects, one first had to be fitted with the right position. Maybe all this was a message to the *Ummah* to stop them from acting rashly; for he was a model to be followed in all respects, and when he would be faced with situations where he needed to be angry, he was to show his *Ummah* how one was to act in such situations.

When he completed his Prayer, he opened his hands high and wide, and started to supplicate his Lord. Zayd was watching him in awe. It was as if he was looking at a great statue made out of light. He listened closely. The Messenger of Allah was saying the following prayer: "My Lord! I offer to Your Knowledge the weaknesses I have, my inability to find solutions and the way people look down on me.

You are the most Merciful among the Merciful!

You are the Lord of the weak and the powerless!

You are my Lord!

Who do you leave me to?

To bloody and cruel enemies, or my brash and ruthless relatives to whom You please to submit my work?

If You are not angry with me, then I do not care for anything in the world; the Wellbeing that You bestow upon me is more important to me than anything else in the world.

I seek refuge in You that You may not treat me with Your wrath, that You may not manifest Yourself to me with your rage.

I seek refuge in You, You who arrange all worldly and otherworldly things, You with whom all darkness turns into light, I seek to enter Your face of light.

I will be at Your gate until I have earned your Contentment!

There is no support other than You, nor any other power one can count on!"

The Messenger of Allah had not finished his prayer when the Truthful Gabriel and another angel, the angel of mountains, descended to his side. It was clear that the supplications of the sad Messenger had shaken the High Heavens and Allah had sent down two of His angels for help. Gabriel was saying: "O Muhammad! Verily Allah the Almighty knows what your tribe said to you and what they did after turning their faces away from you, and here, in order that you may do as you please to those who did these against you, He sent you the angel whose orders the mountains obey!"

The angel keeper of the mountains saluted our noble Prophet and said: "If you should want it, O Muhammad, I will pull down these two mountains over the people of Ta'if!"

It was then that one would witness, once again, the true character of the Prophet of Mercy. Despite everything, his decision would set an example for his followers. That is why the Messenger of Allah said without a moment of hesitation: "No, never! I still hope that Allah the Almighty will create from their offspring servants who worship Him and who hold no false gods!"

One's true nature could be observed on such crucial occasions; the response of the noble Messenger also showed what kind of a man he was.

Then, the angel of the mountains, who had been sent down to pull the mountains over the heads of the people of Ta'if, started to speak in awe: "You truly are merciful and gracious like your Lord has named you!"

They had at last gone far away from this troublesome place and they had taken some time to rest under a tree. Meanwhile, a distant relative of our Prophet who owned the gardens had sent them grapes with his slave named Addas, who accepted Islam after a short conversation. A group of jinns also accepted Islam after watching our noble Prophet pray and listening to the Qur'an he was reading.

Mecca Again

Although Ta'if had not given the expected result, with Addas and the jinn entering Islam, the heart of the Messenger of Allah was somewhat subdued, and he set off for Mecca again. When the road had approached Mecca, he decided to go to the mountain of Nur like back in the days and then he made his way to Hira. The Mecca that had closed its doors to him was there right in front of him, the *Baytullah*, House of Allah, was sad and the believers were orphaned! A silent conversation between them took place. They understood one another very well, for the Messenger of Allah who was known as the "twin brother of the House of Allah" was also orphaned and sad. Zayd, on the other hand, was wondering how they could enter Mecca and could find no solution. He couldn't contain himself and at last he asked: "They have banished you O Messenger, how do you propose to enter Mecca?"

The Prophet of Mercy, peace and blessings be upon him, was self-possessed as always, one could see that he could foresee the outcome of his actions: "O Zayd! There is no doubt that Allah will send a way out, open a new door; there is no doubt that He will protect His religion and He will make His Prophet victorious!"

Later, obeying the need to make use of "causes and means," the Prophet of Allah, peace and blessings be upon him, sent word to some people in Mecca because he did not want to face any problems while returning to his village. The first person he thought of was Akhnas ibn Shariq, but he responded saying: "I have made a pact, a man like me who lives under a pact cannot offer protection for anyone else," thus refusing his request. The same message was then taken to Suhayl ibn Amr known as the wordsmith of the Quraysh. But he responded saying: "The sons of Amir cannot offer protection to the sons of Ka'b," making it clear that he was not yet ready for siding with the noble Prophet. Maybe they were afraid to give a positive answer. But it was clear that Suhayl was a name that our beloved Prophet considered often and from whom he expected many things.

The positive answer came from Mut'im ibn Adiyy.

When the request of the Messenger of Allah reached him, he gathered his children together and advised them in the following way: "Put on your weapons and go and wait for me at the pillars of the Ka'ba, for I have given protection to Muhammad."

Then he himself came to the Ka'ba and said to the people from atop his camel: "O Quraysh! Know well that I have given protection to Muhammad; do not harass him!"

Thus letting the whole of Mecca know that whoever harassed Prophet Muhammad, peace and blessings be upon him, would have him to answer to. Then the Messenger of Allah came to Mecca with Zayd. The first place they wanted to visit was the Ka'ba, and after saluting it, they performed two units of Prayer and then turned towards their happy home. During all this, Mut'im ibn Adiyy was protecting him, not allowing anyone to do him any harm.

On the other hand, Abu Jahl was worried for his own campaign and soon enough he approached Mut'im to ask: "Have you only given him protection or have you become Muslim as well?"

Mut'im turned to his friend and said: "No, I have not become Muslim; I have just given him protection."

This was the answer that Abu Jahl was expecting and so he said: "Then we will not touch someone to whom you have given protection!"

His name was so trusted that his enemies were ready to protect him against his worst enemies at the expense of their whole family. It was clear that to have a say in society and to have one's requests answered, one had to be able to show a sense of humanity in order to have enough "credit" in society. The name of this credit was trust and its source was purity. This credit carried a value that could not be compared to any earthly value, for had they offered the most precious treasures to Mut'im that day, he would not have taken such a risk, he would not have put himself against the whole of Mecca. But the trust he felt for Muhammad the Trustworthy, peace and blessings be upon him, his innocent stance in the face of all that had been done to him moved the likes of Mut'im, and made them feel the need to say "stop" to what was being done to our noble Prophet.

Isra and *Miraj*

10 years had passed since the meeting in Hira. The calendars were showing the 24th day in the month of Rajab. There had been many efforts during this time, but Mecca had resisted in unimaginable ways. There had only been a handful of people who accepted the call to faith. However, when one considered the amount of energy put into this cause, one would have expected them to come running, which had not been the case. The Messenger of Allah was not living for his own sake. He was doing all that was in his power so that even his greatest enemies may have the chance to taste the beauty of submission to faith, knocking on their doors every day, just in case they change their minds.

However these efforts that needed to be applauded were being met by incredible hostility—the attitude of the Meccans after the deaths of Abu Talib and Khadija, what he lived through in Ta'if and the way people received him on his return with a sour face—all these had troubled the Messenger of Allah deeply and he found consolation only by seeking refuge in Divine grace. Had these breezes of mercy not existed, the suffocation in Mecca would have been unbearable. Then one evening, when the Messenger of Allah was at the house of his cousin Umm Hani, it was as if the roof of the house had opened and the Truthful Gabriel had descended upon them.

It was clear that this coming was very different from previous ones. With him he had a mount named Buraq, a mount a little bigger than a donkey but a little smaller than a mule, one that previous Prophets had also used. It seemed there was a Divine invitation and Gabriel had come to escort this most auspicious of guests, the Sultan of Messengers, Glorified Leader, comforter of the afflicted, the commander in the Divine Assembly, Muhammad, peace and blessings be upon him, for he was the special invitee of the Truth and he was being called to the heavens to meet his Lord. This was to be a gift from Allah to comfort the sadness that the Messenger had been through. In order that he may observe with his eyes and ears the truths that he felt in his conscience, Allah the Almighty was going to take His servant, Muhammad, peace and blessings be upon him, from Mecca up to His presence.

And who knew what kind of a mysterious journey He would put him on. But before he could set on this journey, there needed to be an operation, similar to the one he had experienced when he was still with his nursing mother Halima as-Sadia. The Truthful Gabriel cleaved his chest and washed its inside with the water of Zamzam; then he filled it with faith and wisdom that he had in a golden bowl and then closed it. Then Gabriel, the truthful guardian of the skies, took the hand of the truthful guardian of the earth, Muhammad Mustafa, peace and blessings be upon him, and they set off together on an indescribable journey beyond.

The Buraq that he was riding was moving very fast, every step he took was at a further point in the horizon and he was moving at the speed of lightening. The minute he mounted the Buraq, space had changed and they had found themselves in the Masjid al-Aqsa in Jerusalem. The Messenger of Allah tied the Buraq where previous Prophets had tied it. Then he turned towards the mosque to pray. The chosen servants of Allah who had performed the duty of Messengership till that day had gathered together there as well and were waiting for the Personage who was the seal of this chain to arrive. He was greeted and embraced with greetings and salutations. Then they lined up into a row to fulfill the most important business—to perform two cycles of Prayer. They were waiting for the imam, the leader of the realm of Prophets. So the Abrahamic line would be sealed with Muhammad and he would take on the mission for the rest of time. This was the reason why this place had been chosen rather than another. The issue of representing Truth was now to be taken from this place that had been the home of many Messengers and now faces were going to be turned towards Mecca. The step by step process during the *Miraj* and the Prophets encountered one by one along the way can also be seen as foreshadowing the union of the *Ummah* and the positive hopes for the future.

The Sultan of the Prophets walked towards the gathering and took his place at the front of the row. This sequence and order symbolized the fact that when the time came, humanity would go back to the first pure line that Allah had created them in. It was the picture that illustrated that the children of Adam would be united as one again on Adam's earth, and the consolidation of the leadership of the Personage whose intercession everyone called upon when seeking forgiveness. Since all the other Prophets were praying behind him, it meant that the *Ummah*s of those Prophets would one day pray behind him as well!

Surprises did not end with what had happened in the Masjid al-Aqsa. Gabriel then invited the beloved of Allah, peace and blessings be upon him, to a journey that would take him beyond the skies. All of a sudden space transformed and a journey full of mysteries started. He was rising up above the skies level by level and at each level there was another ritual to be observed. Then, the Beloved of Allah came face to face with the *Sidratu'l-Muntaha* (Lote-tree of the Uttermost End), a beauty that was impossible to put into words. It was like a parade ground for colors of all hues. This was a sacred place, somewhere between the "realm" of Absolute Necessity (Divinity), and the realm of contingency (the created) and now the Truthful Gabriel was no longer by the Messenger of Allah, for the realm of contingency had now been left behind. This was the privy chamber, the harem, and there had been no physical or spiritual presence since the creation of mankind that had been blessed by an entry into this chamber. That is to say, the Pride of Humankind and the Pearl of Creation, our noble Prophet, was the one and only, the first and the last guest of this chamber. Just as there had been no one here before him, there would be none after him, for he was the Seal of the Assembly of Prophethood.

The Messenger of Allah was now witnessing the ink of the pen of fate, he could hear the sounds the pen made when writing the *taqdir*, that which had been ordained to happen. Here was also the manifestation of the mystery of *"Qaba kawsayni aw adna" (an-Najm 53:9)*. He had come closer and closer and when he had gone far enough that there was no more space to be covered, he had reached *la makan*, non-space.

Despite all these, the Messenger of Allah was not diverted from his purpose; there was no change with him. All had become light all of a sudden and he had seen that the *Sidra* was encompassed with a beauty that could not be perceived with limited sight and put into mere words.

Everything that was mortal had been enveloped in light; the Messenger of Allah who had become a statue of light himself and was watching the Light of Grace. The Beauty of Allah that is promised to the believers in Paradise was observed here and in this horizon where space became non-space, the Messenger of Allah would meet the Gracious Lord without any mediation. The Great Lord who had exalted Abraham with special intimacy and Moses with His word would throne his Beloved, the last golden chain of the constellation of Prophethood with seeing Him; thus showing time and space how the Messenger of Allah stood with the Lord.

Leaving all this beauty and splendor behind and going back to the land of difficulty and strife was something that only a merciful Messenger like him could do, for he had seen, and he was coming back to show his *Ummah* what he had seen; he had heard and he was returning to us to let our souls hear what he had heard and experienced. He had seen the beyond including the horizon of Sight. He was now returning to share with those who followed him, the harmonious beauty he had seen, in order that he may open the doors of such sight to ready and capable souls. He had gone as himself, had seen and heard as himself and he was returning as himself.

Just as his departure had been a clear lesson for all, his return also contained meaningful messages. Furthermore, the Messenger of Allah had completed this long journey that he had set on in the middle of the night and had returned having crammed all these events he had experienced in a very short period of time. The first people whom he told of his journey were naturally those closest to him. As soon as he performed his Morning Prayer, he turned to his household and started to recount all the events that had happened to him in one moment of the night.

He told people what he has experienced, however they did not believe him. They asked Abu Bakr what his opinion was. He said: "If he is saying all that, it must be true." After that day, he had been called Siddiq, the loyal and faithful one.

The Night Journey (*Isra*) and *Miraj* had made the distinction between faith and denial even clearer. While the deniers turned towards their dark worlds and followed their own traps, those who believed renewed their determination to speak the truth to the most stubborn of people, and wanted more than ever to be foot soldiers of the cause to find new faces who might embrace the faith.

Aqaba Allegiances

Now was not the time to stop. The Messenger of Allah had turned his face away from Mecca once again and was contemplating new openings in other lands. Twelve years had passed since the meeting in Hira. It was the pilgrimage season once again. He was expecting news from the six Ansar from Medina who had come to him and become Muslim the year before.

The time he was waiting for came and our noble Prophet went to Mina in order to meet those traveling to Mecca and to tell them about Islam. He had, in a way, set up camp there, and treated everyone he met as fresh hope, inviting everyone he saw to faith in Allah. There were also those who were looking for him in this crowd. These were the youths from Medina who had become Muslim the year before. They saw him from afar and ran towards him. The place they met in Mina was called Aqaba. But now they had doubled in number. The only name from the year before who had not been able to make it was Jabir ibn Abdullah. Added to those from last year were Muadh ibn Harith, Zakwan ibn Abdulqays, Ubada ibn Samit, Yazid ibn Salaba, Abbas ibn Ubada, Abu'l-Haytham at-Tayyihani and Uwaymir ibn Saida. They had become Muslim and they had come to Mecca for a permanent union. This meeting meant a new opening for Islam, for the grip that was tightening in Mecca would find a release in Medina, and maybe the cause of Allah would take root in a place other than where it had originated. In short, what had been foreshadowed was now taking its course, and the words of Waraqa ibn Nawfal were turning out to be true.

They spoke at length, and afterwards the Messenger of Allah asked for their allegiance. He said: "Come and give allegiance to not holding anything equal to Allah, not to steal, not to commit adultery, not to kill your children, to have control over your hands and feet and not to slander anyone, to obey me in all that is good and beautiful! Whoever stays true to his word from among you and remains loyal, remember that it is Allah who will reward him, and whoever faces difficulty in keeping his allegiance and is persecuted, this will be atonement for him, for those who keep secret what has befallen them will be judged by Allah. He may forgive if He pleases, and He may punish if He pleases."

The Pride of Humankind, peace and blessings be upon him, was standing before them and calling them to virtue, because whatever they had suffered from, it had always resulted from not heeding the issues that they had been warned and informed about. Now, by accepting the Messenger of Allah's call for virtue, they had the chance to attain a quality of life they longed for. Each issue had been addressed carefully and in detail, and now it was time to farewell. However, there was something on the minds of the Ansar from Medina. They had learned some of Islam's rulings while they had been in the company of the Messenger of Allah but Islam was a religion that was being renewed every day, a religion that came to the people with a new message as the need arose. Also, because they had failed to come to an alliance as the tribes of Khazraj and Aws, they could have difficulties in letting the other tribe lead the Prayers, and even this could constitute a problem among them. In the short period of time they had spent with the Messenger of Allah they had not had the time to learn about the verses that had been revealed to that day, so they needed a *murshid*, a teacher, a guide. They spoke of this need to the Messenger of Allah before they took their leave. His benevolent eyes searched around for someone who would go with the Ansar to Medina and to make out of their town a civilized city before the official migration would take place: "Mus'ab!" called out the noble Messenger.

It was decided that this guide would be Mus'ab ibn Umayr, the once wealthy son of a family who disowned him as their child merely because he had become a Muslim. It was a sad departure for Mus'ab because he would now have to part from his Beloved. But duty came before everything else and he set on the road for Medina with all excitement and without hesitation. There, he would represent the Messenger of Allah and he would teach the religion that the people of Medina had only recently been introduced to. This was an honorable duty indeed; it was now Mus'ab who would make Medina ready for the impending "Divine migration"; he would lay the foundations of the civilized city of Medina. Yes, he was alone, but he was going with the power of the cause he was representing. It was As'ad ibn Zurara who opened his doors to him in Medina. He took him in his home and they started to look for ways together to share the beauties in their hearts with the people of Medina. This was where they were performing their Prayers five times a day; they were reading the verses of Allah to a new face every day and were struggling to go deeper in their religion. There was now an ember in the Name of Allah in Medina and there was a hearth for faith.

Mus'ab was the perfect representative. People who saw him admired him immensely. His faith, sincerity, modesty and perfect morals attracted the attention of everyone in Medina! Each day one of the leading men of Medina would come to him, and Mus'ab would speak about the finer aspects of religion. He put all his efforts into Medina, he had almost become like a one man *Ummah*. Of course, as was expected, he also had to face certain difficulties, but these were familiar things for him. Wasn't it the Messenger of Allah himself who had had to shoulder the greatest of difficulties? No one wanted to submit easily! But those who came to him with swords in their hands would return with faith in their hearts. Mus'ab would speak to the future Companions of the Prophet who first came to him in fury in such soft tones, the sternest of them could not resist his nice behavior, and before long they came and submitted themselves.

"My friend, first listen to me, and then you can cut my throat if you like. I will not resist you," Mus'ab would tell them.

Indeed, in the face of a person taking life so lightly and who cared for nothing but for speaking the truth to people, all ice seemed to melt, and the circle of faith around Mus'ab grew day by day.

One day, As'ad ibn Zurara took Mus'ab to the neighborhood where his family lived. They came to a well and stopped for a break. Sa'd ibn Muadh and Usayd ibn Khudayr from among the inhabitants had heard that they were coming and they did not approve of these latest developments. They were talking among themselves. Sa'd pulled Usayd to one side and asked him to banish both of them from their land. Usayd took his spear and approached them. As'ad and Mus'ab who saw him coming could guess what was about to happen. But their concern was different to many others, for once faith had taken root in a heart, and that heart wanted to share its wealth with other people even if they should come with the intention of murder; that heart needed to show its difference. As'ad whispered into Mus'ab's ear and told him who Usayd was. In *tabligh*, communicating one's faith, knowing your interlocutor was very important indeed. Usayd was the lord of his tribe and Mus'ab had to speak to him accordingly.

Usayd started his rebukes the minute he addressed them. He was very angry: "Why do you come here and suggest these things to the weak? If you want to stay alive, leave this place immediately!"

Mus'ab was as gentle as ever: "Will you sit down a while and listen? If you like it, you'll accept it. If you don't like it we will do as you please."

This was a reasonable reply, so reasonable that one had to be fair in the face of such behavior. Usayd was a reasonable man. The situation was clear for him; he thought things would not change even if he did listen. Then what harm could there be in this? If he liked it, he would leave and if he did not like it, they would leave. He set his spear aside and sat down to listen to what Mus'ab had to say. Wisdom was flowing from the lips of Mus'ab like sweet honey. Usayd was very impressed. He was about to submit to the faith as well. He was unable to control the exuberance he felt in his heart. The expressions on his face were mere reflections of the changes happening in his heart. Even before Mus'ab was finished with what he had to say, he intervened and started to say: "What a wonderful thing this is… What beautiful words…" and then he added: "What must someone who wants to enter this religion do?"

Mus'ab spoke to him of *ghusl*, the major ablution. He spoke of how one's clothes had to be clean, he spoke of the words of *tawhid* needed to declare the oneness of Allah, and he spoke to him about the Daily Prayers.

Usayd got up and left. He just seemed to disappear! When he came back to the gathering, one could see water dripping from his wet hair. Usayd had believed and he spoke the words of *tawhid* from his very heart. Faith had changed him so fast and so much that he started to feel Mus'ab's anxiety there and then: "There is someone I know, if he also believes, there will be no one left who doesn't believe in this town. Wait, I will send him to you," he said.

Usayd went straight to Sa'd ibn Muadh. Sa'd and his friends had gathered together and were waiting for Usayd. When they saw him coming they said to one another: "I swear he is not coming in the same way that he went!" Sa'd had understood. When Usayd came, he was asked hastily:

"What did you do?" Usayd responded saying that he had encountered no problems: "By Allah, I spoke with those two men. There is nothing wrong with them. First I dismissed them. Then they said 'We will do as you please'."

Usayd's aim was to have Sa'd and Mus'ab meet each other and so he was trying to convince Sa'd that they were now holding the ropes and that he could go speak to the men if he so wanted. In order for him to see the beauty in all its clarity, Sa'd needed to be in Mus'ab's presence. People didn't like the atmosphere to be so friendly. There were those who wanted to keep the enmity going. They started to say things that would provoke Sa'd. They wanted to make him feel that things were getting out of control and these developments had to be stopped right then and there.

As mentioned, Sa'd was the lord of his tribe and he could not allow such disorder. His veins were throbbing because of the nerves. He was also very angry at Usayd. He had sent him there to see to this issue once and for all and now he had come back speaking about the beauty of what he had encountered. He had to solve this problem himself. He took his spear and went straight to Mus'ab. He was so angry that he was breathing through his nostrils and was saying everything that came to his mouth. He first blew at his aunt's son As'ad who had brought Mus'ab to their town: "Had there been no family bond between us, you would not have escaped my wrath!"

He was throwing threats at Mus'ab and he continued shouting for a while. It looked like the tempests raging inside him were not going to calm down any time soon. But there was no change in Mus'ab's attitude. He was showing the same maturity as always, for he did not care about death. He was only looking for ways to give life even to people who came to kill him: "Please listen! If you like it, you'll accept it. If you don't, then you can do as you like," he said with the same sweetness. The decision lay with Sa'd again.

"You are right," he said, for there was no man on earth who could make him do something he didn't want to. Just like Usayd, he put his spear aside, sat down and started to listen to Mus'ab. He was struck at the very start with the invocation "In the Name of Allah, the All-Merciful, the All-Compassionate" that Mus'ab had spoken! Light upon light was settling on his face. Even before Mus'ab had finished what he was to say, he started to ask questions similar to Usayd: "What does one need to do when one wants to submit and enter this religion?"

Mus'ab told him the same thing he had told Usayd. Everything was clear and out in the open, and to grasp the truth wherever one finds it, was true virtue. Denial had no logic to produce excuses! It had nothing left, nor could it have any excuses any more. In the company of Mus'ab he too would set about the task to find the key that would unlock the hearts of his tribe. He too was not returning back to his tribe the way he had gone to seek Mus'ab.

They understood now the state Mus'ab was in... Sa'd also started to feel the same anxiety, for he had found a value that he had not realized till that day and now he felt the need to share it with everyone he knew!

Something had to be said to the curious looks given by the members of his tribe. Sa'd had no intention to let even one person from his tribe loose. He first asked them: "How do you know me among you?"

They all confirmed his good character. Sa'd meant to turn his standing among his tribe into credit for faith. He shared with them what he got from the source and then invited them to faith. He put everything he had in it and then added: "If you do not believe Allah and His Messenger, I will not speak to any of you, man or woman." When leading men like Usayd and Sa'd accepted, naturally, the others followed. In Medina everyone looked to one another. It would not be becoming of them not to follow when men who had been their guides till that day had submitted: "Come, let us go to Mus'ab! Let us submit as well!"

Amazingly, these voices were now being heard in Medina!

Medina was a very fertile place. The news of Mus'ab was spreading with the speed of light. In a very short time, there were no households left in Medina that had not converted to Islam. Mus'ab was going from house to house, sharing the wealth of his heart and preparing the people to become Ansar, the Helpers. Gradually, the whole of Medina had embraced its name to the fullest and had become a Medina, a civilized city.

The light of faith could not contain itself within Medina and had started to spread to its outskirts. Mus'ab was going to the surrounding tribes and carrying the same beauties to them. The Messenger of Allah had done the very same thing; on the one hand he had addressed Mecca, and on the other he had not neglected speaking about Islam to the surrounding tribes. Mus'ab, who was perfectly trying to represent him, could do no different.

One day, Mus'ab wrote a letter to the Messenger of Allah. There was a request made to him and he was asking his beloved Prophet how he should act. In his reply Allah's Messenger described the *Jumu'ah* Prayer to him and the Muslims in Medina gathered in the house of Sa'd ibn Haythama and performed the first *Jumu'ah* Prayer in Medina. About a year had passed since they had given their allegiance to the noble Messenger in Aqaba. Now when they got together, they formed a big congregation. These were good developments, but the pain of severance was difficult to bear. They knew what the Messenger of Allah was suffering immensely in Mecca and

The Luminous Life of Our Prophet

were asking themselves: "For how much longer will we leave him under oppression between the mountains of Mecca, how much longer will we have him suffer?"

Medina was much nicer, more sincere and embracing. This separation and suffering was not the way to go; they had to find a way to have their routes meet, and this separation had to end. There were two ways to do this; either they were to go to Mecca and be his congregation, or they were going to invite the Beloved, peace and blessings be upon him, to Medina to be their leader. When each option was weighed out, both held difficulties. But these difficulties had to be risked and a solution had to be found, for this separation had to end.

The Invitation from Medina

It was the pilgrimage season once again, and as ritually expected, there was a flow of people towards Mecca. There were also Muslims from Medina among those who were coming to the Ka'ba for the pilgrimage. These were seventy five people, including two women. They came to Mecca after a long and arduous journey. This was the most joyful day for them. But for the Mecca of that day, it was impossible for this many people to come and meet with our noble Prophet in the Ka'ba. They had to find another solution and this meeting had to take place without encountering any problems. That is why they first chose Ka'b ibn Malik and Bara ibn Ma'rur among them and sent them to the Ka'ba. With the influence of a dream he had, Bara had been performing his Prayers facing the direction of the Ka'ba. His friends had censured him, for this meant dissension from our noble Prophet's practices who faced the Masjid al-Aqsa. He was looking forward to asking the Messenger of Allah about the truth of the matter. What was strange was neither of them had seen the Messenger of Allah before and they did not know what he looked like. They started to speak among themselves on the road, wondering how they would recognize him. They asked a Meccan. The Meccan responded: "Do you know his uncle Abbas ibn Abdul Muttalib?"

Yes, they knew Abbas who came to Medina now and then for trade: "Yes," they said. The man said: "Then it is easy! He is the man who sits next to Abbas in the Ka'ba! Go there and you will see."

Now they were walking without hesitation. Then they came to the Ka'ba. Abbas was sitting down and the Pride of Humankind, peace and blessings be upon him, was with him. They approached them and saluted them. When they saw how warm and sincere they were, the Messenger of Allah turned to Abbas and said: "Do you know these men, O Abu Fadl?"

"Yes," said Abbas, "This is Bara ibn Ma'rur; head of his tribe, and this is Ka'b ibn Malik!"

The light of joy was upon the face of the Messenger of Allah because these names did not represent just themselves. There were seventy more people like them behind them and they had come representing them. They asked how they were to meet. The location was once again Mina, the place called Aqaba, like in previous years. They went back to their friends and let them know of the situation.

But the other people they had come with from Medina did not know of this. That is why they would camp with them the first night and they would meet with our noble Prophet in the late hours of the night.

When the time of the meeting had come, they got up without making a sound and came to the place of the meeting. Our noble Prophet was once again accompanied by his uncle Abbas. When the Messenger of Allah saw seventy five people in front of him, he was overjoyed beyond words. Mus'ab, the one and only representative and guide of the Messenger had left and now he had returned with seventy five people! Never in the thirteen years of strife in Mecca had so many people been welcomed into Islam at once. The troubles in Mecca seemed to have transformed into a shower of blessing in Medina. This was the product of one year, and now they were speaking of the process that led them here. Mus'ab had another piece of good news that would make his Beloved, peace and blessings be upon him, happy. This was in fact the good news that was awaited from every believer! He was very emotional as he recounted his good fortune: "O Messenger of Allah! There is no household in Medina left in which Islam is not spoken about," he said with great modesty.

For a believing soul to live and be present in any part of the world meant that that place had already been conquered in the name of the cause. The Messenger of Allah had provided the goal, and Mus'ab had received the message. That is why people had come running after the steps he had taken; he had reaped the harvest of the sincerity he had sown.

They had a joint request; they were inviting the Rose of the Hearts, Muhammad the Trustworthy, peace and blessings be upon him, to Medina. The reasoning was valid; Medina seemed much more favorable for an Islamic way of life. Its people were also warmer and more welcoming to a religious way of life.

Yes, there was an invitation, but there was a great price to be paid in order to accept it. Our noble Prophet's hijra alone would not solve the problem; everyone who believed would have to immigrate to Medina. For the ones who stayed in Mecca, the Quraysh would devise various plots and they would suffocate them with their harassment. This presented them with a great problem; they would have to leave their houses and possessions, relatives and friends here. For some, immigration would also mean leaving parents and children behind, and leaving the fields and orchards in the hands of the Quraysh. In short, this would be like leaving for the grave, for everything with worldly connections would be left in Mecca. On the other hand, one would have to start anew and with nothing in Medina, they would have to set up new homes and start new businesses. While one lived one's religion freely, one also had to find a way to earn a living so that one's family and children would not have to suffer poverty and scarcity. It wasn't just a couple of families; there were about 180 of them! If these problems weren't solved soon, there would be very serious social problems and this could cause further problems in the future.

It was clear that the Messenger of Allah now had decided to leave Mecca. For thirteen years he had strived for the faith of his community but he had always been met with violence. But now before him were people who were actively supporting his cause. His uncle Abbas, who watched from afar what was happening, felt the need to say something to these people who were inviting the Messenger of Allah to their land. He said: "O people of Khazraj! As you know, despite everything, Muhammad is among us and we are protecting him despite all interferences. But now he means to join you and go with you to your land. Accept this only if you will able to be true to your word, if you will be able to protect him against those who contradict him as you protect your own life and possessions. But if you will leave him alone after you leave this place and hand him over to his enemies, if you will hurt him in the end, then give up the idea right now and leave him with us.

Despite everything, he lives here with his own tribe with honor and dignity and performs his duties as should be."

With this statement, Abbas wanted to remind them what their invitation meant. He wanted them to understand the real nature of what they were getting themselves into and to make sure that they would protect his nephew with a strong will despite all the obstructions they may face. He could see that he would soon be separated from his nephew and he was not going to hand him over to other people without seeing the same kind of determination in their eyes.

The people coming from Medina were equally brave and they turned to Abbas to say: "We have listened to what you say and we know what you mean."

They then turned towards the Messenger of Allah and said: "O Messenger of Allah! What do you want from us in the name of your Lord and for yourself?"

Then the Pride of Humankind, peace and blessings be upon him, took word. He first thanked Allah and then read verses from the Qur'an. Then he started to speak about the general aspects of Islam and compared the customs of yesterday with today. He then added: "I want absolute obedience both at times of welfare and wellbeing and at times of trouble; both when you have little to eat and in times of abundance. I want you to give alms! You will never hold any other thing equal to Him, perform the Prayers and give alms! You will advise people to do good and warn against the doing of evil! You will take all your steps for Allah without fearing that some people might censure you. When I come to stay among you, you will protect me like you protect your children and your women and help me."

Bara ibn Ma'rur, held the Messenger of Allah by the hand and said: "Yes, I swear by He who has sent you with Truth that we will protect you as we protect our children and women. We promise you and we swear allegiance to you O Messenger of Allah! I swear by Allah that we are people who know what war is and we can hold our weapons, this is our heritage from our ancestors who always lived on the battlefields."

Here, Abu'l-Haytham came to the fore. It was clear that he too had something to say: "O Messenger of Allah! We have a problem with a tribe over there and we keep warring with them. While we fight with them on this issue, should Allah give you victory and should your cause start to be accepted by all, will you then leave us and go back to Mecca?"

The Messenger of Allah started to smile. Then he said: "No. On the contrary, the rule is blood for blood, possession for possession! Now I am a part of you, and you are a part of me. I will fight who you fight, and I will live in peace with those you have come to an agreement with!"

As'ad ibn Zurara also came to the fore, held the hand of the Messenger of Allah and said similar things. Things were much clearer now. As'ad was told by his own tribe to let go of our noble Prophet's hand, so that they may too hold it and swear allegiance to him. Upon that the Messenger of Allah asked them to form a representative delegate of ten. While doing so, he was making references to Moses and Jesus, telling them that both Prophets had chosen certain people with whom they took their cause further. Each delegate would represent a tribe; they would organize their friends, and they would also act as a catalyst when they returned to Medina to ensure that Islam spread faster in their town. These people were As'ad ibn Zurara, Sa'd ibn Rabi, Abdullah ibn Rawa-ha, Rafi ibn Malik, Bara ibn Ma'rur, Abdullah ibn Amr, Uba-da ibn Samit, Sa'd ibn Ubada and Munzir ibn Amr from the Khazraj and Usayd ibn Khudayr, Sa'd ibn Haythama and Rifa'a ibn Abdulmunzir from the tribe of Aws. The Meccan Muslims were represented by the Messenger of Allah himself. Things were now going to be wrapped up.

Abbas ibn Ubada came to the fore and said to his friends: "O people of Khazraj! Do you realize what you are doing by swearing allegiance to this man?"

"Yes," they said. His aim was to make people realize the responsibility of their word and to make them hold on to it faster and stronger. He continued: "You stand now against all, the red and the black, declaring war on all! If you think you can hold onto your word when your possessions and family become targets, then all is well; then happiness in this world and the next will be yours. But if you fail to show loyalty when you face difficulties tomorrow, then this will spell your defeat in this world and the next."

"We are entering this cause at the expense of our property and at the risk of bringing trouble on the heads of our family; we invite him in full knowledge of this," the responded.

They then turned to our noble Prophet and asked: "If we prove ourselves to be loyal to our word, what will we gain, O Messenger of Allah?"

He answered without hesitation: "Paradise."

It was now time to take the last step. With great respect they said: "Give us your hands, O Messenger of Allah. We will swear allegiance to you."

They then came to the Messenger of Allah one by one, held his hand in *musafaha*, a gesture in which both hands enveloped the hands of other, and thus sealed their allegiance. The two women from Medina, Nasiba bint Ka'b known as Umm Umara and Asma bint Amr who had come all the way with the group, also sealed their allegiance from afar through a gesture.

The Permission for Hijra

Meanwhile, the Truthful Gabriel had come and brought the permission for hijra. This meant that the oppression and violence in Mecca would end and he would continue his life in a healthier environment. The Companions would start one by one to set on the road and they would leave Mecca without provoking anyone. They knew that there was the Ansar and a blessed city waiting for them with open doors.

A new process had started. In a short while, everyone who could set off for the road would start their journey and would reach a new region, a new world. But this would not be as easy as they thought.

The hijra of the Muslims was not easy for the Quraysh to accept; when they learnt of the Muslims' plan, they did all that was in their power to stop them, to prevent them from getting out of their control and go to another land. The Quraysh already resented the fact that they had failed to change the course of events in the previous two hijras to Ethiopia so they wanted to do all they could to prevent Islam from spreading in other regions.

That is why they would stand guard on the road and try to turn people back from their journey. They arrested and imprisoned some of them and subjected them to torture, trying to make them recant their faith. Sometimes they even pursued them all the way to Medina. In short, Mecca was displaying all the characteristics of a repressive regime, and as deniers they made it clear that Hell itself was not in vain.

Despite all the pressure and obstruction, the hijra to Medina continued. Three months had passed after the hijra which had started with Abu Salama. Among the Muslims, only slaves and imprisoned ones, along with the Messenger of Allah Abu Bakr and Ali remained in Mecca. It was none other than the Messenger of Allah himself who had postponed Abu Bakr and Ali's hijra. Now it was their turn.

Things were not irreversible at the moment; they could solve the problem right now. That's why they needed immediate precautions. It was the twenty-sixth of the month of Safar, and it was a Monday.

Late this morning they gathered together to discuss their final strategy. As usual, they went to Daru'n-Nadwa, their advisory assembly place inherited from Qusay ibn Kilab. They wanted to solve this issue that had continued for fourteen years; they were treating the issue in such secrecy that they were not allowing people younger than forty years of age to attend; they were doing all they could to prevent what was being spoken inside to reach outside those walls.

An old man with rugged clothes whom they didn't know, who said that he was from Najid, came to them and were waiting to join them at the door.

"Who is it?" They asked anxiously.

"An old man from Najid, I am among your uncles' sons! I have heard that you have gathered here together for a very important business and I came thinking that I may be of some use. I will leave if you do not want me."

"If he is our uncles' son, then he is from us! He wouldn't come from Najid to spy against us! Anyhow, he is not from Mecca," they said and so they let him in.

And then the conversations started. Abu Jahl was leading the discussion. He started the sitting: "You know the position of this man of yours; if he leaves you and goes elsewhere to gather strength and attack you, this will cause you much headache. Tell me what you think we can do to avoid this situation and let me see whether you can come together to devise something."

Abu'l-Bakhtari took word: "Tie him up in chains and imprison him; lock the doors on him and wait. One day he too will grow old like other poets before him and die."

The old man from Najid intervened: "I am not of your opinion. This will never solve your problem! If you imprison him like you suggest, his cause will go over the walls you build around him and reach his friends. Then they will attack you and take him away from you and build their strength outside. This is not a solution, you should think of something else."

Aswad ibn Rabia then spoke: "We have to tear him away from our society, kick him out of the country, and let him go wherever he wants! Then we will be rid of him! We will not care where he goes or settles after we have got rid of him."

This idea did not please the old man either, he took word and said: "I swear this is not a solution! Do you not see the beauty in his words, the intellectuality in his logic and the grace in his actions? These will affect the hearts of people and he will reappear among you one day. If you do that, the day will come when he will move the masses with his virtues and you will find yourselves facing the tribes that have given him his word! He will come and want to have what you have, and then you will not be able to do anything against him. You should find another solution."

There was something strange indeed with this old man's position; the Meccans had come together to find a solution to the problem but this man from Najid was even more eager than the Meccans! They were happy to have included him in this assembly.

Abu Jahl, who was chairing the meeting, was also pleased with the contributions of the old man from Najid. For him, the solutions suggested were not valid either. But he himself could not think of another option. The eyes turned towards Abu Jahl who was consolidating the old man's stance. He was waiting for his turn to speak: "I also have an opinion on this matter that you are trying to resolve," he said.

"What is it, O Abal Hakam?" they asked. He continued: "I believe the ultimate solution lies in raising a group of able young men from each tribe who are active and good marksmen. They should attack him with their swords and kill him at one strike, and thus we will be rid of him! When he is killed in this way his blood will be on the hands of all the tribes, and the sons of Abdimanaf won't be able to confront all these tribes. They will only have the option of demanding blood money; we will pay it and the issue will be solved."

The old man from Najid entered the conversation at this moment and this time, he was nodding his head in agreement, and the last thing he said was: "The word spoken by this friend is the right one! I cannot think of any other solution!"

They had now made their decision and were going to put their plan of killing Muhammad, peace and blessings be upon him, into practice. They left the Daru'n-Nadwa in secrecy just as they had gathered there and each went to his own home.

The Holy Migration

On the other hand, the Messenger of Allah now had the permission for hijra, and he was about to leave Mecca. One of the verses that the Truthful Gabriel had brought was continuously on his lips, at every opportunity he was supplicating: *"My Lord! Cause me to enter in a manner sincere and faithful to the truth, and cause me to exit in a manner sincere and faithful to the truth, and grant me from Your Presence a sustaining authority!"* (al-Isra 17:80), and now these prayers had been answered and the Messenger of Allah was about to set out for Medina for the holy hijra. The Truthful Gabriel told him of the traps that the Meccans were setting: "Do not always sleep in the same bed, O Messenger of Allah."

And then he told him the strategy he should use when he left Mecca in order to escape Quraysh's traps. In short, the hijra started in between the conspiracies of the Quraysh and the precautions provided by Allah, the All-Knowing. Our noble Prophet asked Gabriel, after he had brought him the good news of the hijra:

"Who will be my Companion on the hijra?"

"Abu Bakr," he replied.

Abu Bakr had been eagerly waiting to be the Prophet's Companion on this journey. Then, unexpectedly at noon time, when everyone else was relaxing in their homes, the

Messenger of Allah came and knocked on Abu Bakr's door; he was asking leave to enter. This was strange indeed! The most beloved servant of Allah, peace and blessings be upon him, was at Abu Bakr's door, waiting to enter.

"May my mother and father be sacrificed for you! There must be something really important since he comes at such an hour," Abu Bakr mumbled to himself.

Before long he ran to the door and welcomed in the Messenger of Allah. He was waiting anxiously, for the Messenger of Allah would normally come in the cool hours of either the morning or the evening. Before long, the Messenger of Allah asked the members of the household—Abu Bakr's daughters Asma and Aisha—to leave the room. Abu Bakr said: "Do not fear, O Messenger of Allah! They are my daughters; they are like your family! May my mother and father be sacrificed for you! Is there something wrong?" He asked trying to understand the reason of his visit.

The reply was not late in coming: "I have been given the permission to leave Mecca and go on the hijra."

Abu Bakr was now even more excited and asked: "Are we to go together, O Messenger of Allah?"

The following words flowed from the Messenger's lips towards the face that was waiting eagerly: "Yes, together."

Abu Bakr was overjoyed! He had prepared for that day and was waiting for the order to go. When he had asked for permission to migrate with the other Companions, he had received the reply: "Do not make haste! One hopes that Allah will give you a Companion!"

Afterwards, they started the preparations for two. For four months he had been preparing two camels for this long trip. He had been expecting these very words from his Beloved. This was the start of the next phase that would change the course of events. Being the Companion to the Messenger of Allah on this historic journey! Could there be a greater fortune than this? Abu Bakr, may Allah be pleased with him, had been unable to control himself and was crying out of joy.

Before long, he brought two camels to the Messenger of Allah and said: "O Messenger of Allah! I have prepared these two rides for our journey."

But the Beloved of Allah, peace and blessings be upon him, had to be an example in all respects and so said to Abu Bakr: "Only under one condition: If I pay the price of the camels," Thus making it clear that on such an important journey as this, one could not make use of something, the price of which one had not paid.

The Precautions concerning
the Hijra

Since everything had already been communicated, it was time to set on the journey; Abu Bakr would prove that he was *siddiq* and would take precautions to make the road safer as befitting to his name. One had to be on guard at all times. Going on such a long journey with camels was not going to be easy. So, they first made an agreement with a polytheist by the name of Abdullah ibn Urayqit who knew the road well.

Abdullah had the same mentality with the Quraysh in regards to Islam, but Abu Bakr and the Messenger of Allah trusted him in the matter of the road. Abdullah ibn Urayqit could have been tempted by the money that they had put on their heads and could give the Quraysh information about the direction they were going to go. But the Messenger of Allah knew very well the character of the people he dealt with. Even though he was a polytheist, Abdullah was a man who did not care much about the gains of this world and was a man of his word.

He was a man who knew the road they were going to take very well. Even in such risky circumstances, what mattered were the capabilities of the person in question. They were to meet at Thawr three days later and Abdullah was going to bring the two camels that Abu Bakr had bought for the hijra, and thus the journey would start.

Abu Bakr had told his daughter Asma to prepare their food and to send it to Thawr while they would be staying there. There was another precaution that Abu Bakr took; he called his shepherd Amir to his side and asked him to herd the sheep after them so that their tracks would be covered by the tracks of the sheep. He knew very well that the Meccans were very good at following tracks and so they could easily use this to their advantage.

Abu Bakr's son Abdullah would come to them together with Amir and bring them the food that Asma prepared along with the news of the Meccans during the period they stayed there. Abdullah would come to the cave at night and would leave in the early hours of the morning, and during this time, Amir would come to graze the sheep in *Thawr*, and this scheme was to be followed every day during their stay there. Thus, the travelers on this blessed road would also have met their need for milk.

Another precaution that one had to take was on the part of our noble Prophet, peace and blessings be upon him; he had left his nephew Ali in his place so that he would take care of the things that had been entrusted to him by people and return them to their rightful owners. His greatness was such that he was not going to let even the people who tried to kill him, lose their properties. He was very careful about the things that were left in his care and was appointing his beloved nephew to see to it that everyone got what was rightfully theirs.

These measures were not unnecessary; they were all approved by the Messenger of Allah for he was sent as mercy to all his *Ummah*. He knew very well that Allah would protect him even if he didn't do all these and take all these measures, for Allah the Almighty had told him that He would protect him from all dangers that could come from people, and he kept reciting this comforting verse of the Qur'an in his Prayers.

The matter was different indeed; the Messenger of Allah was a guide, a model for people, a model according to which they could rearrange and reshape their lives. If he had declared his hijra like Umar, then the whole of his *Ummah* would have felt the need to follow his steps exactly, and this would have meant encouraging people to take a step that they might not have been ready to take. He would thus take into account the weakest of his *Ummah* and would arrange his business according to these conditions. That is why he took all the precautions possible and gave the most excellent lesson about taking the means for the end into consideration.

On the other hand, the Quraysh thought that they were about to reach their solution. The people they had chosen from among themselves had come together and surrounded the house of the noble Prophet. These unfortunate people who had been blinded by rage had surrounded the Messenger of Allah's house, and were counting the minutes to deal the final blow.

Now they were waiting for the moment when they would resolve the matter quietly. But Allah the Almighty was powerful over everything and He knew all that was happening. All things in the heavens and earth were subject to the force of His hand and He would do what He wanted when He wanted, and no one would be able to say or do anything against it. Things being thus, the traps that the Quraysh set and the death commando they had prepared had no importance! This would be proven soon.

Under normal circumstances, when the Messenger of Allah performed the Evening Prayer, he would lie down for a while, and when the Ka'ba became peaceful and quiet, he would go there and worship his Lord alone in peace. But this evening things were different; when the Messenger of Allah heard of the situation, he called Ali to his side and said: "Wrap yourself up in this green mantle and lie on my bed. Do not fear, lie down and sleep, for they will not be able to harm you at all."

Then the Messenger of Allah recited the first nine verses of the Surah Ya-Sin and then stepped outside his home. The Quraysh were keeping vigil outside. At that moment he was reciting the verse: *"And We have set a barrier before them and a barrier behind them, and (thus) We have covered them (from all sides), so that they cannot see"* (Ya-Sin 36:9).

He then threw the earth and dust he picked up from the ground over those who had surrounded his house, and accompanying this act he was saying: "Let these faces turn black and become blind!"

The earth he threw touched every one of them and miraculously, it was as if they had gone blind. He was walking among them and yet none of them could see him. Yes, these people had set up a plan to deprive the most beloved servant of Allah of his home and had come to kill him; he who had done nothing to them except inviting them to the Truth. However, Allah the Almighty who had sent him as a Prophet of mercy to all realms also had a plan. It was clear that even if something as wrong as denial may be exacerbated there was no way to stand before the will of Allah, and what He says would always come to pass.

The Messenger of Allah had already left. After a while someone else approached the people who had been waiting outside his home. When he saw them in that state he asked: "Why are you waiting here?"

They answered without hesitation: "We are waiting for Muhammad."

The man was enraged. The men they had chosen to kill Muhammad, peace and blessings be upon him, were acting like tame cats; they had not even noticed the earth that had been thrown upon them! While Muhammad the Trustworthy, peace and blessings be upon him, had gone his way, they were lazily waiting at his door, contemplating plans to kill him! This was stupidity loud and clear! When berating them, the man said: "Woe unto you! You dummies! He has already thrown earth over you and has gone his way."

"We swear we did not see him," they said.

They were dumbfounded and helpless! It was as if their ability to see had been taken away from them and they had not been able to see the Messenger of Allah although they had been looking straight at him! They touched their heads to see whether what the man was saying was true. Yes, they were covered in earth, and looking at each other in disbelief they started to shake the dust from their clothes.

Before long, the news spread among the Quraysh, the other leading men who had been awaiting news of Muhammad's death were devastated to hear that the Messenger of Allah had already gone on hijra! All the elders of the tribes ran to his home. When they opened the door and entered, they held their breath for a second, for the bed was not empty! The men who had waited outside were saying: "Here is Muhammad under that blanket! You have caused uproar for nothing."

But this respite did not last long, for Ali sprung up to his feet after hearing so many people enter the room he was sleeping in. This was the second shock for them. They asked with rage: "Where is Muhammad?"

Ali answered rather calmly: "I do not know anything in regards to your question."

It was them who had lost once again; they had been even more enraged by the answer they got and they were throwing threats around. They did not want to leave Ali, so they harassed him for a while and then they took him to the Ka'ba. They imprisoned him hoping that he would tell them the whereabouts of the travelers, hoping that he would give them some kind of a clue to go by. But they understood that they would not be able to get the answers they wanted however much they forced him. Not letting Ali go would be against their interest because he had been left behind to distribute the things that had been entrusted to the noble Prophet, peace and blessings be upon him, and now he was going to give everything to their rightful owners.

The Pharaoh of the *Ummah*, Abu Jahl, showed once again how deserving he was of his title when he said: "I will give a hundred camels to he who brings me Muhammad, dead or alive!"

They were about to lose sight of our beloved Prophet and Abu Bakr altogether at a moment when they thought they had them in their hands. It was clear that they were not going to able to gain control of the situation on their own, and so they supported Abu Jahl's example and the prize on their heads, dead or alive, was officially decided as hundred camels each.

Turning Towards Thawr

It was the 27th day of the month of Safar. The blessed immigration had started from the house of Abu Bakr in the dead of night. The direction, however, was not the direction of Medina as the other Companions had taken, but Thawr, in the direction of Yemen. They went for about eight kilometers and they were going to climb Thawr which was high, full of great rocks and rugged roads. While doing this, the Messenger of Allah was trying to tiptoe so that the people following him would not have traces to pursue them with. He had to maneuver with precaution; he was going to stay there for a while and watch what was happening in Mecca from there, for the Messenger of Allah knew that they did not want to give him breathing space even outside Mecca; he knew that they would try to stop him reaching his goal the minute they realized that he had left his village. The Quraysh knew that the Companions of Muhammad had gone to Medina and they had been pursuing those who directed themselves towards that city. Abu Bakr's sensitivity and effort was not lacking; he was taking great care of the Messenger of Allah fearing something might befall him, sometimes keeping his back and sometimes walking in front.

Abu Bakr wanted to be the first to enter the cave. He wanted to extinguish whatever evil it may harbor and thus protect his Beloved, peace and blessings be upon him, from any harm. This was sensitivity peculiar to Abu Bakr. All his efforts stemmed from his care for the Pride of Humankind that he shouldn't be harmed in any way. That is why he tore off his clothes, and was covering the holes in the cave to prevent wild animals from entering. However, there were two holes left that he could not cover, but he had a solution for these as well: He put each of his feet in the two separate holes and thus invited the noble Prophet in. Years later Umar would speak of these efforts and say "I would have given all I had, and done anything to have Abu Bakr's night at the cave with the Messenger."

Inside the cave, the Messenger of Allah placed his glorious head on the blessed knees of Abu Bakr and started to rest his eyes. Abu Bakr sat there, completely still, with both of his feet covering the two holes of the cave. After some time had passed, Abu Bakr felt a sting on one of his foot. It was the bite of a snake. Despite cringing with pain on the inside, Abu Bakr did not move or make a sound in order to not disturb his beloved Messenger. What great love! What great devotion!

Eventually, the tears that came down from his eyes and the cold sweat pouring from his forehead alerted our noble Prophet and he asked: "What is with you, O Abu Bakr?"

"May my mother and father be sacrificed for you, O Messenger of Allah, a snake has bit me," was all Abu Bakr could say. He was rather embarrassed to be saying this at all, for he did not want to discomfort the Messenger of Allah with such things. He didn't want to waste his precious time with such an issue he thought was insignificant! Upon that the Messenger of Allah placed a little bit of his saliva gently on the wound and then asked his Lord to heal his faithful Companion. All of a sudden, with the will of Allah, things returned to normal as if the incident had not taken place at all. There was no pain left in Abu Bakr.

In the meanwhile, a spider had set to work and was weaving its web at the entrance of the cave. Two pigeons had come to nest at the entrance as well. A tree also started to blossom and was acting as a curtain for our noble Prophet. It was clear that Allah the Almighty was not going to leave his Beloved to anyone else's devices, and was going to protect him Himself. The track followers had climbed Thawr, and they were scanning the cave. When they saw the pigeons, the blossoming tree and the spider web, one of them naturally said: "Look at this spider web! It looks as if it was weaved even before Muhammad was born."

The others were thinking no differently. Even though the spider's web provided only a very thin curtain between them and the Messenger of Allah it had protected him and now the Quraysh were returning empty handed.

Inside the cave, Abu Bakr had seen that the polytheists had closed in on them at a spear's length; he could hear them speak and was breaking out in a cold sweat. He could see the feet of these men and almost hear them breathe and gasp like enraged cows, and he whispered: "O Messenger of Allah! If one of them should kneel and look inside from the viewpoint of his feet, he will see us easily!" It was once again up to the Messenger of Allah to calm his friend down in the cave, a faithful friend whom he had called "my brother."

"Why do you fear about the outcome of two people whose third is Allah, O Abu Bakr?"

It was the Messenger of Allah who was saying this. He was the most beloved servant of Allah, and Allah the Almighty had promised him protection from the evils of men. He was speaking sure of himself for he knew that even if the Quraysh did not understand, Allah the Almighty would help His Last Messenger like He had helped all his Messengers; He would support him, give him peace of heart and help him with armies that eyes could not see.

Abu Bakr knew this as well, but knowledge was not enough to dispel the anxieties that one felt when one actually had to live through this process. All his worry was that something would happen to the Messenger of Allah, for he knew that any harm that fell upon his own head would be limited to one person only, but if something should happen to the Pride of Humankind, peace and blessings be upon him, this would affect the whole of humanity.

At last, the people who had come to the entrance of the cave returned and now the road promised a degree of safety. They waited there for three days. During this time, Abu Bakr, may Allah be pleased with him, stepped out to keep vigil. When all was peace and quiet, his son Abdullah would come to them and bring them news of what was happening. Later came Amir and their guide Abdullah ibn Urayqit; bringing with them the camels that were to take Allah's Messenger and Abu Bakr to Medina.

The news that came from Mecca revealed that the attempts to look for the Messenger of Allah was somewhat abated. This meant that it was time to set off. It was to be with the first light of the month of Rabi al-awwal, another Monday morning. They would leave the cave very early and first would go towards west on the side of the coast, and then through the direction of the Red Sea they would turn towards Medina, their ultimate destination. This was an unusual route between Mecca and Medina. This difficult route would start from Thawr and would take a whole week. Abdullah ibn Urayqit, Amir ibn Fuhayra and Abu Bakr as-Siddiq were with him.

The Messenger of Allah turned towards Mecca one last time; it was clear that he was saddened to leave Mecca which had been a passing point for Prophets and in which the first building on earth had been constructed; a building which was known to be his twin. It was as if he was leaving his heart in Mecca as he left for Medina. He had waited for forty years for revelations to come, and during that period he had often climbed Hira, and prayed that the Ka'ba would one day embrace the kind of worship that it deserved, and contemplated the future. It was not easy; the most beloved of Allah's servants and the last in the chain of Prophets, the Illustrious Beloved of Allah, peace and blessings be upon him, had to leave the house of Allah, setting sail to another land.

These were the last looks he would cast upon Mecca, and it was as if our noble Prophet was speaking to it. Abu Bakr was watching him intently, observing this silent conversation. The following words flowed from his lips: "Mecca I swear, I was forced to leave you! There is no doubt that you are the land that is most pleasing to Allah; He has special gifts for you! I swear by Allah that had your people not forced me to get out, I would not have taken a single step outside!"

After that, the Messenger of Allah led his group on to the journey, followed by his loyal friend Abu Bakr and the Meccan polytheist guide Abdullah ibn Urayqit. They took the coastal route and started to make their way towards Medina.

Suraqa's Pursuit

Even though many people had already given up trying to get the reward money for the Messenger of Allah some still persevered. One of them was Suraqa.

It had been three days since the travelers had left Thawr. The journeymen of this blessed immigration saw, unexpectedly, a cloud of dust approaching from behind them. Abu Bakr was filled with the same worry that he had in Thawr. This time, there was no cave to take refuge in and they had no means to defend themselves.

"O Messenger of Allah! The man following us is about to catch up with us!"

But the Beloved of Allah, peace and blessings be upon him, was calling with the same stance and trust in Allah: "Do not worry! Allah is with us."

They would not be able to cause harm to someone who was only doing his duty, and the Divine mercy was the safest place they could seek refuge in. But Abu Bakr was worried more than ever, and thinking that they had come to the end, he was shedding tears. The Messenger of Allah saw his state and asked: "Why are you crying O Abu Bakr?"

"I swear I am not crying for myself; I fear he will harm you in some way, O Messenger of Allah."

When the silhouette came close enough, it was clear that it was Suraqa who was following them. While Abu Bakr continued to be worried, the Messenger of Allah turned around and looked intently on Suraqa. It was clear that he was trying to maintain eye contact with him, and hold him captive with his eyes to render him incapable. There was also a drift towards the Divine hearth. The lips of the Messenger of Allah were moving and he was praying: "O my Lord! Concerning this man who is approaching us, give us succor the way You see fit," continuously, keeping his gaze fixed on Suraqa.

When the Prophetic gaze touched Suraqa, the feet of the horse he was riding got stuck in the sand. Consequently, he was thrown meters away from where he was, and one could see a cloud of smoke emerging from where he was seen last! First he thought this was an accident. But it did not look like one. When one looked at the causes, one could see nothing that could have caused it. Had what he had heard about him been true? Was Muhammad the Trustworthy, peace and blessings be upon him, truly a Prophet? What if it were true? Suraqa contemplated the thought for a while. There seemed to be no other answer. He started to size up the Pride of Humankind, peace and blessings be upon him, with his eyes. He said to him: "Pray to Allah for me so that I may be released from here," and then added, "I promise if I can get away from this, then I will stop following you."

The request was made to a Prophet; how could it be that he should be faced with a request and he should not answer? Even if the person who had asked was his sworn enemy!

Suraqa was freed from the ditch like nothing had happened. It looked as if the prize put on the heads of the travelers were holding his feelings captive, and when he got on his horse again, he wanted to gallop it once more towards the rewards.

But the same gaze followed him and the front legs of the horse got stuck in the sand once again. A great cloud of dust rose from where he fell. He was in great shock; the front feet of the horse had stuck even deeper this time although there was no reason for it to do so, and he was unable to get them out!

He could not understand what was happening, he had ridden his horse around here for years, but this was the first time such a thing had happened to him. Maybe it was not Abu Jahl but Abu Bakr this time that was right. Then he knew that it was futile to try to do evil to these men who were under Divine protection. Now he was calling out sincerely from the heart: "O Muhammad! I understand that what has befallen me is all due to your prayers. I have camels in such and such place; take whichever you want of them, but please pray that I may get out of here. I promise, truly, that I will not follow you any longer."

The Messenger of Allah first said: "I do not need your camels," and then he prayed for his release. Suraqa was up again with his horse.

As he stood up covered in dust, who knows what was happening in his inner world, for it was not difficult to see the change in his demeanor when he stood up for the second time. Abu Bakr was watching the developments with alarm and awe; and was thanking his Lord to see that the Messenger of Allah had been protected once again. After his stumbling horse, Suraqa was about to go on his knees in front of the Messenger of Allah. One could see the traces of submission in him; he was slowly coming to his presence. The Messenger of Allah looked at him as if saying "You too?"

"Yes, me too, O Messenger of Allah," responded Suraqa, and then promised him that he would go back and divert all his enemies who might mean to follow him into the wrong direction.

Each had to show their loyalty in their own way, through their own self-sacrifice. Now he was also bound on the road of Allah, and was one of the few protectors of the noble Messenger. Then the Messenger of Allah gave him the following good tidings: "I wonder how you will be when you take possession of the two bracelets of Chosroes of Persia, O Suraqa!"

Suraqa had paid no price for his own release and he had also been honored with Islam, and now he was receiving good news about his future! This was the news that one of the two most powerful states at the time would soon be defeated and that the bracelets that symbolized the power of the king would be Suraqa's. He could not believe it!

"You mean Chosroes, the son of Hurmuz?" Suraqa tried to clarify.

Our noble Prophet replied: "Yes."

This also meant the appointment of a new goal for the *Ummah*, starting with Suraqa himself.

And so Suraqa, who had set off with the intention of killing the noble Prophet, had now become a Muslim in his presence, and what's more, he had also received the decree of the Messenger of Allah and was returning to Mecca as a new man.

This man who meant to take our noble Prophet's life only a short while ago would now become a hero of the instantaneous bonding that took place in the Prophet's presence. He would take a stance that would divert people from following Allah's Messenger and he would tell everybody that there was nobody to be caught in the direction where he came from.

The Excitement of the First Meeting

Meanwhile, Medina was experiencing a great sense of excitement, waiting for our noble Prophet's arrival. That is why they had gathered at the place called Harra, and they were gazing at the road. The general name of this place was Quba.

They knew the day that the journeyers had left Mecca and they could estimate the day that they would arrive in Medina, so with the first light of day they would go out of town to wait for them. They would wait there till the hottest time of the day, and when they saw that he did not come, they would retire to the shade and wait there till the afternoon. They did not know how long they had spent at Thawr, and so they did not know how much they would be delayed. This wait continued for three days. It was the eighth day of the month of Rabi al-awwal, again a Monday, and the third day of waiting. When noon came, they had once more retired to the shade. At that moment they heard the voice of a caller. They looked towards where the voice was coming from; it belonged to a Jewish man from Medina. Allah the Almighty had given the mission of giving such good news to the Ansar (the Helpers) and the Muhajirun (the Migrants) with this lucky Jewish man. Maybe He was also pointing to a fact with this, that the Jewish people comprised the majority of the population in Medina.

The Jewish man was shouting at the top of his lungs: "O sons of Qayla! Here, the friend you have been waiting for has come!"

Medina was engulfed with a wave excitement and had become one beating heart. They ran to and fro in order to meet and welcome him, their cries declaring the greatness of Allah resounding through the town. The journey that started on the first day of Rabi al-awwal in Thawr had ended, after a long and tiring week, in Quba.

The Ansar of Medina got their weapons; they were taking their precautions lest any problems should arise. They gathered to meet the beloved Messenger with a great ceremony in Harra.

Since the Beloved's arrival in Quba, people were racing each other to be his host, for they all wanted to invite him to their homes. He would choose to stay with the sons of an-Najjar, for the sons of an-Najjar were the relatives of his grandfather Abdul Muttalib. People had formed a human chain on the road and were welcoming and embracing the Messenger of Allah a treasure who the Meccans could not bear to the degree that they had wanted to kill him. Some people were standing on rooftops in order to see his beautiful face, some were hanging from windows!

It was as though the Ansar had been living a life of drought and had been left thirsty for years, and it was as the Messenger of Allah who was the water of life and good fortune that was about to rain down on them. It was clear that when they pronounced his name they were feeling him to their very bones.

People had come in great numbers to the see the noble Messenger. He had come all this way to be with them, how could they stay where they were and not embrace him? Some of them had even dreamt of meeting him for years, and dreamt of this special day; they were exuberant with celebratory songs. He was now very close.

Where they were staying as guests was the neighborhood of Kulthum ibn al-Hadm. But just as in Mecca, he would not stay put and would reach out to people. That is why he went to the house of Sa'd ibn Haythama and spoke with the youth there at length. It was well known that the house of Sa'd ibn Haythama was where the unmarried young men gathered. That is why some even say that this was the house that our beloved Prophet stayed at in Quba.

Not all of the Ansar had seen the Messenger of Allah yet and that is why the people who had come to welcome him did not know for certain which one he was. They were going to meet him for the first time! Abu Bakr, may Allah be pleased with him, was standing, and the Messenger of Allah was sitting in silence. The people coming to meet them directed themselves towards Abu Bakr. Abu Bakr, modest as he was, was very embarrassed because of this misunderstanding; that is why he pointed to the Messenger of Allah by shading him with part of his garment. People now knew who was who, and they all said with the one voice "welcome O Messenger of Allah."

Ali, who had been given the duty to give all entrusted belongings to their owners in Mecca, had also made his hijra three days later on foot and today he would meet our noble Prophet and Abu Bakr once again in Quba.

Ali, who had taken care to travel by night, had large wounds on his feet. The Messenger of Allah who saw him in this state first opened his arms to embrace him and then shed tears of compassion. Then he put his saliva on the wounds, and prayed for a cure. Before long all of Ali's difficulties were over.

The Messenger of Allah and Abu Bakr stayed in Quba for four days and they built a *masjid* there. Later this *masjid* was known as the Quba Masjid, and it was the first *masjid* in Islam.

When it was Friday, the Messenger of Allah brought people together in this *masjid* and had them pray the Jumu'ah Prayer for the first time.

Four more days had passed and again, on a Monday, our noble Prophet had turned towards Medina with his loyal friend by his side. This destination would start a process that would last for ten years.

Permanent Home: Medina

Then one afternoon, the Messenger of Allah came upon Medina like the full moon, from where the sons of an-Najjar lived. He was in the front, followed by Abu Bakr. Now Yathrib would become one with the Messenger of Allah and would take the name Medinatu Muhammad, meaning "the city of Muhammad," and from then on, it would remain as Medina.

Now there was real celebration in Medina, some youths had gathered together and were dancing in a circle, and others were singing songs of welcome to our noble Prophet.

Now everything looked brighter, there was a joy in Medina the like of which had not been experienced before. There was a smile on every face.

One could hear the voices of children reach to the skies in Medina, in a way that made one forget what had transpired in Mecca: "Here, the Messenger of Allah has come," they were saying, and then they were singing the following song: "O White Moon rose over us, from the Valley of Wada, and we owe it to show gratefulness, where the call is to Allah. O you who were raised amongst us, coming with a work to be obeyed. You have brought to this city nobleness, Welcome! Best caller to Allah's way." And thus the cradle of civilization, Medina, was embracing the Messenger of Allah with such lovely melodies.

On the other hand, there were some people who were playing the *daf*, tambourine.

"We are the neighbors of the sons of an-Najjar. How fortunate we are that Muhammad is our neighbor," they all said.

The Messenger of Allah would respond: "Allah knows that I love you, too!"

The excitement that had been felt in Quba was being felt here among the inhabitants of Medina as well. People had lined the roads and were all inviting our noble Prophet to stay at their home. Each household who saw him approach their house was hoping that he would stop there, inviting him even more heartily.

But instead, the Prophet of Mercy, peace and blessings be upon him, responded to all the invitations by saying: "Let the reigns of my camel free, for it has the duty to decide," and thus he had left the decision as to the where he would reside in Medina to fate in great submission. This would also prevent the plans of those who might have had other intentions. The blessed camel named Qaswa was walking through the streets of Medina with a great number of people eagerly following in his trail.

The daughters of the sons of an-Najjar were also very excited. They were welcoming the Messenger of Allah and were saying from where they were: "We are the children of the neighbors to the sons of an-Najjar; how fortunate we are that now the Messenger of Allah is our neighbor."

The Messenger of Allah turned to them and asked: "Do you love me?"

The word love was hardly sufficient for what they felt for him. They cried out: "Yes, O Messenger of Allah! Yes, O Messenger of Allah!"

In response to this sincere declaration of love, the Messenger of Allah said: "I swear I love you too! I swear I love you too! I swear I love you too!"

Then suddenly Qaswa stopped in front of a house and looked around it. Then he moved a little and continued to walk. He then turned back to where he had first stopped. It was clear that he was striving to fulfill the role that fate had given him. He waited for a while more and then sat where he was.

The Ansar, people of Medina, and the Muhajirun, the Migrants of Mecca, were all looking at each other, for the house that the Messenger of Allah was going to stay at had thus been decided. Tears were flowing down Abu Ayyub Khalid ibn Zayd's cheeks, for closest to where the camel had sat down was his own home. The Messenger of Allah asked: "Whose is the closest house?"

"My house, O Messenger of Allah," said Abu Ayyub. "This is my house and here is its door."

"Then let us stay at your house," said the Messenger of Allah and thus started a guest stay of seven months.

This house had an interesting feature about it. It was the house that had been built by the King of Tubba, As'adu'l-Khimyari, who had decreed that the Last Messenger should live in it when he came to Medina.

The Messenger of Allah was now the guest of Abu Ayyub, but the excitement was shared by all the Ansar, for he was now the guest of them all, preferring the warmth of Medina after the aggressive atmosphere of Mecca. Now the house of

Abu Ayyub had become a place of regular visits; each evening there would be at least two or three people from the Ansar at Abu Ayyub's door bringing plates of food, so that they could show their hospitality to the Messenger of Allah and to people who came to visit him.

The Ties of Brotherhood

The Beloved of Allah, peace and blessings be upon him, had arrived in Medina safe and sound but his arrival was now calling for many provisions to be made. The people who had come with him were not a handful, and there were also people who had remained in Mecca although they were Muslims. Each of those who came had come with their families, or was sending for their families afterwards. There was no alternative.

They were now a hundred and eighty families, and the families were not small; each family was large in size with many children. How were all these families going to be housed and how would they be provided for? One could find short term solutions but this was not a stay that would last two or three days.

In order to find a solution to all these problems, one of the first things that the Messenger of Allah did was to forge the ties of brotherhood between the Muhajirun, the Migrants of Mecca, and the Ansar, the Helpers of Medina. This was like a sister-family project in today's terms, and thus the housing and other social problems for forty five families had been solved. He had come together with his Companions in the house of Anas ibn Malik and was saying the following: "Become brothers in pairs for the love of Allah!"

The idea of brotherhood to further the feelings of unity among the Muslim community was not being raised for the first time that day. Even during the Meccan years our noble Prophet had already declared people like Zubayr ibn Awwam and Abdullah ibn Mas'ud brothers, and thus he had sought a way to alleviate the burden of all kinds of difficulties in a period of great oppression. He would be the first to put the idea in practice, so he raised the hand of his nephew Ali and said: "This here is my brother."

He was not leaving his nephew Ali, who had stayed with him since his childhood days and who had grown up with the upbringing of the Prophet, so the Messenger of Allah was declaring him to be his brother. Then he declared his uncle Hamza the lion-hunter and Zayd ibn Haritha who had been enslaved due to the wrong conceptions of the period of ignorance, but who had later been freed and had the good fortune of serving our noble Prophet, brothers. It was clear that he wanted to keep these two men by his side.

In this excitement of brotherhood that was sweeping Mecca, every member of the Ansar was looking out for the Muhajirun who would be declared to be his brother. Before long, this number reached a hundred and fifty and then it encompassed all the one hundred and eighty six families of the Muhajirun.

The Muslims were now settled in Medina but there were still many problems to be solved. First of all, they needed a place where the believers could come together to share the verses of the Qur'an, where they could perform the Prayers and listen to the advice and *tabligh* of the Messenger, peace and blessings be upon him; where the issues of the day would be discussed and resolved; in short a place where they could come to the awareness of being a community, and this meant they needed to build a *masjid*. They no longer had the Ka'ba where they could seek refuge in. That is why they were performing the Prayers, when their time came, wherever they happened to be.

First they decided where they needed to build the mosque. It was where the camel of the Messenger of Allah had first sat, and it belonged to two brothers Sahl and Suhayl who were under the protection of As'ad ibn Zurara who was the envoy of the sons of an-Najjar. There were sheep sheds, old buildings and a few graves in this piece of land.

Our noble Prophet called the sons of an-Najjar who were his relatives and requested to buy the land from them for its price. They on the other hand said: "We swear we do not want any payment for this, we believe Allah will give us our compensation."

They wanted to be one of the pioneers in taking the cause further. But the Messenger did not want to be a burden on them with such an important issue. He called out to Abu Bakr and they bought the land for ten dinars. Then they built the Prophet's Mosque on this land.

Another issue that needed to be addressed was the demographics of Medina, ethnicities and differences of religion. There was a need to establish the foundations of a framework within which all these different lifestyles could live together. At the time, Medina had a population of about ten thousand people. There were around one thousand five hundred Muslims, four thousand Jewish people, and four thousand five hundred Arab polytheists. The shared values among these populations had to be brought to the fore and the town of Medina had to become a shared living space on the basis of these values.

First of all, he had the physical borders of the city of Medina determined; and the area within those borders would then on be called the Haram. Afterwards, a census was carried out in Medina for the very first time, and the city was being restructured.

The first treaty in Medina was between the tribes of Aws and Khazraj. For the first time in centuries, Aws and Khazraj were being bound with an agreement and the century long dispute between the two tribes that had now both become Ansar was coming to an end. Then, a similar agreement with the Jewish people, who comprised an important 40% of the population in Medina, was also made.

The Battle of Badr

All that was happening was proof of the beginning of a new era. Yathrib was dressed in its new civilized character, and people who visited it were benefiting from its peaceful environment. But Mecca was not going to let things go so easily; it was full of hatred and was making plans to catch and kill those that had immigrated to Medina. The Meccans came together often to discuss this issue and were making decisions to reach their ultimate goal, staying true to their own nature. Their attitude presented a threat to Medina. They did not accept the immigration of the Muslims, and they also tried, through propaganda, to turn other people against the emigration as well. This had become a matter of honor for the Meccans.

All the developments showed that the Quraysh were making great preparations for war in Mecca. Furthermore, they had confiscated the possessions of the Muhajirun. They wanted to take these possessions to Damascus and sell them for a profit. In short, they were planning to attack Muslims with the money they would make by selling their goods. The caravan they formed was basically a huge treasure trove on camels. There were around forty people in charge of the caravan which was worth fifty thousand *dirhams*. This was going to give the Meccans an overwhelming power in war and this power was going to be used directly against Medina. The

Muslims could see the danger approaching; and the seed of this danger, the caravan, was going to pass very close to Medina and then reach Mecca. Thus the Muslims now had the opportunity to prevent this threat before it came to pass.

On the other hand, Abu Sufyan, who had returned from Damascus, had heard of the activity in Medina and had changed his route to reach Mecca. He also sent Damdam ibn Amr, paying him twenty *mithkal*, as a messenger to the Meccans to let them know what was happening on the road. This news was like a spark ready to be ignited by the Meccans, and it was presenting brilliant opportunities for the likes of Abu Jahl. This gave them the lead to prepare for war. The rich were providing with means those who were not equipped to fight, telling everyone that they had to participate in this war.

Whatever was needed for a battle was brought together in a very short period of time. Manpower, horses, camels, weapons and money... The non-believers had not wasted any time and had set out from Mecca with an army of 1,000, whereas there were only a mere 300 gathered around the Messenger of Allah. Even worse, the Muslims had very few horses and their weapons were terribly insufficient.

The army led by Abu Jahl and the caravan led by Abu Sufyan met each other somewhere along the way. Abu Sufyan said, "As you can see, none of the goods have been damaged. I managed to escape their pursuit. There is no need for battle. Come, let us go back now."

"What are you saying Abu Sufyan? We have come all this way from Mecca with such a magnificent army. We cannot return without destroying Muhammad and his friends," roared Abu Jahl!

Abu Sufyan was much calmer about the situation. "Didn't you come here to save the caravan? You have seen that the caravan is safe. There's no longer a need to fight," he repeated.

"Not at all, there are plenty of reasons for us to fight. Until we have gotten rid of Muhammad there will be plenty of reason for us to fight," roared Abu Jahl once again.

This time Abu Sufyan's answer was crystal clear. "My duty was to return the caravan safe and sound back to Mecca, and that is exactly what I will do. I am not coming with you to fight, I am going to Mecca," he said.

As he ordered the caravan to take up speed once again, he looked over at Abu Jahl and the others with him and said, "You will do nothing but perish yourselves." With that he mounted his horse and rode on towards Mecca.

On the seventeenth day of Ramadan, one Friday evening, our noble Prophet came to Badr with his Companions. He had been informed that the polytheist army had started out of Mecca, and so he had found it suitable that they wait for them near the water wells at Badr. When the army reached the water well nearest Badr, our Prophet consulted with the Medinan Muslims on where they should set up the army headquarters. Hubab knew the water wells in the surroundings very well. He shared his opinion, saying, "O Messenger of Allah! This is not a very suitable location to settle down. Let us go to the water well closest to our enemies. Let us dig a pool there and fill it with water. Then, let us close up all the other wells. This way, we can drink water from our own pool during the battle, and they will be left without water."

Our Prophet and his Companions liked this idea very much. The plan was implemented in exactly the same way.

They settled down and set up the headquarters right next to the water well they had spoken of. That night, in his tent, the Messenger of Allah prayed until the morning light and supplicated to his Lord, saying, "O my Gracious Lord! There the Quraysh stands before us with all their self-esteem and pomp. They dare to challenge You, and they accuse Your Messenger of being a liar. My Lord, I ask of You to grant us the victory which You have promised us, against them. My Lord, early tomorrow morning, rub their noses against the dirt in the battlefield!"

Meanwhile, it had started raining in Badr, as a kind of messenger of mercy before the start of the battle. Together with the rain, the Almighty Allah had also sent down a peaceful and relaxing sleepiness over the Muslims, and they had all fallen into a sweet slumber behind the shelter of the trees. This sweet slumber had been a kind of Divine aid for the Muslims so that they could forget the fatigue and hardships they had endured up until then and become refreshed and energetic for the following day. With the same rain, the non-believers found themselves struggling with many hardships difficult to overcome, having trouble even walking as they sank into the mud and dirt.

In the morning of that night, our Prophet gathered his Companions at Badr and lined them up in rows, ready for battle, before the polytheist army even had a chance to arrive and get settled.

Meanwhile, a wind, unlike any other they had seen before, passed by. A second and third gust of wind followed shortly after and passed by. With the first wind, the Archangel Gabriel, with the second, the Archangel Michael, and with the third, the

Archangel Israfil, upon them be peace, took their places next to our Prophet, each accompanied by a thousand Archangels. The Archangels had wrapped their heads in green, yellow and red turbans, leaving one end of the cloth flowing down their backs. There were signs made of wool adorning the foreheads of their horses.

Despite all the efforts of individuals in the Meccan army about not wanting to fight against their own brothers and relatives, the desire for revenge and feeling of hatred from Abu Jahl and those like him had won out in the end. When the efforts to prevent battle had proved futile, the first thing the Messenger of Allah did was turn towards the *qiblah* and perform two *rakah*s of Prayer in supplication to Allah the Almighty, for Him to help them overcome the enemy who outnumbered them greatly. Then he opened his blessed hands and pleaded to his Lord, "O my Gracious Lord! Grant us that which You have promised us! O my Almighty Allah! If you are to destroy this mere handful of believers, then there will be no one left in this world to worship and glorify You!"

Just then, because his hands were raised to the sky, a part of his dress slid off his shoulder. Abu Bakr put it back in place and did not leave our Prophet's side. The Messenger's supplications had grown so intense that Abu Bakr couldn't stop himself from saying,

"O Messenger of Allah! All this supplication to your Lord is enough! He will, without a doubt, fulfill His promise to you!"

It was at that moment that Allah the Almighty sent down this verse to our Prophet; "When you were imploring your Lord for help (as a special mercy), and He responded to you:

"I will help you with a thousand Archangels, coming host after host. "Upon this, our Prophet turned to his faithful Companion and said, "I have glad tidings! O Abu Bakr! Allah's help has arrived! That over there is Gabriel! Atop the Naq Hill, holding the rein of his horse, equipped with his weapons and coat of armor! Ready for battle!"

They could hear more neighing of horses and clinking of swords than there actually was in the valley of Badr now. In such an atmosphere, the strength of the opposing forces had gradually decreased while the strength of our Prophet and his respected Companions gradually increased. These tidings had spread throughout the Companions in a very short period of time and faces shone with delight. The Messenger of Allah had one more piece of glad tidings to share with his Companions. He turned to them and said, "I feel as though I can see the very point in which each non-believer will be killed by the end of today!"

After a series of fighting and rigorous battles against each other, the Muslims wiped out the enemies of Islam and gained a glorious victory. There was nothing left of the Qurayshi army in the valley of Badr other than the lifeless bodies laying in the battlefield and the captives tied up and waiting in one corner. The Quraysh had come all the way from Mecca to Badr with such high hopes, and now they had no other choice than to go back with disappointment and casualties. Abu Jahl and many other Qurayshi leaders lost their lives in this battle named the Battle of Badr. Aside from the seventy non-believers who had been killed in the war, seventy more were held captive. There had also been a total of fourteen martyrs in the believers' side. Though they had gained victory over the non-believers, still, a sorrow had fallen over Badr on account of the fourteen martyrs. Allah's Messenger himself led the Funeral Prayer for those who came to Badr and who became the first ones among them all to be blessed with the honor of martyrdom. He prayed for them and accompanied them in their last journey.

Because this had been their first battle ever fought, what they would do about the captives was going to be a whole new experience for them. There was no other similar practice which would serve as an example to resolve the situation about the captives. To make it worse, no Divine command had been sent to show them the proper way, either. The Messenger of Allah immediately called his Companions together so that they could discuss and consult each other on what to do about the situation. He said, "What do you think we should do about the captives? Even if they were your brothers yesterday, today, Allah has made them dependent of the decision that you will come to."

As an outcome of the consultation, the general opinion was that the captives be freed in exchange for ransom money. Those who did not have the means to pay the ransom would be freed in exchange for teaching ten Muslims to read and write. Still there were those who could neither pay the ransom nor knew how to read and write. The Muslims did not leave them stranded like that, though. They too would be set free on the condition that, from that day on, they would not speak badly of Islam or help, in any way, those fighting against the Muslims. Many people from both Mecca and Medina became Muslim after this incident.

The Battle of Uhud

Victory had been won at Badr but it was clear that matters were not going to be settled in Badr, for as they fled the field of Badr, the hatred of the Meccans was no less than when they had gone there in the first place. When one considered the population at the time, with seventy dead and just as many prisoners of war meant that the impact of war had touched every household. The people who had gone to Badr reluctantly were now filled with hatred against Islam and the Muslims, saying that they would take revenge as soon as possible. People who had witnessed that day took oaths not to sleep in their beds, to continuously wail or to never to touch anything new until revenge was taken. In short, on their way from Badr, they had already started to make plans for a new attack, swearing that the business was not finished there.

Three years had passed since the Hijra, and it was a Thursday in the month of Shawwal. Our noble Prophet received a letter that Abbas had sent when he was in Quba. After listening to Ubayy ibn Ka'b read him the letter, the blessed Messenger told Ubayy to keep the contents of the letter a secret and then went to see Sa'd ibn Rabi.

It appeared shortly after that the Quraysh, who were getting help from neighboring tribes, had left Mecca to take revenge on the Muslims and to redress the injuries they had suffered in Badr. The Quraysh had given the newly formed army their goods that were in the caravan that Abu Sufyan had led to Damascus before Badr, and had contributed in other ways to the army in order to take revenge on Medina.

The Meccan army had come to the vicinity of Uhud. Uhud meant Medina; the Meccan army that had come there with great pomp and grandeur was now looking upon Medina with the desire to burn everything to the ground.

The leading Companions had gathered together. The Messenger of Allah, peace and blessings be upon him, was consulting with them. This was a development that was different to Badr. They had consulted with each other before going to Badr as well and they had decided on a plan of action together. The same had to happen that day, for the verse that had been brought by Gabriel was explaining that our Prophet had to consult with his Companions, pointing to the general fact that consultation should be the action taken by the entire Ummah.

They first discussed the current state and situation of the Meccan army. They knew that a force of three thousand was approaching them. Especially the Companions who had not been able to attend Badr or those who had become Muslim after Badr, were saying that they would fight with the Meccans and defeat them.

The blessed Messenger, on the other hand, was saying that they should not leave Medina and that they should defend the city from the inside. The leading men of the Ansar and the Muhajirun did not agree with this impulsive attitude, and were saying that it would be better to do what the Messenger of Allah said. But the overriding view was that of the men who had not yet had the chance to fight in the previous war. Abdullah ibn Ubayy, especially, was discontent about where the discussion was going and kept saying that he thought that they shouldn't fight. But this was a consultation, and our noble Prophet wanted to institute consultation in the lives of the Muslims, which was an order direct from Allah. The fundamental point of establishing consultation among the people was more important than the decision made at that juncture, and that was why everyone could speak their mind freely. He was a Messenger, a Messenger who was informed by Allah the right and wrong decision and the consequences of each decision, but the overriding view was that they should engage in war outside Medina, and so he complied with this view and decided to meet the Meccan army outside of town.

After the Afternoon Prayer, the Messenger of Allah, peace and blessings be upon him, entered his home with Abu Bakr and Umar. He had put on his armor, wrapped his turban, and was holding his shield in one hand and had his sword by his side.

They were about one thousand people. Only one hundred of them wore armor. Zubayr ibn Awwam was leading the cavalry, and Hamza was the leader of the men who were running towards Uhud with no armor.

Meanwhile, about three hundred men, including Abdullah ibn Ubayy ibn Salul, the head of the hypocrites, returned home, leaving the army that was supposed to protect Medina. This meant that in the face of three thousand men on the enemy front, the Muslims were going to fight one man against five. This was a deliberate act to hurt the Muslims from within and its aim was to shake the Muslims' spiritual resolve.

The blessed Messenger would now position himself facing Medina, with the mountain of Uhud behind them. Morning had almost broken and he prayed the Morning Prayer with his Companions. He then turned to them and spoke to them at length. This was his last sermon before the battle began. Then, he chose around fifty archers, and appointing Abdullah ibn Jubayr as their leader, and advised them as follows: "Keep these horsemen away from us; do not let them come from behind us to surround us! Even if we should come victorious, stay where you are!"

The Meccan army was prepared and they had come to Uhud very sure of themselves. Khalid ibn al-Walid was keeping the right flank with two hundred horsemen. These were the horsemen that our Prophet had drawn the archers' attention to.

That day, the cavalry of the Meccan army had attacked three times in a row, and every time they attacked, they had been pushed back by the group of archers located on the hill. The horses could not advance with the arrows coming directly at them. They could now see why our Prophet had insisted that they keep their position at all times. But the moment when the polytheists were defeated and started running away, there was a divergence of opinion on the hill of archers. Some of the archers who saw the battle progressing in the favor were calling out: "O you people! Come to the spoils! Allah the Almighty has helped you defeat the enemy but you stay there doing nothing. Look, your brothers have come victorious over the enemy, go after the polytheists and collect the spoils with your brothers!"

These words were the first point of fracture in the resolve needed in Uhud. They seemed to have forgotten the aim of the directive given by the Messenger. They interpreted the directive as meaning "stay at your post till the end of the battle" however our Prophet, peace and blessings be upon him, had said to "stay at your post till I order you to come," emphasizing the importance of this strategy.

The two hundred strong cavalry force led by Khalid ibn al-Walid, who were waiting for the perfect moment to attack, realized what was going on with the archers on the hill and they prepared to attack the handful of men that were left. Khalid ibn al-Walid was supported by Ikrima ibn Abu Jahl.

This negligent act, one that seemed to be small at first, was about to change the entire course of the war. It was a bitter experience, but maybe through these archers, Allah the Almighty was giving a lesson to those that would come later. This proved that they had to comply with the orders that their leaders gave them without forced interpretation. When and if they diverged from this practice, they had to at least let the person who had given them the orders know their new course of action.

As there were no longer any arrows blocking their progress, the cavalry attacked the Muslims from behind. First, they killed the handful of archers that remained on the hill along with their leader Abdullah ibn Jubayr. And then all of a sudden they attacked the Muslim army who were pursuing the fleeing polytheists from behind, as well as the Muslims that were busy collecting the spoils.

A dust cloud the likes of which had not been seen in Uhud was now rising up to the mountains. The Muslims were now engaging with the enemy that had come from behind, and the polytheist army that had been fleeing a second ago turned back and started to attack as well: The Muslims were now caught straight in between two fires.

The main goal for the non-believers was, without a doubt, the Messenger of Allah, and, even amongst all this chaos, they had him especially in target. A non-believer named Utba ibn Abi Waqqas had thrown four stones one after the other, and one of them had struck our Prophet's blessed face. As a result, his lower right tooth had broken and his blessed lips had also been wounded.

Mus'ab ibn Umayr was carrying the banner of the Messenger of Allah that day, and he was fighting like a lion. The scattering of the Muslims, for an instant, had saddened him deeply. He was fighting with all his might, with the banner in one hand and his sword in the other. Meanwhile, the non-believer Ibn Qamiah had taken an oath to kill our beloved Prophet. Mus'ab looked very much like our Prophet when inside his coat of armor. So, Ibn Qamiah found Mus'ab and stood against him to fight. After a fearsome struggle between the two, Mus'ab was martyred. After his martyrdom, the banner of Islam did not fall to the ground. An Archangel, in the form of Mus'ab, carried the banner of the Muslims in his place.

Ibn Qamiah, on the other hand, thought that he had killed Allah's Messenger. He returned to the Quraysh and cried out in joy, "I killed Muhammad!" These words echoed throughout Uhud. This news devoured whatever strength the Muslims had left. There were ones who dropped their swords and cried out frantically when they heard of the news echoing throughout.

Amidst the turmoil, Ka'b ibn Malik was the first to see and announce to the believers that the Messenger of Allah was living. He cried with a strong voice, "I saw the Messenger of Allah with these very eyes; there was blood streaking down from under his headpiece but he was alive! O Muslim men and women! Good tidings to you! The Messenger of Allah is right over there," and announced that our Prophet had not been killed to everyone that he came across.

With these cries of joy, Uhud had found life once again. Everyone turned to where the voice came from and life had filled Uhud once again.

Meanwhile, our Prophet's headpiece had broken to pieces and two of its rings had sunk into his cheeks. One of his teeth had been broken, and his lips and face were wounded and bleeding. This situation brought unbearable pain to our Prophet's Companions. Blood was oozing down the face of the Messenger of Allah, for whose sake they were willing to sacrifice their lives. The beloved Prophet of compassion, on the other hand, had opened his hands to the skies and was praying for those who had wounded his head and broken his tooth.

"O my Gracious Lord! Show my people the rightful path! For they do not know," he prayed. He was so full of mercy and compassion, even towards those who wanted to kill him.

There was another great sorrow that awaited our beloved Prophet on that day of Uhud. His uncle, Hamza, had been martyred by a slave named Wahshi. Hamza had been known as "the lion of Allah" when he was alive, and he handed in his soul as "the master of martyrs."

The Companions of our Prophet were trying to protect Allah's Messenger with all their might, on one hand, and were retreating towards and gathering at the foothills of the mountain, on the other. This was the first step in turning the battle at Uhud to the advantage of the believers. Following that very challenging and tough period in the battle, Allah the Almighty sent down a feeling of Divine peace and serenity over the Islam army to assure that the believers both reach a state of inner comfort and physical rest. The Archangel, who had taken over Mus'ab ibn Umayr's duty of carrying the banner of

Islam after he had been martyred, continued to wave the banner of Islam in the air at Uhud.

Both sides had suffered great casualties, and the commander of the Meccan army, Abu Sufyan, found it dangerous to attack the Muslims once again. The retreat of the Muslims towards the foothills of Mount Uhud, and the way they gathered together has startled him a bit. Therefore, he called his army to return back to Mecca in order to, at least, not harm the victory they had achieved up to that point.

As Abu Sufyan and his soldiers were starting to turn back, the Messenger of Allah wanted to be certain that they were not planning something evil against them, for he was worried that they might enter Medina to harm the women and children on their way back. Thus, he called his leading Companions to his side and instructed them to follow the polytheist army.

After being instructed by the Messenger of Allah, the Respected Companions started their pursuit of the enemy. They were so close that they could even hear the things that the polytheists were talking amongst themselves. A group of polytheists wanted to plunder Medina while they had the chance, but others, like Safwan ibn Umayya, said, "Don't even let the thought cross your mind! Don't you see how they've come back together and how fearlessly they walk into the eyes of death! There is no way that we can reach Muhammad before killing them all. Let's get out of here before turning our victory into a pathetic defeat."

And so, the Meccan army mounted their camels for the long journey and set off on the road. The fearlessness and determination of the believers in honor of the cause they believed in had discouraged the Meccan army and forced them to leave Uhud with a rush.

When the non-believers decided not to take the risk of continuing in battle and retreated out of Uhud, the Respected Companions of our Prophet walked back to the battlefield among the bodies of the dead and wounded. The wounded were to be taken and the martyrs were to be trusted over to Mount Uhud. Testifying on account of his Companions who sacrificed their lives for the sake of Allah the Almighty, our beloved Prophet declared, "The Messenger of Allah testifies that in the Day of Judgment you will also be martyrs in the eyes of Allah!"

Then, he turned to the Muslims and said, "O people! Come here to visit them on different occasions! Send greetings to them. I swear to Allah, whose Hand of Power bears possession to myself, that they will accept and respond to the greetings of every believer that greets them until the Day of Judgment."

After the Muslims returned to Medina, every believer took sanctuary in their own home and started to take care of their wounds. Before long, Bilal shouted the call for the Evening Prayer. Upon hearing the call, the believers gathered in the masjid and performed the Prayer altogether. The Night Prayer was also performed in congregation in the *masjid*. The Battle of Uhud, which had started in the morning of that Saturday, ended by the Evening Prayer of that very same day.

The believers retreated into their homes to rest and heal their wounds that Saturday night, and on Sunday morning, with the call to Prayer from Bilal, they all gathered again in the Masjid an-Nabawi.

The Messenger of Allah was not sure whether the non-believers were going to come back or not because they were returning from the battle with nothing in their hands. It was highly likely that they change their minds while on their way back, and come back to Medina to attack once again. They had to prevent such a possibility from arising. Also, they needed to let everyone know that Medina was the authority once again after the battle of Uhud. Surely, a short while later, our Prophet's worries were justified. After having advanced a bit on their journey, indeed, the Quraysh evaluated their situation. Talking among themselves,, they decided that it was wrong for them to return empty-handed and that they needed to attack Medina once again, this time to wipe the Muslims out altogether. They had fought but now had nothing in their hands to show that they had won the battle.

When the Messenger of Allah heard of this news, he first consulted Abu Bakr and Umar. They decided to follow the non-believers to keep an eye on them.

Meanwhile, despite the fact that there were some who insisted on going back to Mecca, the majority had agreed on the idea to attack Medina once again, and the Meccan army was just getting ready to take off. Just then, news that the Muslims were coming after them reached the army. Seeing that they had been mistaken in thinking that they had heavily beat the Muslims, the non-believers started to panic when they learned that they were being pursued, and so decided to return to Mecca.

After intimidating the enemy, the Muslims returned to Medina having bandaged the wounds from Uhud. Thus, the victors of Uhud were the Islam army once again.

The Battle of the Trench

The Quraysh had not been able to come to the second Badr that they had made a promise to fight. This cowardly behavior had cost them a lot of face and they had been censured by their friends. Their weakness and lack of bravery were being talked about all over Mecca. Now they had the chance to regain the reputation they had lost, and the Jews of Medina were offering to work with them. This was a great opportunity for both sides; they decided on the time they would gather and disbanded having made their pact.

Afterwards, Abu Sufyan chose men from various branches of the Quraysh tribe, and having gathered fifty leading men of these tribes, he made his way to the Ka'ba. Entering underneath the cloth of the Ka'ba, he swore that they would fight till their last drop of blood.

The Jewish group who left Quraysh now came to Ghatafan and were making the same offer to them. They were saying that they would give half of their yearly produce and gains of Khaybar to them, promising them the riches of the world if they attacked Medina. They told them that the Quraysh would be with them too, trying to make them understand that they too had to be where all the other tribes had promised to be. They accepted. Before long, they went to the Banu Sulaym and convinced them as well. The plan seemed to be going well, and they started touring all the Arab tribes. They gave the date to all the tribes that they negotiated with and told them to be ready by that date. They had convinced almost all the tribes to fight against the Messenger of Allah and the believers. That is why the Battle of the Trench was also called Ahzab, the Arabic word for the plural of "group" since the army was made up of various different tribes.

Then, the time came to deal the first blow in this last confrontation. It was the month of Shawwal and the fifth year of the Hijra. In the assembly of discussions called Daru'n-Nadwa, they bound the standard and gave it to Uthman ibn Talha. Now everything was ready and the four-thousand strong Meccan army started on its way to Medina under the leadership of Abu Sufyan. The army had three hundred horses, one thousand and five hundred camels. The tribes who heard of this move started to act and came to join the army of Abu Sufyan. The Banu Sulaym joined with seven hundred men, the Banu Fazara with one thousand men, Ashja with four hundred men, the Banu Murra with four hundred men. Before long, the total number of the Meccan army reached ten thousand men. The numbers were such that there was one soldier to almost every single person in Medina, including old men, women and children.

They were coming at the Muslims once again; these men whose only goal was to maintain their iniquity had no intention to reform themselves. What had Medina and the Medinan people done to them? But iniquity and denial had no logic! They wanted to kill and their reasoning had become a slave to their hatred. Their vision was small, and their minds had frozen; they were doing what was in the nature of their own character.

On the other hand the Messenger of Allah, peace and blessings be upon him, was following on how the Jewish community had gone to Mecca and how they were provoking the Arab tribes against him. Every movement in Mecca was reported back to him through his intelligence network and he developed his course of action according to this information. Four days before Abu Sufyan set off on the road, the blessed Messenger had received news that the army would be on its way and had already started to discuss the matter with his Companions. Although he did not want to fight, the reality was that the Quraysh had already gathered together and were coming towards Medina to fight them; and he needed to find a way to avert the misfortune that battle might cause.

He asked every one of his Companions about what sort of strategy they should use. He asked whether it would be better to stay in Medina and fight the enemy in the streets, or to go outside of Medina and fight a battle in the field. The discussions held before the Uhud war was still fresh in memory and so this time, everyone was approaching the issue very carefully.

Everyone spoke their mind and each suggestion had its own risks. Then they heard the voice of Salman al-Farisi: "O Messenger of Allah," he said, "In the lands of Persia when we are confronted with the threat of cavalrymen attacking out cities, we dig trenches around our settlements and protect ourselves thus!"

This was the kind of suggestion that our noble Prophet had been waiting for; and the Companions liked this idea as well, and after speaking about it for a while, they accepted the idea to dig trenches.

The Prophet went to the outskirts of mount Sal and set up camp there. Then they determined where the trenches were going to be; because Medina was encircled by mountains, the enemy could only come from the north and this is where they would dig the trench.

They were racing against time and everyone would dig their own portions and the trenches would be finished before the Meccan army came. While the Companions were busy with the digging, at the very same time the Messenger of Allah started to wield the pickaxe. He too carried earth on his back—such that his clothes were covered in earth and dust. Children who had not yet reached puberty were coming to help our noble Prophet dig the trench. The blessed Messenger, who was working hard amongst his Companions, was at times helping them with the digging, carrying milk to the workmen, and reciting motivational words to the men in order to keep their spirits high.

The digging of the trench, which started with poetry and songs and which was made even more joyful with the food that was offered, was almost finished. Those who had finished their task early were helping the ones who lagged behind and thus they were showing that they were one body in the face of the enemy. The digging continued for six days and now the polytheists were going to be faced with a wide and long obstacle when they came! When the digging of the trench was finished the Meccan army had come close to Medina, they had made it almost to Uhud. War was now close at hand and the Messenger of Allah, peace and blessings be upon him, sent the women and the children who had helped with the digging back to secure parts of town.

War was now close at hand and the Messenger of Allah, peace and blessings be upon him, sent the women and the children who had helped with the digging back to secure parts of town. He had an army of three thousand; Zayd ibn Haritha was carrying the standard of the Muhajirun, and Sa'd ibn Ubada was carrying that of the Ansar.

All the preparations had finished and they were now waiting for the moment that the enemy would come. Not a lot of time had passed when the ten thousand strong Ahzab army came to face the beloved Companions—it was as if the earth and heavens were filled with soldiers.

In fact this scene was one that should have frightened them, but the believers had been given news about what would happen beforehand and were spiritually ready for it, and so no anxiety touched them; on the contrary, because they were living through an event that had been promised by Allah and His Messenger, their faith grew even stronger. What the blessed Messenger said was slowly coming to pass! As long as they had the noble Prophet by their side, what care could they have? The messages brought by the Truthful Gabriel were vivid in their minds and the Great Lord said the following in the revelations that Gabriel brought:

> Or do you believe that you will enter Paradise without having experienced the difficulties and trials that those before you went through? Distress and affliction befell them and they were shaken violently, so that the Messenger and those who believed with him said: When will the help of Allah come? Now surely the help of Allah is nigh! (al-Baqarah 2:214)

The polytheists had come sure of themselves and with the intention of revenging the previous defeats, and they had made it all the way to where the trench was. And then they were confronted with the trench! What was this? It was something they had not encountered before. They looked at each other dumbfounded and said: "This was a trick that the Arabs have not played before."

One of them came to the fore and said: "There is a Persian among his friends; this must have been his idea."

They had come with such hopes but now there was a deep and wide trench in front of them which prevented them from entering Medina. They thought the trench must only be in the stretch in front of them and so they went left and right to see where it ended. But it did not yield any results, for all entries into Medina had been obstructed by the trench.

They were experiencing a great shock even before having wielded their swords; they had planned to enter from one end of Medina with ten thousand people and then come out the other side having exterminated all the Muslims including the Messenger of Allah. That is what they had come there for: they were going to occupy Medina and not leave anything standing. But now their plans had been stalled, and they had met an end they had not expected. What were they going to do now?

They had no choice but to try to attack the Muslims by shooting arrows from afar and try to go across from the weaker points of the trench. They got hold of their bows and started to shoot arrows at the Muslims. Thus, a war, which was clearly going to last long, had started.

The Moment the Trench
is Breached

The tense wait in front of the trench had been continuing for days. There were raids on certain days and night but the Ahzab could not cross to Medina. There had been no further engagement other than throwing stones and shooting arrows and spears between the two sides.

There seemed to be no progress; Abu Sufyan, Ikrima ibn Abu Jahl, Dirar ibn Khattab, Khalid ibn al-Walid, Amr ibn al-As, Nawfal ibn Muawiya, Nawfal ibn Abdullah, Amr ibn Abdiwud, Uyayna ibn Hisn, Harith ibn Awf and Masud ibn Ruhayl and the leaders of the Banu Asad had agreed, they were going to determine the weakest point of the trench and then attack it and cross to the other side at all cost.

Finally, they found a narrow passage; Ikrima ibn Abu Jahl, Dirar ibn Khattab, Nawfal ibn Abdullah, Hubayra ibn Abi Wahb and Amr ibn Abdiwud, spurred their horses and jumped, thus crossing to the other side. The others were looking at them from behind.

"Why are you not crossing?" asked those that crossed over to those left behind.

"You have already crossed over, for now we will wait for you to tell us when there is need, and then we will cross over."

These men who had crossed the trench and thus shown their valor were now riding their horses towards mount Sal. They were going to make up for the days of waiting which they had not been able to use their swords, attack the Muslims and damage their forces considerably. But it did not transpire as they would have liked it; the Muslims who saw them crossing the trench ran there at once and held this weak point, making it impossible for further enemy forces to cross over.

Maybe this was part of the strategy of the Messenger of Allah; maybe he had left certain points "passable" so that the enemy would come in a dispersed manner. For in this raid, the valiant polytheist Amr ibn Abdiwud had been killed by the sword of Ali and those who had seen him fall could do nothing but run away.

When Amr ibn Abdiwud was killed and those who had crossed the trench with him had been forced to flee, the polytheists decided to launch an attack that would leave no one behind and started to make preparations for this; everyone was encouraging each other for this last push.

With the first lights of the morning they started a total attack. The Messenger of Allah, peace and blessings be upon him, had prepared his Companions for battle as well and they were keeping file just behind the trench, waiting for them; when they received news that the polytheists had prepared for battle, our Prophet gave them the promise of victory if they continued to fight with patience.

They were mounting attack upon attack and there was great worry. It was impossible to tell who would attack from where. The polytheists seem to pop up like mushrooms from everywhere, when they got rid of one, when they had finished

The Luminous Life of Our Prophet

off a group; another one came and around the trench was a battle that seemed to have no end.

Meanwhile, a group of two hundred men led by Khalid ibn al-Walid were approaching the tent of our noble Prophet; they were blinded by hatred and did not think twice about death.

This scene would continue till late hours of that day; the Messenger of Allah, peace and blessings be upon him, and his Companions had not had time to pray in this chaos, they had failed to fulfill their duty towards Allah during a battle which they were fighting in His Name.

The polytheists had come with a purpose and had fought to the death and yet had not been able to get the result they wanted, and so they started to draw back slowly; before long everyone had retreated back to their own line. Usayd ibn Khudayr had been appointed to keep guard on the polytheist side of the trench with a group of two hundred men.

In the meanwhile our noble Prophet was performing the Prayers he had missed. He had come all the way to the place called Buthan and there he would first perform the Prayers he had missed and then pray the Evening Prayer. After completing his Prayer he said: "Just as they have prevented us from performing the middle Prayer, I hope Allah will fill their homes and graves with fire."

For a believer the Daily Prayers was everything and the blessed Messenger, peace and blessings be upon him, had opened his hands to the skies and was asking his Lord to punish those who had kept him away from such an important duty.

The Banu Qurayza, who had annulled the agreement they had and thereby had declared war on the Muslims, continued to provide support for the polytheists on the other side of the trench. However, the supplies of the Ahzab were rapidly depleting.

Divine blessing made itself felt once again; the Messenger of Allah, peace and blessings be upon him, saw the Truthful Gabriel and turning towards his Companions, he repeated three times: "Take care; rejoice at the news that comes from Allah"

And just as he finished his words all was chaos in the Trench, there was a great wind and tents were flying in the air, one could hardly see anything from the dust. The Ahzab army was already asunder because of inner conflict, and they were fighting a great storm that hit their side of the trench; their cauldrons were overturned, their fire had gone out and their settlements were completely destroyed! It had become quite dark and there was a frightening noise where the trench was! It had gone so dark that they could not even see the tips of their fingers. The polytheists who were already shivering because of the cold were now totally desperate because of the storm.

They were faced with armies they had not seen till that day! Sand and dust was everywhere and it was difficult to tell who was doing what! They were trying to tie up the ropes of the tents that had broken away, trying to dig the poles back into the ground but each time a gale took them away and they could not succeed. They were now shivering with fear and the leader of each tribe was calling his men to his side—still this was not enough and they feared that they would be assassinated at any moment. They were continuously crying out for help, driving the men near them to desperation.

Now the ruler of the trench was the wind that Allah had sent as a blessing. He had filled the eyes of the polytheists, who had come to attack Medina with the intention of getting rid of our noble Prophet and the believers, with sand and the enemies of Allah were writhing in pain. The frightened hypocrites were asking to leave, speaking of their unprotected families as excuse and were leaving the battlefield. But the believers who anticipated the blessing of Allah felt themselves to be stronger than before. The wind had supported the spiritual standing of the believers whereas it had frightened the polytheists.

Now it was time for the Ahzab army to leave before they had the chance to stay around. The polytheists, who had not forgotten Uhud and Hamrau'l-Asad, feared that the Muslims would follow them from behind and so they had left an army of two hundred cavalrymen under the leadership of Khalid ibn al-Walid and Amr ibn As by way of protection. When the morning came, there was not a single enemy soldier left on the other side of the trench!

Now that the polytheists had retreated, there was no need to stay by the trench any more, and that is why the blessed Messenger, peace and blessings be upon him, gave the order for his people to return to Medina. But because he was thinking of the Banu Qurayza, he did not want his Companions to be unduly overjoyed; for there were still some accounts to be settled. On the other hand, the hypocrites who had backed away from fighting with petty excuses had no idea that the Ahzab army had retreated and they were saying: "They still have not perished," thus eagerly awaiting the defeat of the believers. They were the ones, along with the Banu Qurayza, who were expecting retaliation for their betrayal, who would be devastated to see the blessed Messenger and his Companions return home safe and sound. Now that the Ahzab army in whom they had put their trust had retreated, they were left alone. Only three polytheists had been killed as a result of this war which had gone on for almost a month, and eight of the Companions had fallen martyr. The Truthful Gabriel then descended and spoke about what had happened at the Trench, summarizing the real intentions of the parties who had been fighting.

The noble Prophet, peace and blessings be upon him, had returned to Medina. The Banu Qurayza surrendered after a siege.

The *Peace Treaty of* Hudaybiya

While during the days people daydreamed about being in Mecca, in the evenings they dreamed of worshipping in the Ka'ba. Our noble Prophet also had a dream; in it some of his Companions had shaved their heads, and some had had their hair shortened and they were walking around the Ka'ba in peace and safety; he too had taken the keys of the Ka'ba and walked around it and performed the minor pilgrimage, *umrah*.

When the morning came, our noble Prophet shared his dream with his Companions; there was great joy in Medina and the Companions felt the peace of being promised that they would soon be going to the Ka'ba—they were going to go and this longing would come to an end. The blessed Messenger felt the very same thing.

They started to make their preparations. Nobody could claim the Ka'ba for themselves; their ancestor Abraham had built it and had entrusted it to the people so that they may worship Allah in it. Now this trust was squandered in the hands of those who were not fit to be its trustee. It was our noble Prophet who would give it back its original purpose and glory. He was going to go there and demonstrate himself how Allah was to be worshipped.

Meanwhile, Busr ibn Sufyan had come to Medina and become a Muslim. When he wanted to return, our beloved Prophet said to him: "O Busr! Do not make haste in going! Maybe we will go all together! For we are planning to set off for the *umrah*."

The aim was not war but worship; that is why they only took small daggers with them in order to protect themselves from wild animals. On this journey a number of sheep and camels were accompanying them in order to be slaughtered. The blessed Messenger had taken a camel with him for this purpose.

It was another Monday in the month of Dhu al-Qadah and the calendar showed the sixth year after the Hijra. The Messenger of Allah went into his blessed room, put on two layers of clothing and mounted his camel Qaswa and set off on his way. This was the start of the journey towards the center of the world. This time our mother Umm Salama was accompanying him.

When they reached Dhu'l-Hulayfa, they prayed the Noon Prayer. Then the blessed Messenger started to mark the seventy camels that had been brought there to be sacrificed; he was turning the sacrificial animals towards the direction of the Ka'ba and marking them on the right side.

There, a further two cycles of Prayer were performed; the atmosphere was unbelievable and the joy of worship could be seen on every face, in every tear. The main goal was to circumambulate the Ka'ba so our noble Prophet put on the piece of cloth called *ihram*. He wanted to share with his Companions the determination of spirit that should accompany their dress: "*Labbayk Allahumma labbayk. Labbayka la shari-*

*ka laka labbayk. Inna'l-hamda wa'n-ni'mata lak; wa'l-mulk la
sharika lak*," he started to say, "Dear Lord, here I have come
to Your presence. You have no partner. Thanks are due to
You and all things are Yours."

Our mother Umm Salama also spoke the intention of
getting into ihram, which was more a state of being than a
mere piece of cloth.

This was their first introduction to the concept. They
were following closely what the Messenger of Allah was doing; whatever he did was repeated by his followers. The honorable Companions who followed his every step also dressed
in the ihram there.

The journey continued, the one thousand four hundred
strong mass of people were walking towards Mecca, they took
extra care that nobody would be hurt in the slightest. The
caravan did not disturb the people of the lands they passed
through—the farms and orchards were left untouched. The
journeyers were like angels that descended from the heavens.
Humanity was for the first time experiencing an understanding that prioritized rights and justice.

They did not want to confiscate anyone's property. People who watched them from afar could see their difference
and they would want to offer presents to the Messenger of
Allah. Ima ibn Rahda had come with his son and given the
blessed Messenger, as present, two hundred sheep and two
camels with udders loaded with milk. The Messenger of Allah, peace and blessings be upon him, first said: "I hope Allah will grant you more bounty," and then distributed this gift
among his Companions.

This was one indicator of being accepted in the world with open arms, and this respect would not be limited to this either. Each tribe that they came across appreciated their peaceful journey and so gave them what they had in their hands—bread, gherkins and herbs. During this journey, the Messenger of Allah was given a herb that had a nice smell and a delicious sap, and he sent some of it to our mother Umm Salama to taste as well.

The Attitude of the Meccans

The news that the Messenger of Allah was coming to Mecca with his Companions in order to do *umrah* and visit the Ka'ba, had reached Mecca, and the Meccans were overwhelmed with fear. The blessed Messenger was coming upon them at a time when they least expected it. Even if war did not seem to be the intention of the Muslims, the reactions of the Meccans showed their weak psychological state. They gathered their assembly together and started to discuss the issue: "Muhammad wants to come with his army and perform *umrah*. The Arabs who hear this and who have seen how we have warred with him until recently, what will they think? As long as we breathe we should not let them enter Mecca!"

There were of course those who believed that the *umrah* was just a cover up that the Muslims were using and that they really wanted to make war with Mecca. The discussions revolved around the necessity of not letting the believers into Mecca and the job of organizing this stance was given to Safwan ibn Umayya, Ikrima ibn Abu Jahl and Suhayl ibn Amr.

The journey continued. At last they approached the place called Hudaybiya and were faced with a situation they did not expect. Qaswa had sat down, and he would not get up. The Messenger of Allah could not understand the reason why his camel was not standing up despite the efforts by him and his

Companions. They said: "Qaswa is being very stubborn," and he replied: "No it is not! Qaswa is never stubborn! The One who once stopped the army of the elephants enter Mecca has stopped him."

There was no space for coincidence in the universe; each movement was a message from Allah for him. This was also better than walking into Mecca and starting a chain of events they could not predict. The atmosphere was very tense and this could cause a lot of bloodshed.

Then there were those in Mecca who had become Muslim and yet were hiding it. If there should be a war, Muslims could kill Muslims without knowing. Besides, there were potential Muslims in Mecca who could meet the true religion the next day themselves, or following generations from their family could indeed declare their loyalty to the Messenger of Allah. So this was the time to seek peace and the Messenger of Allah said: "I swear by He who holds Muhammad's life in His hands that today, whatever plan is asked for me that will exalt Allah's name, I will accept it."

The Messenger of peace was once again choosing peace over war.

Our noble Prophet, who had understood the message, changed Qaswa's direction and tried to get it up. It was as he expected; Qaswa got up and started to walk! This validated the meaning of the message. They had now reached the furthest point of Hudaybiya; the weather was very hot and people needed water. The developments showed that they were going to stop there for a while. That is why the Messenger of Allah went to a well that had some water and set up camp there. There were no other wells around.

Where the Messenger of Allah had camped was outside the boundaries of the Haram, or the Sanctuary. For his Prayers he went a little way further and entered the Sanctuary Zone and performed them there. It was now time for the Afternoon Prayer and the Messenger of Allah took a jug of water for his ablutions. The honorable Companions watched him as he took ablutions. There was something strange. He looked at them and asked: "What is with you all?"

"We are perished, O Messenger of Allah!" they said.

The Messenger of Allah, peace and blessings be upon him, turned to them and said: "As long as I am with you, no one will perish."

Who could perish as long as they had the Messenger of Allah in their heart?

But they wanted to explain what they really meant: "O Messenger of Allah, we have no water to take ablutions or to drink except for what is in your hand."

The shortage of water was extreme and it seemed that the Companions expected the blessed Messenger to work a miracle. He told them to pour the jug of water into a bowl and then he placed his blessed fingers inside it and started to say a prayer. Then he said: "There you have it! *Bismillah.*"

The honorable Companions waited to see what would happen. And what did they see? Water was miraculously running from the fingers of the Messenger of Allah! People ran to get their water skins. They drank from this water, took their ablutions and also gave it to their animals. Smiles covered the faces of the Companions once again at Hudaybiya, the water skins were full and they had satiated themselves with water, even if it was only for the time being. The blessed Messenger, who was also smiling after seeing these developments, opened up his hands to pray: "I bear witness that there is no deity but Allah and that I am His Messenger," thus thanking his Lord.

That day a rain that soothed the hearts rained on Hudaybiya, the dry grass found life and the insects that lived on the land were refreshed. This was a manifestation of Divine grace for the believers.

The Envoys of the
Blessed Messenger

Things were still not clear and our noble Prophet took a step and chose Hirash ibn Umayya from among his Companions, and giving him his camel named Salab, he sent him to the Quraysh. His aim was to make clear once again that his intention was not war and that he had come solely with the intention of *umrah*.

As soon as Hirash arrived, Ikrima ibn Abu Jahl drew his sword and slashed the camel on the legs; he was filled with so much hatred and rancor that he was also about to kill Hirash. The tribes of Ahabish, who saw such an outburst of anger, intervened at once and did not let him kill the envoy of the blessed Messenger; they set Hirash free and let him return. Hirash came back to our noble Prophet at once and spoke to him about how he had been treated.

The sensitivity of the situation was growing each passing day and at such a juncture every step taken was very important indeed. The Quraysh were very nervous; they were acting without thinking things through and causing much problem.

Our noble Prophet on the other hand, was determined to get his message to the leaders of the Quraysh. He was going to speak to their hearts and minds and somehow convey to them that they should get out of the way of people who had no other aim than gaining the contentment of Allah by visiting the House of Allah. This time he called Umar to his side to send as envoy to the Quraysh. When he learnt of the blessed Messenger's intention, Umar said: "O Messenger of Allah! I fear that the Quraysh will try to kill me, for they know my enmity towards them. And there are none among them from the sons of Adiyy who may protect me! But despite all that, O Messenger of Allah, if you want me to go to them, I will go without any hesitations!"

Umar's worry was not for his life, but he knew that should he get killed, the killing of such a respected envoy as himself would be cause for war—and under such circumstances who knew what would set off the first spark. Our noble Prophet was thinking as he listened to Umar: "O Messenger of Allah!" continued Umar. "I can recommend you someone who is more respected by the Quraysh, and who will be more protected among them, who had stronger connections, Uthman ibn Afwan."

Foresight was an important quality for a believer, and these suggestions of Umar were full of foresight and wisdom. Upon the advice of Umar, the blessed Messenger called Uthman to his presence and said: "Go to the Quraysh and tell them that we have come to do *umrah* and not to make war! And invite them to Islam."

The mission that was given to Uthman was not limited to that. He was also to go to those who had become Muslims after the Hijra and give them the good news of the imminent conquest of Mecca, that soon Allah would make His religion victorious there. He was to give them this news so that they may be able to live their religion out on the open, without feeling the need to hide it.

After receiving orders from our noble Prophet, Uthman set off on the road. When he arrived to Baldah, he was confronted by the Quraysh: "Where are you going?" they asked. He was cautious and said: "The Messenger of Allah sent me to you. I invite you to believe in Islam and Allah; enter His religion altogether—Allah the Almighty will make His religion and Messenger come victorious over you. Stay out of his way so that you may not be of those who oppose him! And if the Messenger of Allah should be defeated, well then, that is what you want! If he should be victorious, then the choice will be yours; you may come and choose Islam like other people, or you can resist him and fight him! You know what war always brings you; you are weak and exhausted and you have lost leading men of your tribe! What's more, the Messenger of Allah is not coming to fight; he comes with animals marked for sacrifice, with only the intention of doing *umrah*, and he wants me to tell you that he will return after he had offered these animals in sacrifice."

"We hear what you are saying. But this is something that cannot be. He can't come here suddenly like that. Go and tell your friend that he cannot come upon us!"

It did not seem possible to get the Quraysh to open their doors; even before meeting the leading men of Quraysh they had been faced with the reaction of the people on the street and Uthman could not perform the mission that had been entrusted to him satisfactorily. It looked like he was not going to be able to speak to them as he wished and so he was about to return. Just at that moment, Aban ibn Said came up to him. After a quick exchange of civilities, he said to Uthman: "Whatever you need, just tell me without hesitation."

He had come down from his horse and was asking Uthman to mount it; he would get on behind him. Umar had been right; at a juncture where the routes seemed to be blocked, old friendships would come into play and many doors that seemed locked would open. On the other hand Aban was saying: "Go to the left and right and do not fear anyone, for the sons of Said are the most honorable and respected of the Haram," thus making clear with the language of poetry that Uthman would be under his surety. First, they came all the way to the Ka'ba and Uthman started to visit the leading men of the Quraysh. He was visiting every single one of them and bringing them the news of our noble Prophet. They were all saying: "Muhammad will not come upon us like that," and then were closing their doors.

But they were not able to banish Uthman altogether and said to him: "You can come by yourself and circumambulate the House of Allah if you like." But he answered: "I will not circumambulate the House of Allah unless the Messenger of Allah does," thus refusing their offer. He understood the intentions of the Quraysh and so he went to the believing men and women of Mecca who had been oppressed: "The Messenger of Allah says," he began, and those who saw a Companion such as Uthman realized that they would be receiving some news from our noble Prophet and hence were overjoyed. There were those who had been waiting for this for six years: having found him, it had been very difficult to live away from him! But the reason Uthman came was not solely to bring them his greetings. There was good news: "I will place you under my wings and protect you very soon and no one will have to hide their faith in Mecca anymore."

This was like receiving gales of spring in winter! They longed to be able to express themselves freely! Now that such an envoy like noble Uthman had come to them, this good news would come to pass as well. As they saw Uthman off, they waved at him in tears and asked him to bring their greetings to our beloved Prophet. Uthman's efforts continued for three whole days.

While Uthman continued his Mecca visits, the anxious wait of the blessed Messenger and his Companions continued. Although the Quraysh were challenging them, they could not flat out declare war on them because of their previous experiences in war. That is, although they were incensed by the developments, they were also afraid to take any wrong steps; they were weighing every development to a reasonable conclusion.

On the other hand, the honorable Companions were worried about Uthman who had gone as envoy and had not come back. Some of them were saying: "Uthman has gone and we believe that he must have reached the House of Allah and done his circumambulation."

To which the Messenger of mercy, peace and blessings be upon him, said: "I do not believe he will go and circumambulate the Ka'ba while we wait here."

The Companions said: "What should stop him," seeing that he has gone so far and for so long.

Our noble Prophet, who knew his friend well, turned to them and said: "This is what I believe of him; even if he should have to stay there as it is for a year, he would not circumambulate the Ka'ba without us."

Because of the tension in the atmosphere, our noble Prophet had asked his Companions to keep sentry at night and Aws ibn Hawli, Abbad ibn Bishr and Muhammad ibn Maslama rotated among themselves for this job. This was something that had been suggested by the blessed Messenger and before long it would become clear how right he had been in suggesting such a measure. While Muhammad ibn Maslama was keeping guard, fifty men of Quraysh led by Mikraz ibn Hafs had come to where the honorable Companions were in a seeming mission of reconnaissance, to see if there would be an opportunity for them to catch the Muslim unawares and raid their camp.

Muhammad ibn Maslama, who noticed the men immediately, set to work at once; he took the Qurayshi men prisoner—only Mikraz had been able to escape. As Maslama was taking the men to the presence of our noble Prophet, Mikraz was running to Mecca to inform the Quraysh of what had just happened.

On the other hand, Companions such as Kurz ibn Jabir, Abdullah ibn Suhayl, Abdullah ibn Hudhafah, Umayr ibn Wahb, Abu'r-Rum ibn Umayr, Hisham ibn As, Abu Hatib ibn Amr, Abdullah ibn Abi Umayya, Ayyash ibn Abi Rabia and Hatib ibn Abi Balta'ah came to our noble Prophet and said that they wanted to go to the Ka'ba in secret and the blessed Messenger had given them leave upon their insistence. But when the Quraysh saw that these men had broken into their ranks, they were thoroughly displeased and had taken the said Companions as prisoner. When they learnt that Muhammad ibn Maslama had taken their men prisoner, the atmosphere got even tenser. A group from the Quraysh ran to Hudaybiya and started to pelt the Messenger of Allah and the honorable Companions with stones and arrows. The honorable Companions had been on their guard. In the confusion, twelve more cavalry men were taken prisoner from the Quraysh, Ibn Zanim who had been shot with an arrow while he was at some high place was killed.

Although neither side really wanted to fight, it looked like war was close at hand once again; at such a juncture even the smallest spark could set a great fire and lead to unforeseeable consequences. That is why the Quraysh got together to assess the situation once again. They decided to send Suhayl ibn Amr, Huwaytib ibn Abdiluzza and Mikraz ibn Hafs to the blessed Messenger as envoys in an attempt to lessen the tension. But the news that Uthman had been killed along with ten other Companions on their way back changed everything at once; there was a new development and things had to be considered accordingly.

The Alliance at Ridwan

When the news of the martyrdom of Uthman and the ten Companions reached our noble Prophet, he said: "It seems we will not be able to part from this place without having fought the Quraysh," asking his Companions to swear allegiance to him. He had come to where the houses of the Banu Mazin ibn an-Najjar were and he sat under a tree: "Allah the Almighty orders you to swear allegiance to me," he said.

Upon that, the honorable Companions started coming to our noble Prophet and to swear allegiance to him one by one; they were putting their lives at stake, and swearing that come what may, they would not stay away from the field of battle, and that they would defeat the polytheists.

At one point our noble Prophet lifted up one of his hands and supplicated: "Verily Uthman had gone in pursuit of Your and Your Messenger's business!"

And then with one of his hands he took the other in lieu of Uthman's and said that Uthman had also taken the oath of allegiance in absentia. He then turned to his Companions and said: "You are the best on earth," and told them that the people who put their trust in him under that tree would not be touched by Hell fire.

Among those who had come all the way to Hudaybiya were Jadd ibn Qays who had not sworn alliance; he had been unable to get rid of the dissension in his heart and he had hidden under his camel in order not to be seen and to not swear allegiance.

Everyone, including the Messenger of Allah, had donned what weapon they could find. The forces on both sides were not equal but the honorable Companions had a faith that could overcome anything. Umm Umara had taken one of the poles that had been supporting a tent and tying a knife at its tip, she had made it into a weapon in order to defend herself in case of danger. Our noble Prophet, who until then had deemed it not appropriate to light fire at night, allowed people to light fires after this point saying: "Light fires and prepare food; because no one will be able to come close to you in measure of good deeds."

Suhayl ibn Amr, Huwaytib ibn Abdiluzza, Mikraz ibn Hafs and the Qurayshi's around were watching what was happening very closely. They felt a little intimidated; it would not be possible to fight such determined people who were running towards death with such open hearts. For them, it was impossible to see another group of people like them; this was a different and unbelievable kind of loyalty, one that bonded stronger than blood ties or tribal connections! The Companions were united in showing the Meccan polytheists how to really show respect to a leader, how sensitive one could be in living by their leader's orders, and how, when the going got rough, they could exercise physical and spiritual self-sacrifice.

These were action that the Quraysh had neither seen nor heard. That is why the envoys believed that they had to find a way of agreement at all events, and they were debating as to how they would get out of this situation with minimal losses. Before long, news would come and they would learn that the information about Uthman and the ten other Companions being martyred was false—and so the Muslims would rejoice.

The Agreement

Suhayl ibn Amr and his friends returned to Mecca and they spoke about the scene they saw at Hudaybiya as clearly as they could. They spoke of the way that the Companions reacted to the news of their friends' being murdered and how they ran to swear their allegiance when our noble Prophet invited them. They spoke of their determination to fight the polytheists despite their difficult circumstances. The Qurayshis, who finally used some common sense, converged on the following decision: "For us, the best would be to make peace with Muhammad on the condition that they will not visit the House of Allah, but come back and do so next year. Thus the Arabs and those who have heard about his arrival here will know that we have deterred him! They can come next year, stay in Mecca for three days, offer their sacrifices and return. Thus they will not have entered our land without our permission and have stayed only for a couple of days!"

Upon this decision, they sent Huwaytib and Mikraz led by Suhayl ibn Amr to our noble Prophet once again. They said to Suhayl: "Go to Muhammad and make an agreement with him! But be sure the place the condition of not entering Mecca this year; we swear that we will not let the Arabs say that we have been pressured into letting him enter our land."

As planned, Suhayl and his friends set off on the road again and came to Hudaybiya. The Messenger of Allah, peace and blessings be upon him, who saw them coming from afar, said: "Since these men have been sent again, the Quraysh want peace."

He was hopeful; this was what he wanted as well. He also knew that the Meccan polytheists and the Jews had made a pact at Khaybar to have a joint stance against Medina. Now they would at least be able to come to an agreement with one party of this alliance, and this could weaken the force of the enemy. This opportunity had to be taken in the name of Islam, the religion he had been sent to communicate to humankind.

Suhayl came close to our noble Prophet, who was sitting on the floor. He knelt down. Abbad ibn Bishr and Salama ibn Aslam ibn Harith were keeping guard next to the blessed Messenger, dressed in their helmets and armor. The honorable Companions had formed rings around the blessed Messenger, trying to follow what was happening. They spoke for a long while. There was intense negotiating; the voices kept increasing and decreasing. At one point Suhayl raised his voice so much that Abbad ibn Bishr found this difficult to tolerate and warned him: "Keep your voice down when you are talking to the Messenger of Allah!" reminding all that one should not raise one's voice higher than that of our noble Prophet. After these long and heated talks, some articles had been agreed upon and it was time to put them down in writing. The articles were as follows:

1. They were to not fight among each other throughout a period of ten years.

2. People were to be safe and secure from any possible dangers from either side.

3. Our Prophet and his Companions were going to go back this year, but, the following year, they would be able to visit the Ka'ba.

4. Those who were to flee from the Quraysh and seek refuge in the Prophet, without permission from their guardians, were to be returned to their guardian, even if they had accepted Islam as their faith. On the other hand, if one of the Muslims were to take refuge in the Quraysh, they would not be returned.

5. Condemnation and reproach from both sides were to be eradicated, and incidents such as treason and robbery would not be permitted whatsoever.

6. All other tribes and communities aside from the two were free to make agreements and unite with whichever side they pleased at any time they wished.

This article and the circumstances seemed very dire to the believers; on the one hand was Suhayl who did not want to negotiate and on the other hand were the believers who thought that the Muslims had conceded too much. At that moment, some of the Companions were not yet able to comprehend some aspects of the agreement. Thus, they were not very much pleased with the covenant that had been made.

Suhayl ibn Amr turned to the blessed Messenger and said: "Now have these written on paper."

Upon that our noble Prophet called Ali to his side and said, "Write!"

"*Bismillahirrahmanirrahim!*" (In the Name of Allah, *Ar-Rahman* and *Ar-Rahim*.)

"What do *Rahman* and *Rahim* mean," asked Suhayl.

He hesitated when asking, for although he felt a pang in his heart as he said this, he was there to represent the Quraysh and this role made him look sterner than he really was. Suhayl was not a man who did not know what Ar-Rahman (the All-Merciful) and Ar-Rahim (the All-Compassionate) meant. From the very first days his three siblings, his son-in-law and daughter, and then two of his sons had become Muslim and had preferred to be with the blessed Messenger. He had subjected his youngest son Abu Jandal to various pressures and tortures; he had left him locked up thirsty and hungry and come to the presence of the Messenger of mercy. That is why he insisted: "I do not know what they mean, so instead you should write, "in Your Name, O Allah", *'Bismikallahumma!'"*

The believers who saw his insistence said: "We swear we will not write anything other than *Bismillahirrahmanirrahim.*"

Once again, there were claims on both sides. They were thinking only of the present moment and they were acting impulsively without thinking of the gains to be made tomorrow. Our noble Prophet, who did not want the issue to be bogged down in details, turned to his son-in-law Ali with great self-confidence and patience and told him to erase *Bismillahirrahmanirrahim* and write *Bismikallahumma*.

Another hurdle was thus over, and the Companions were silent in the face of this determined stance of our beloved Prophet. The blessed Messenger was about to say: "This is the agreement made between the Messenger of Allah and Suhayl, the son of Amr," when Suhayl stopped him again and said: "I swear, had we believed that you are the Messenger of Allah, we would not have stopped you from circumambulating the House of Allah and we would not have fought you! Write in this document things we know; write, Muhammad, son of Abdullah."

This was the extent of his intolerance! Suhayl was the representative of denial of the day, and he was being very stubborn. He was not going to let slip any detail when it came to advancing his own cause, and he tried to turn each step to his advantage. Even though Suhayl wanted this title erased, he was still the Messenger of Allah. And so the Messenger of mercy turned to Ali and said: "Erase it..."

The words had been spoken but the atmosphere grew very tense. Companions such as Sa'd ibn Ubada and Usayd ibn Khudayr held Ali's hand and said: "Either you write the 'Messenger of Allah' or the issue between us and them will be solved by the sword," making it clear that they would not tolerate his blessed name to be rubbed off and anything else written.

Ali was of no other mind; he had just erased "*Bismillah-irrahmanirrahim*" and written "*Bismikallahumma*", but he did not want to erase the name of our noble Prophet, he wanted this form of address to remain in the document like a seal. He did not want to obey this order of the blessed Messenger either.

Meanwhile, voices were being raised more and more in the presence of the blessed Prophet, and a commotion had started. The Messenger of Allah gestured with his hands to quiet his Companions. Then he turned to his son-in-law with grace that was becoming of him; it was clear he had a few words for him: "Tomorrow, you will find yourself in a similar position and you will have to compromise as well!"

He had once again opened the curtain of the hidden realms, foreshadowing the chain of events that would start with the assassination of Uthman and end with the assassination of Ali himself; particularly with the incident of Tahkim in which Ali would have to make a critical and life-changing choice. Then he gestured: "Give it to me," and then erased his noble title "Messenger of Allah" with his blessed hands and then asked "Muhammad, son of Abdullah" to be written instead.

This wish was also obeyed and another situation of conflict was avoided.

They then started discussing the article "A person who leaves Mecca and seeks refuge in Medina will be handed back to Mecca even if he should be a Muslim." Again voices were raised: "Glory be to Allah!" they were saying, "How can you have that written down? How can we hand over someone, who comes to us as a Muslim, over to the polytheists?"

"Yes," was all the blessed Messenger could say.

Again, there was something he knew that the others did not. As the Qur'an puts it; the speech of our noble Prophet was nothing other than revelation. He had opened up the curtains of the hidden and was speaking to his Companions thus. He continued his words in the following fashion: "Allah the Almighty will distance the person who leaves us and goes to them from His grace; but when it comes to those who leave them and come and seek refuge with us, Allah the Almighty will bestow upon them a way out and well-being."

Now the agreement had been completed to the full and one of the Companions, Ibn Maslama, had made another copy of the document under the order of the blessed Messenger and given it to Suhayl ibn Amr, the representative of Mecca.

The Journey Back to Medina

Till that moment, the honorable Companions had no doubt that the dream of the blessed Messenger would be realized; that is why they had come all the way to Hudaybiya—they were anticipating their own dreams of circumambulating the Ka'ba after all those years to come true. What they had lived through for twenty days, the harsh conditions of the agreement that had been signed and lastly the state of Abu Jandal had shaken them profoundly. They found themselves in a state of hesitation. They were sad about the death of Companions such as Ibn Abbas and about not having been able to go and circumambulate the House of Allah. Even the camels that had been kept away from going there had started to moan, making sounds they usually make out of love for their offspring.

Now everything had come to an end and the agreement had been signed. Now a new era was beginning; now they had the opportunity to share the beauties of Islam with other people without having to worry about the state of war. But the honorable Companions had not quite grasped the meaning of this opportunity yet, and they still could not come to terms with the fact that they had to leave without having circumambulated the Ka'ba. As they were getting ready to return, the blessed Messenger called out to them: "Stand up, slaughter your sacrifice animal and cut your hair," but none of them moved to obey the orders of the blessed Messenger.

They could not give up the idea of visiting the Ka'ba and they did not want to be in a situation where they would seem disobedient to the blessed Messenger. But circumstances now called for a choice. They also hesitated as to whether what our noble Prophet said was an order or an encouragement. It is probable that they hoped that the Truthful Gabriel would come and abolish the peace treaty; for revelations kept coming and such a change of course was still possible and then they could go and circumambulate the Ka'ba that very year. They were in very deep thought, and they were not quick enough to show the usual sensitivity they had towards the orders of the Messenger. That is why the Messenger of Allah, peace and blessings be upon him, repeated his request three times, and still no one moved to sacrifice their animals and cut their hair in order to get out of ihram. Our noble Prophet was rather disappointed by this and he went to our mother Umm Salama and said: "The Muslims have perished. I have told them to sacrifice their animals and cut their hair and yet they do not do so." He wanted to discuss the issue with his soul mate and he sought her view on the matter. Umm Salama looked kindly at the blessed Messenger: "O Messenger of Allah," she started. "Do not censure them as yet, since they are experiencing a great shock at the moment. The problems you have faced concerning the articles of the agreement, having to return without the conquest they were hoping for—these have taken a great toll on them. O Messenger of Allah! Best is if you go and slaughter your animal without saying anything, and then call someone to shave your head."

Our mother Umm Salama was speaking as one of them; everyone had a mission, and she, for her part, was fulfilling the duty of being with our noble Prophet on this journey and was suggesting the best solution at such a historic moment. It was evident that at such moments the actions of people who were at the forefront of society would be more effective than verbal encouragement or force.

Our noble Prophet got out of his tent; he had thrown his ihram over his shoulder leaving one shoulder open and he had taken a knife in his hand making his way towards where the camels were. Everyone's eyes were locked onto him. Before long they all heard our noble Prophet say: "In the Name of Allah, the Greatest," it was clear that the Messenger of Allah was slaughtering his animal.

How could the Companions remain seated after seeing the blessed Messenger slaughtering his animal; everyone went to where the animals were. Our mother Umm Salama's suggestion had worked; people were now running to and fro in Hudaybiya, and all the Companions were slaughtering their animals.

The blessed Messenger, who had just sacrificed his animal, was about to leave his ihram; he called Hirash ibn Umayya to his side and had him shave his head. The honorable Companions were rushing not to let a single hair strand of our noble Prophet fall to the ground. Umm Umara had got hold of some of his hair.

Some of the honorable Companions also had their heads shaved, and some had only shortened their hair. The Messenger of mercy looked out of his tent and said: "Let Allah the Almighty's mercy be on those who have their heads shaved."

The Companions who had shortened their hair were worried: "O Messenger of Allah, how about those who have it shortened?"

They feared that they had not properly withdrawn from their state of ihram. The blessed Messenger said once again: "Those who have it shaved," and he repeated this three times.

The Companions were now in great doubt and they expected the blessed Messenger to say something good about those who had only shortened it. The Messenger of mercy said:

"And also those who have it shortened," thus making the matter clear and putting everyone out of their misery.

Then a strong wind blew towards Hudaybiya and the hair cut from the Companions was carried towards Mecca. Now, having postponed the circumambulation of the Ka'ba by one year, it was time to leave Hudaybiya. It had been twenty days since they had arrived there and with the intention of coming to Ka'ba next year and performing their Prayers in peace and security, the Messenger of Allah, peace and blessings be upon him, ordered them to start their journey back to Medina.

The Muslims were returning home with great gains; however, the noble Messenger had heard some talks going around. Some were saying that Hudaybiya was not a conquest. The Messenger of Allah, peace and blessings be upon him, who heard these rumors turned to his Companions once again and said: "These are such bad words! Quite the contrary, this is the greatest of conquests, for the polytheists have put their swords in their shields and have resigned from driving you away from their land. They sat down and made a pact with you, for they felt they had to confer with you for their own safety! Because when they saw you and estimated your strength, they realized this was a scene not to their liking and that Allah the Almighty had made you victorious over them. Now you are returning home in safety, having gained good a deed—this is the greatest of conquests! How quickly have you forgotten Uhud! That was when although I called after you, you kept climbing up high without even looking back. Remember the day of Ahzab when they all came attacking you; they were attacking you from below and above, and your eyes had opened wide thinking it was your last, and even then, you had certain doubts concerning Allah and His help."

These words of the blessed Messenger weighed heavy on the honorable Companions and they all said in unison: "Allah and His Messenger tell the truth; indeed this is the greatest of conquests."

Now the Companions were comforted. They had found out that the objections they made now and then by raising their voices had been forgiven and so were content. They also understood well that the choices made by the Messenger of Allah were none other than within the Will of Allah the Almighty and that to seek alternatives to his decisions were not becoming of a believer.

The blessed Messenger was now walking day and night with his Companions, as he wanted to reach Medina as soon as possible. A month and a half had passed since the Messenger and his Companions had left Medina with the purpose of performing *umrah*. Nearly half of this period had been spent in Hudaybiya and the rest on the way and back.

The Period of Ambassadors
and Opening Up

A new era started in Medina. With Hudaybiya, the danger that could come from Mecca had been averted, and now was the time to take the enlightening message of Islam to people who were living without knowledge of religion. The wars that had occurred had always been ignited by the Meccans and it was always them that had been the cause of the conflict. Each time, the Muslims had taken the position of defense, and they had not had the opportunity to portray the Divine message—which was as essential as water and air to people who were living without an aim. The real goal of a believer was to take the Name of Allah to hearts who were in need, to let them know their Lord.

In fact, with Hudaybiya started the conquest of Mecca; the people now had the opportunity to get to know Islam in this atmosphere of peace, and they got a chance to see the beauties in the heart of Islam. New ways and routes between Mecca and Medina were established, and these ways and routes were now pathways used to take Islam to hearts in need. This is what the blessed Messenger did and he encouraged his Companions to do the same. Now was the time to conquer the hearts within and without, for he had been sent as Prophet to the whole of humanity, not only those who he could directly address. He was a Messenger whom all should recognize and for this to happen, the Muslims needed to reach out to other people. On the basis provided by Hudaybiya, Allah the Almighty was now giving the believers this opportunity.

Six years had passed since the Hijra, and they were about to enter the seventh. One day after Hudaybiya, the Messenger of Allah addressed his Companions, and after giving thanks to Allah and praising Him, he said: "O people, there is no doubt that Allah the Almighty sent me as mercy to all mankind. Fulfill your duty towards me so that Allah the Almighty may treat you with His mercy. I will send some of you as ambassadors to kings; do not act like the Children of Israel and oppose me as they opposed Jesus, son of Maryam!"

The Companions were surprised: "O Messenger of Allah! In what way did the disciples oppose?"

On that question he answered: "He had invited his disciples to do the duty that I ask of you today. When Allah sent him the revelation 'Send your men to the kings of the earth' he had sent them to a number of places. The disciples who were sent to places that were close-by consented whereas those who were sent a long distance objected. Then Jesus opened up his hands and said: 'My Lord! I have conveyed what you have sent me to the Disciples; but they waiver.'

Upon that Allah the Almighty said: 'I know how to deal with them.'

The next day they woke up speaking the language of the country they were to be sent to. Upon that Jesus said to them: 'This is something that Allah has deemed and verified for you; now don't lose time and be on your way.'"

With this story it was obvious the blessed Messenger was preparing his Companions for something important; for his Messengership was not limited to a particular region like Prophet Jesus, it contained all.

And so his Companions had to show even more determination than the Disciples and not falter in their obedience to their Messenger. And so it would be! The Companions who listened to the Messenger said: "O Messenger of Allah! We swear by Allah that we will not contradict you on any matter; you can send us wherever you like, without a doubt we will obey your orders!"

They were thus mentally prepared; and when our noble Prophet received such a firm answer from his Companions, he chose some of them to send to tribal chiefs, sovereigns of states and kings around the area. He was writing letters to them and handing the letters to the Companions he was sending to the determined lands. The Companions who had heard of these missions were excited; when they heard that they were also going to be sent to the Byzantines, the Persians and the Abyssinians, they had a few concerns and they shared their concerns with our noble Prophet: "O Messenger of Allah!" they were saying. "They do not read letters unless they are sealed."

It was true; it was important to know your addressee when communicating the message. In order to not be faced with a negative outcome from the start, they had to take care of these eventualities. The Messenger of Allah, peace and blessings be upon him, had a ring made. On the ring was written: "Muhammad, Rasul of Allah." From then on, this signature would be stamped at the end of all the letters sent!

On the same day he called six of his Companions to his side and sent all of them to different places. Amr ibn Umayya would go to the Abyssinian king (the Negus) Ashama ibn al-Abjar; Dihya ibn Khalifa al-Kalbi would go to the Byzantine emperor Heraclius; Abdullah ibn Hudhafah as-Sahmi would go to the Persian (Sassanian) king (Khosrau II) Khusraw Parviz; Hatib ibn Abi Balta'ah would go to the Egyptian vicegerent (the Muqawqis) Juraij ibn Matta; Shuja ibn Wahab would go to the king of Damascus, Harith ibn Abi Shamir al-Ghassan; and Sulayt ibn Amr al-Amiri would go to the chief of Yamama, Hawdha ibn Ali. All of the chosen messengers knew the languages of the lands they would be going to.

Slowly but eventually there came an atmosphere of peace. Our noble Prophet was sending letters with envoys in all directions in order to perform his duty of communication to a greater geography. He wanted to be able to help everyone—to the extent that he did not want a single moment to be wasted. He wanted to abolish all the obstacles between people and their Lord and he wanted to take everyone to the exalted level of being a good subject to Allah. This was his duty as the Prophet whom all had been waiting for in this late period of history, and the blessed Messenger was performing his duty in an excellent manner.

Khaybar: The Point of Contention

It had been twenty days since the blessed Messenger, peace and blessings be upon him, had returned from Hudaybiya—with the agreement signed, the troubles that could come from Mecca had somewhat been averted. For with Hudaybiya, the alliance that the Meccan polytheists and the Khaybar Jews had made was annulled, at least for some time. Still, the Banu Qurayza, the Banu Qaynuqa and the Banu Nadir who had been exiled from their homeland and who had come to live in Khaybar presented a clear danger—it was difficult to know what reaction they would give to different developments.

Especially leading Jewish men such as Sallam ibn Abi Huqayq, Kinana ibn Rabi and Huyay ibn Akhtab had come and settled there, saying that they would seek revenge with the help of their friends in Khaybar, throwing threats all around. They had also played a great role in provoking the surrounding tribes and encouraging the Meccan army to come all the way to the Trench. The delegation that had gone to Mecca to provoke the polytheists included nineteen of the eminent men of Khaybar, they had also gone to the surrounding tribes, and they had promised a great portion of their produce should these tribes attack Medina! They acted on feelings of revenge and were keeping their eyes out for any opportunity.

When they returned empty-handed from the Trench where they hoped to be victorious, they had become anxious. They knew that they would be held accountable for their actions and so they wanted to be the ones to act first. They had decided to act quickly, so before the Messenger of Allah and his Companions came upon them, they were planning to make a surprise attack on Medina with the help of the Jews of Tayma, Fadak and Wadi al-Qura.

Usayr ibn Zarim, who had become their leader after Abu Rafi, was particularly swearing challenging oaths and seemed to be provoking his community. He had also spoken to the people of Ghatafan and had been able to convince them in this business of attacking Medina. His efforts were being well received by his community as well and they were applauding him as a leader who would help them avenge their friends' deaths. In short, Khaybar had become the center of sedition and was ready to explode any minute.

The Messenger of Allah, peace and blessings be upon him, was following all that was happening very closely. To be better informed of the situation, he had appointed three of his men to go and find out what was happening in Khaybar and then to report back—their investigation confirmed what they had been hearing. The same was true regarding the experience of Harija ibn Husayl who, among them, had come all the way to Medina. The "bounty" that had been promised in the verses before the conquest was becoming clearer and clearer.

Our noble Prophet ordered his Companions to make preparations; but he also warned that no one should act with the wrong assumption of getting the spoils of Khaybar, and made it clear that those who were joining the campaign for that purpose would not be given any spoils whatsoever.

The Jews of Medina, who lived in Medina according to the pact that they had signed with the Muslims and who now understood that the blessed Messenger intended to lead a campaign against Khaybar, were quite anxious, and in order to weaken the hand of the Muslims they did not ask them to pay all the debts owed to the Jews. People like Abdullah ibn Abi Hadrad, who was trying to pay the debts he incurred before Khaybar, had had to sell the clothes off his back, and had gone to war with borrowed clothes! The Messenger of Allah himself had had to help Abu Abs ibn Jabr, who had no means to join the campaign. The Jews of Medina, who did not think the conquest of Khaybar was possible, were speaking of the castles, the great rivers and variety of fruits to be found there, along with the courage of their warriors—trying to weaken the morale of the believers.

Despite all this, one day our noble Prophet and six thousand six hundred people—two hundred of them cavalry—set off from Medina and made their way to Khaybar! The Messenger of Allah had left Siba ibn Urtufa as his representative.

On this journey there were ten Medinan Jews with our beloved Prophet. There were also about twenty female Companions who were to act as nurses, spin thread, cook food and carry water.

Meanwhile, the leader of the hypocrites was at work; he was trying to send the news of the campaign of our noble Prophet and his Companions to Khaybar so that the Jews may be warned. When our noble Prophet reached a point between the Khaybar castles of Shikk and Natat, he gave the order to camp. It was a rough, bushy place and yet they were to stop and perform Prayers.

When they started on the road again and came to a point where they could see Khaybar, the blessed Messenger called out to his Companions: "Stop!"

These people, who were the epitome of obedience, had all stopped in their tracks and waited to see what the Messenger of Allah would do. Maybe he was going to turn to his Merciful Lord once again in all earnestness and present his position to Him. He lifted up his hands and started to pray in the following manner: "Dear Lord! The Lord of the seven heavens and all that they cast a shadow on; the Lord of the earth and all that it shoulders, the Lord of the devils and those who are led by them; the Lord of the wind and all that it scatters around! We ask for the good of this land and its inhabitants; and we seek refuge in you from this place and all harm that could come from its inhabitants."

When they came to Khaybar it was the middle of the night and the Messenger of Allah, peace and blessings be upon him, chose his place to camp and they started to make preparations for the following day. Because it was night, this was when our noble Prophet would perform his Tahajjud Prayer, and with the first light of day he had started his Morning Prayer, and his Companions were right behind him. They raised their hands in prayer and asked for victory from the Great Lord.

As usual, the people of Khaybar had left their homes to go to their fields and gardens, and they were totally shocked to be faced with an army that was waiting for them: "Woe is us! Here is Muhammad and his orderly army!" they said and started to run away.

They were running away on the one hand but on the other they were still trying to belittle the army of faith that they held in deep enmity: "Muhammad will dare fight against us? What a strange thing!" and they believed they would come victorious despite everything.

The fact that things had become so serious had divided them into two camps: one camp was saying that they should stay inside the castles and be on the defensive, the other camp was saying that they should come out to the field and fight one on one. They trusted their big and strong castles, they were filled with provisions and rivers ran through them to satisfy their needs. Leading men such as Sallam ibn Mishkam were saying: "Do not shy away from fighting with him here; it is better for you to die fighting then to be left alone here."

They took their valuables and families to the castle of Katiba and placed their provisions in the castle named Naim. All those who could hold a weapon had gathered in the castle of Natat and were promising each other that they would fight till the last drop of their blood.

As expected, the first spark came from them; with the first rays of sun they started to shower arrows onto where the Messenger of Allah and his Companions were. They were shooting so fast and in such succession that by the end of the day fifty Companions were wounded. The arrows that they shot became ammunition for the believers—as soon as the arrows fell on the ground the Companions would collect them and shoot them back at the castle of Natat. A siege that would continue for days had thus started; when night fell they moved to the place determined for their headquarters and this place would bear witness to the fall of the Khaybar castles one by one.

The Khaybar siege was continuing but our noble Prophet had fallen ill and was not able to come out among his Companions. It seemed that fate was preparing the Companions for difficult circumstances. Our beloved Prophet called his loyal friend Abu Bakr to his side and gave the white standard to him—this meant that now Abu Bakr was commander of the army in front of Khaybar. Night fell that day as well and no results had been obtained; it seemed as if each day was an exact replica of the previous one. The shower of arrows that started in the early hours of the morning would cease during the evening, and the same routine would be repeated the next day. The morning of that day the Messenger of Allah would call Umar to his side and give the standard to him. The following day, the standard was given to someone from the Ansar—the standard kept changing hands every day!

In the meantime there was close combat as well—some groups who came out of the castle would be confronted by the Companions and these confrontations would last until one party triumphed over the other!

At last the Messenger of Allah, peace and blessings be upon him, turned to his Companions one day and said: "I will give the standard to such a person who loves Allah and Allah loves him," and he also gave the good news that Khaybar would be conquered the next day. Our noble Prophet was bearing witness—the commander who would take Khaybar was an important person who loved Allah and who was loved by Allah. For the Companions who had no expectations of acceptance other than by Allah thought this to be a very exalted and important position indeed and so everyone was expecting to be handed the standard the next day. There was a special kind of tranquility and peace in their hearts knowing that the conquest would happen the next day, and so the Companions passed the night in remembrance of Allah.

Morning broke, and after the Prayer the blessed Messenger turned to his Companions once again, and after giving them advice, he asked for the standard to be brought to him. The honorable Companions were standing up in ranks to see which lucky person the standard would be given! Then our noble Prophet asked: "Where is Ali?"

"O Messenger of Allah, Ali's eyes are aching," the Companions responded.

"Call him to me," he said and so Salama ibn Akwa went to call Ali. Salama was holding Ali's hand to aide him, and thus they came to the presence of the blessed Messenger.

The Companions had thought that he would not be able to come at all because of the pain in his eyes that he had been suffering from for days. When they saw him approach, they started to point out to him and say: "There he is, Ali is coming."

And the blessed Messenger said: "He will be the means through which the conquest will happen," pointing to his son-in-law.

"Come near me," he called out. Ali said: "O Messenger of Allah, I have pain in my eyes to the degree that I can hardly see where I am stepping."

Upon that our noble Prophet started to say a prayer of healing for Ali's eyes. He had also taken a little bit of his blessed saliva and was putting it over his son-in-law's eyes, supplicating to Allah to heal them. They were experiencing another miracle!

It was as if these were not the eyes of Ali that had been aching until a moment ago. There was no pain left, and Ali could see clearly now. It was as if he had not been ill at all!

Then the blessed Messenger put the sword and armor on Ali, the Warrior Lion, and handing him the standard he said: "Take this standard and advance! Fight till the moment Allah will make you victorious and do not turn back."

"What shall I fight the people on?" asked Ali, and our noble Prophet answered: "Fight them till they bear witness that there is no deity but Allah and that Muhammad is His subject and Messenger. When they accept that, they will have saved their lives and possessions from you—their accounts are held by Allah! Advance towards their homes and wait a while; invite them to Islam and tell them about the responsibilities they have towards Allah and the Messenger of Allah. I swear by Allah that should a single man become Muslim because of you, this is better for you than valleys full of red camels."

The compassion of the Messenger of mercy was to such a degree that he wanted to lay out principles for people who had been showering arrows and stones at them, with whom they had been fighting at close quarters. After giving orders, he started to pray to Allah that He may help Ali and his friends. Ali, who had bravely taken the standard from our noble Prophet, started to walk confidently towards the castle and came to the front of the Khaybar castles; the honorable Companions were walking with him. Then he erected the standard in front of the castles. The people inside the castles were watching the developments—having seen him come and erect the standard had caused anxiety among the people of Khaybar and they called out: "Who are you?"

"I am Ali, son of Abu Talib," answered Ali.

The name Ali was not foreign to them; it seemed that in the books they had in their hands there was mention of this name as the one to conquer their castles, and when they heard his name their anxiety grew. One of the people who had heard the name 'Ali' started to call out: "O community of Jews, I swear by what has been revealed to Moses that your end has come, and you will be defeated today!"

Meanwhile, a tough war was raging. Marhab and Ali who had taken out their swords were sizing each other up and were making moves. In front of Khaybar one could only hear the clashing of swords and challenges thrown at the other side. At one moment there was a great noise, everyone understood that a deathly blow had been struck. They wondered about the result. When the dust settled they could see that it was Ali who had been left standing, and then the believers started to call out *takbir*s.

When the Messenger of Allah, peace and blessings be upon him, saw that Marhab too had been killed after Yasir, he gave the following good news to his Companions: "Rejoice; Khaybar is easier now!"

And just as the blessed Messenger said, it became easier. With the death of Marhab, the place was a battlefield in the real sense of the word. The Khaybar were giving it their all in order to defend their castle which was about to fall, and they were attacking to death! For them, each conquered castle meant another space that they had to leave. They were fleeing towards the castles remaining in the back and were trying to protect themselves there.

During this conquest, Ali's shield fell from his hand and he had nothing left to protect himself with. He looked to both his sides and then saw the door of the castle. He reached for the door and yanked it loose and used the door of the castle as his shield—and he used it till the end of the battle. Ali and the Companions were pursuing the Khaybaris who were fleeing towards the castles from behind. Now the sound of "Allah is the Greatest!" was echoing throughout Khaybar. The voices of *takbir* frightened the people of Khaybar even more and they felt weak—there was nothing left that they could do. However much they would try to seek refuge in their castles they could see that their end had come.

With the conquest of each castle there were spoils and prisoners in their custody. But the warriors still did not give themselves up.

Now the Companions had also started to use catapults with the order of the Messenger of Allah. This machine, which was made by the people of Khaybar themselves, was now raining stones on them. During the chaos, an arrow hit the blessed Messenger and got tangled in his dress. He got a handful of dust from the ground and threw it in the direction of the Khaybar. The people of Khaybar seemed to be shaken as if there had been an earthquake and started to fall down one by one.

The castles of Watih and Sulalim were now also under siege, and the Khaybaris understood that they were about to face extinction, and so they took the decision to surrender.

Our beloved Prophet had conquered the castles of Khaybar and another threat against Medina had thus been dealt with. Of course the issue was greater than Khaybar; they were now going to deal with other elements that were causing threat.

Meanwhile, they performed their *Umrah* according to the terms of the Hudaybiya Agreement, on the month of Dhu al-Qadah, the seventh year of the Hijra. So the dream of a year ago had become reality.

Mecca's Beloved Ones

It was clear that the language of the heart and the manner of behavior left very deep impressions on people. To represent the ideas that one adopts to the best degree was much more effective than explaining it with words to others. The Messenger of Allah, peace and blessings be upon him, was doing both. He made use of every opportunity for his cause and he always wanted more. When he entered the grounds of Ka'ba and started to worship Allah, there were those who were watching him with curious eyes just as there were those who fled in order to not come in contact with him. He knew all of them and he wanted to leave his doors open to all. And so he was sending messages to people he had not been able to see that day and was trying to make them think.

Khalid ibn al-Walid was one of those people. He must have been one of those people that the Messenger of Allah wished would come and submit to the will of Allah, because he asked his brother Walid ibn al-Walid who had already become Muslim and come to Medina: "Where is Khalid ibn al-Walid?"

That day Walid would not be able to find his brother Khalid even though he looked for him everywhere. But he had to reach him at all cost because our noble Prophet had a message for him, so he wrote his brother a letter. In his letter Walid was talking about the meeting he had with our noble Prophet and that the blessed Messenger said, concerning Khalid: "It is not possible for a man like him to know about Islam and to not recognize it. I wish he had entered all his battles on the side of Muslims and against polytheists! This would have been best for him; and so we would prefer him above others and treat him like the apple of our eye."

He finished his letter with: "O my brother! Make use of these opportunities that come to you in the most perfect time, and thus compensate for the opportunities that you have missed!"

Khalid ibn al-Walid had made his decision; returning from the wars he fought against the Messenger of Allah he always had a feeling of sourness inside which he could not give any meaning to. Since Hudaybiya he had been thinking deep and hard. Now he was looking for a Companion to pour his heart out—if he spoke about it to Abu Sufyan, Ikrima or Safwan ibn Umayya, he would not get a favorable response. But he was adamant. After a long period of hesitation he tried to speak of his thoughts to Uthman ibn Talha. When he saw that he too was ready to meet the blessed Messenger and embrace the faith, they made plans to go and set off on the road the next day. When they came to the place called Hadda, they ran into Amr ibn al-As:

"Welcome," he was saying to them.

"And you too," they replied and asked,

"Where is it that you are going?"

Amr would choose to answer the question with question: "And where is it that you are going?"

There was no need to prolong it and they replied: "To enter Islam and follow Muhammad."

Amr ibn al-As said: "I am like you, too."

Then the long-standing friends directed their quick steps to Medina. They stopped at a place near Medina in order to rest and change their clothes; they wanted to go to the presence of our noble Prophet in the best of appearances!

Meanwhile the blessed Messenger had already received the news of their coming, and turning to his Companions, he said: "Mecca is sending its beloved ones to your lap!"

Walid was too happy for words to hear his brother's coming—his brother whom he had not been able to find in Mecca. He wanted to go out and meet him on the way. It was true, Khalid ibn al-Walid was really coming! He said: "Make haste, the Messenger of Allah has received the news of your coming and is very happy, he is waiting for you."

They too were excited and they started to speed walk. When they came to the presence of the Messenger of mercy, there was no way to describe the smile on his face—his radiant face was shining bright like the sun!

First Khalid saluted our noble Prophet; the blessed Messenger was so warm that Khalid could feel his response to his salutation deep in his heart. His arms open and inviting, the warmth in his smile and the love in his heart—with all this the blessed Messenger had conquered them. His arms opened wide were inviting him, his smile so warm was embracing him, his love so deep was melting him. All he could say was: "I swear that there is no deity but Allah and that you are His Messenger." The blessed Messenger who was happy at the arrival of a hero who had found his place replied: "Thanks be to

Him who has given you guidance. I saw great reason in you and I was hoping that one day this reason would carry itself to goodness!"

Khalid realized that now after all those years he felt like the real Khalid; he was met with compliment over compliment and he was ruing the time he had wasted before this moment.

"O Messenger of Allah," he said. "As you can see and know I have acted against you and against Truth at every turn. I ask you to pray for me to Allah that He may forgive me!"

Amr ibn al-As and Uthman ibn Talha were experiencing the same emotions.

Amr ibn al-As reached out for the hand of the blessed Messenger, but then took it away for a while. The blessed Messenger would ask the reason why he withdrew his hand: "I have conditions," said Amr ibn al-As. Our noble Prophet asked: "What are they?"

The great man had lowered his head—he was being crushed under the faults of his previous life: "Being forgiven."

Our noble Prophet held Amr's hands inside his own hands and said: "Islam cleanses the faults one has made before becoming a Muslim."

Now everyone could see that Hudaybiya had been a conquest; it was true that they had not been able to enter Mecca that day but now hearts had been opened to Islam and even the most eminent men were directing themselves towards Medina. From then on this process would continue at great speed.

The Battle of Muta

It was the Jamazi al-awwal month of the eighth year of the Hijra; the conditions of peace were being put to best use and the developments were closely watched in the name of communicating the message of Islam. To that end our noble Prophet sent another letter to the governor of Basra with Harith ibn Umayr. But something that they had not witnessed before would happen that day and Harith, the envoy of the blessed Messenger, would be brutally killed by Shurahbil as he was passing a place called Balka. After cutting his way, Shurahbil had tied Harith down and when he found out that he was the envoy of the Messenger of Allah, he had murdered him. This was a crime that could not be forgiven and meant an open declaration for war. Because even under the harshest circumstances envoys were meant to be under protection.

When the news that Harith was murdered reached the blessed Messenger, he was very sad and he encouraged his Companions to fight against Shurahbil who could not even tolerate an envoy going his way, for he was there to put an end to such acts of banditry and those who had made this a profession had to be stopped. The direction they were about to go was under Byzantine rule and so they were handling the matter very carefully and were thinking of every eventuality.

Soon there was an army of three thousand people. Such a big army had been gathered only in the Trench before. It seemed as if the Messenger of Allah, peace and blessings be upon him, could sense what was going to happen. He had put Zayd ibn Haritha, his freed slave, at the head of this army by handing him the white standard. He told him to go all the way to where Harith ibn Umayr was murdered and invite the people there to Islam. Should they not accept it, then he told him to trust in Allah and to do what they had to do to reach the result. With the appointment of his slave, the blessed Messenger was also uprooting certain understandings, showing that a slave could indeed be a commander, and that in the sight of Allah everyone was equal. He knew that this raid would not end with Zayd and so he said: "If Zayd should fall martyr, then Jafar ibn Abi Talib should be commander, and should Jafar fall martyr, Abdullah ibn Rawaha should be the commander," letting them know the gravity of the situation. Many of the Companions had already understood from his words that the said commanders would fall martyr one by one and their farewells with these friends became more emotional than usual.

As he saw his army on its way, the Messenger of mercy gave the following advice which still echoes in our ears today: "Fight in the Name of Allah, fight against those who deny Allah and rebel against Him in the way of Allah! But do not wrong anyone! Do not oppress anyone forgetting your covenant! Do not kill women and children, the old, or people who have devoted themselves to prayer in the temple! Do not cut a single tree, nor destroy a single date grove! Do not burn the buildings!"

The blessed Messenger would see them on their way till the hills of Wada, and would gaze after them for a very long while. On their way they would receive the news that Heracles had prepared an army of one hundred thousand, and although they hesitated for a moment about letting the Messenger of Allah know about this, they decided to continue on their way even though certain death may be awaiting them.

After a two-day stopover at Ma'an they continued on their way. In the place called Masharif the two armies met. There was a sea of soldiers in front of them that seemed to have no end. War seemed inevitable. The army of Zayd decided to camp at the place called Muta and prepared for war there! The right wing was commandeered by Qutba ibn Qatada, and the left by Ubada ibn Malik.

With the first rays of sun the next day, swords had been drawn in Muta and the three thousand army of faith was confronting the Byzantine army of two-hundred thousand. This was not a war of equal forces; if this strong army had just walked on straight to trample the army of Islam, they would be victors. But that is not how things happened. In this war that lasted seven days, just as the blessed Messenger was saying, Zayd, Jafar and Abdullah all fell martyr. Thabit ibn Akram took the standard and after a long search he gave it to Khalid ibn al-Walid.

Khalid, who was now commander of the Muslim army, had continued to fight without breaking the course of the war and had left his entire prowess to the dark of the evening. Such a numerous army had not been able to defeat an army of three thousand in five full days—an enemy that should have been like a handful to them! This was because in the evening Khalid had deployed a completely new tactic in the organization of the army. The ones who had been fighting in the front were now pulled to the back, the ones on the right exchanged with the ones on the left—and thus this gave the impression that fresh troops had been sent.

The next morning when the enemy formed their lines, they could understand the rattle they had been hearing during the night. A fresh new force had been added to the ranks of the Muslim army, for the men they had in front of them were different to the men they had been fighting for the last six days. They were experiencing a great shock; how could this army that had not been able to deal with three thousand soldiers deal with an army that had fresh troops? They seemed to have accepted defeat even before fighting that day and Khalid wanted to make use of this situation. He was trying to widen the distance between the enemy that had retreated and his troops. The Byzantine army saw this and thought it was a new tactic on the part of Khalid. They conjectured that should they attack, they would be encircled by the Muslim army and suffer great losses.

This situation continued till evening of that day and it meant the end of battle for both sides. For the Byzantines did not want to appear weak by losing even more men to a small army, so they started to retreat! This had been Khalid's intention from the start. He wanted to bring back to Medina what the Messenger of Allah had entrusted to him. In this war that they had fought for seven days—chest to chest—they had given twelve martyrs including three commanders—this was the sign of true heroism! They had fought against a state that had a say in the world affairs of the day, and in a confrontation where there was no balance of power, they had only suffered twelve losses. This could not be explained with anything other than Divine help and all tribes that heard of this would regard the army of the Messenger of Allah in another light. This also meant the first hole to be opened in the Byzantine walls.

There had been some tribes that had posed problems to the Muslim army on the way and shed blood. Khalid decided to pay them a visit and teach them all a lesson on his way back to Medina.

Our noble Prophet would call out to his Companions: "Gather together to go and meet your brothers," and they would all go out of Medina, children and all, to welcome them. He had taken the children of Jafar on the back of his own mount and came all the way to the place called Juruf. The heroes of Muta were now standing in front of him! Allah the Almighty had helped them in all their helplessness; they had returned without being defeated. But not all was aware of this fact and some of the Companions were saying: "You have abandoned the battle?" These were bitter words that hurt and so they asked: "O Messenger of Allah! Have we abandoned the battle? Are we runaways?"

They wanted to know for certain what their status was.

"No, quite the contrary, you are those who get up and prepare to fight the enemy again," said the blessed Messenger and set their minds at rest. Then he turned to his Companions and said: "They are soldiers who did not run away from fighting in the way of Allah but are, by the will of Allah, those who have retreated ready to run to the front again."

These were words that settled the matter and some of the soldiers who had felt the need to hide themselves because of censure were breathing a sigh of relief to hear that they had not committed an error in the eyes of Allah and His Messenger.

The Conquest of Mecca

Twenty-two months had passed since the agreement of Hudaybiya, and the Meccans had kept to their side of the bargain. The calendars were showing the month of Shaban, the eighth year of the Hijra.

The blessed Messenger, peace and blessings be upon him, had led the Morning Prayer when Amr ibn Salim, from the Huza'a, came to him with forty horsemen by his side. He was trying to let them know what had happened to them by reciting a poem at the Masjid an-Nabawi, asking for help from the Messenger of Allah.

It appeared that the Quraysh had come together with the Banu Bakr and the Banu Nufasa, and had attacked the Huza'a who had led a peaceful and quiet life since Hudaybiya and killed twenty-three people, most of them women, children and old men. Safwan ibn Umayya, Ikrima ibn Abu Jahl, Huwaytib ibn Abdiluzza, Shayba ibn Uthman and Mikraz ibn Hafs had taken part in this cold blooded raid.

They had been so blinded by hatred that the Huza'a people, who had sought refuge in the Haram area, had not been spared their wrath! They had taken matters so far that some of them had to raise objections. Those who had a little bit of humanity left in them were now saying out loud that they did not approve of what was happening.

When morning came and the gravity of what had happened came to light, the Quraysh regretted what they had done—yes, this looked like a clear violation of the Hudaybiya Agreement. Now the die had been cast. They were making impossible suggestions to save themselves or to justify themselves.

On the other hand the Messenger of Allah, peace and blessings be upon him, listened to what was being said: "You will be helped, O Amr ibn Salim," and comforted the leader of Huza'a.

But he was very sad and angry—what conscience could rest calm after twenty-three people had been brutally murdered in the night, most of them being children, women and the elderly? And especially if the attackers were people who had promised "We will not make war with you or your allies for ten years?" It seemed that the Quraysh would not stop acting impulsive. At that moment a cloud appeared in the sky and there was very loud thunder. The Messenger of Allah, who did not take much account of statements made other than the revelations, would know how to listen to the message given to him by way of phenomena and said: "This cloud is giving me the good news of the Banu Ka'b's victory."

Since there was no place for coincidence in the universe, this had to be a sign of Divine wrath.

The blessed Messenger, who had from the very beginning tried to institute peace in Hijaz, was sending campaigns to other places in order to stop acts of banditry—and here was the Quraysh committing a despicable crime in Mecca—something he had not been expecting: "I will help those people; if I do not help the Banu Ka'b today, Allah will not help me. I swear by He who holds my life in His hands I will protect them as I protect myself, my family and my house," thus showing his determined state of mind to all.

He then called a Companion named Damra to his side and asked him to give the matter some consideration— through a different perspective.

Damra, who received the blessed Messenger's order, went straight to Mecca and spoke to the Quraysh, but the last word he would get was: "We tell him that we are rescinding our agreement with him," and thus the Quraysh would be the side who preferred war.

Although the Quraysh denied committing the act, they were still worried and were trying to find a way to get out of this situation with minimal losses. In order to voice their worries, Harith went to Abu Sufyan.

Ibn Hisham and Abdullah ibn Abi Rabia would warn their leader in the following manner: "This is a wrong that you have to make right—if you do not correct this error and find another ground for peace, then Muhammad will most certainly come here with his Companions and will break our backs."

Abu Sufyan who had been listening to them started to think deeply: "This business is something that I am neither totally involved in nor totally out of."

Meanwhile the leaders of the Quraysh had come to his side. He was experiencing a very critical moment as leader, and turning to the Meccans he started to say the: "This is not a responsibility that you can lay solely on me! I have not been consulted on this matter, I did not know about it, and I did not authorize it. I swear by Allah that if my feelings are not misleading me Muhammad will surely declare war on us; and

I fear my feelings have never been wrong. I do not see any option other than going to Muhammad and asking him to renew and extend the agreement."

More and more people among the Quraysh were regretful. These people who, till yesterday, had not thought of an option other than defiance were now realizing the gravity of the issue and were becoming more timid.

"You speak the truth!" they were saying.

And at last they decided to send Abu Sufyan to Medina to speak to the Messenger of Allah and extend the period of the agreement. Before long, Abu Sufyan was on the road to Medina with his slave!

On the other hand our noble Messenger had turned to his Companions in Medina and said: "Abu Sufyan is about to come to you with the intention of renewing the agreement and extending its period, but he will return angry and empty handed," sharing with the people around him what was happening in Mecca.

This was a critical turning point and a process which had to be followed through delicately—there was no room for fault. He was going to go to Mecca which Allah had promised him, but he did not want there to be any bloodshed; he planned to surprise them and catch them unawares. That is why he would hold all the routes and he would see to it that everything that happened in Medina would not be known in Mecca. Intelligence was the most important thing in war; in the most unpreventable wars a little piece of news could change the whole course of hostilities and make the impossible possible. And so they had to be very careful about the dissemination of news until he entered Mecca. For this reason he placed men at all the important passages and gave the duty of the control of these passages to Umar. Umar was going around to the guards and telling them to question anyone who traveled on this route and not to let anyone pass before they understood what the traveler's purpose was; and afterwards their job was to report this back to the Messenger of Allah.

The blessed Messenger had another precaution at this juncture: he sent Abu Qatada ibn Rab with a unit to a place called Batn al-Izam on the way to Damascus, and thus gave the impression that they army that was being prepared was going to take to that route, countering the news and rumors that the army was meant for the direction of Mecca. Meanwhile he was sending envoys to all directions and spreading the news: "All those who believe in Allah and His Messenger should be ready in Medina by the month of Ramadan."

Now the Companions were coming to Medina in droves; the headquarters had been set up by the wells of Abu Inaba and everyone coming in was settling there to wait for the order to move. Meanwhile people like Hassan ibn Thabit were encouraging the Companions with poems in the struggles to be staged against the enemies of Allah.

Taking off from Medina

Eight years had passed since their arrival in Medina and now believers had to leave the city because of the Prophetic invitation. Everyone who had become a Muslim to that day had responded to the invitation of the Messenger of Allah and had run to Medina. It was a Wednesday, the first days of Ramadan. Naturally, everyone was fasting. The Messenger of Allah first turned to his Companions and said: "Those who want to may continue with their fast, those want to, may break it," he called out. He himself was one of those who would not break their fast.

Meanwhile, he sent a scout force of two hundred under the leadership of Zubayr ibn Awwam. Then he prayed the Afternoon Prayer with his Companions and then gave the order to move. Around him was an army of ten-thousand people, made up of the Ansar, the Muhajirun and other tribes. Because the road was long, they had taken their horses with them but were riding their camels. They came to a place called Sulsul without stopping and here the blessed Messenger pointed to a cloud above and said: "I see that this cloud is giving me the good news of the Banu Ka'b victory."

The weather was quite hot and when they reached Arj, our noble Prophet poured some water over his head and washed his face in order to cool down a little bit. This route was also the route that he had taken on his migration. He then continued to advance in the direction of Talub. While the journey continued, the Messenger of Allah, peace and blessings be upon him, separated a hundred horsemen from his Companions and told them go ahead before them.

Before long, these horsemen would meet a man from the Hawazin and they would catch the man and bring him to the Messenger of Allah. When the blessed Messenger questioned the man to learn that the Hawazin was gathering soldiers against him, he said: "Allah is enough for us, what a beautiful aide He is!" and calling Khalid ibn al-Walid to his side, he told him to make sure that no one hears about their campaign.

Meanwhile, he noticed a dog that was suckling its young a little far away; it was snarling at the people that had gathered around him and was showing its teeth to them. Prophetic compassion would answer to this compassion of the mother and he would call Jamil ibn Suraqa to his side. He told him to wait beside this dog that was suckling its young until everyone had passed and to make sure that neither the dog nor its young would be hurt, telling him to keep the caravan of people away from them.

As they made their way on the road, people kept joining them. There were also those who came and became a Muslim. The strange thing was that most of the Companions did not know who they were going to go to war against. There seemed to be three alternatives: Quraysh, Hawazin and Thaqif. Even Companions such as Ka'b ibn Malik who seemed to be in the front would come to the Messenger of Allah and try to learn which out of these three they would be fighting.

When they came to Kudayd, they ran into Sulaym. There the Messenger of Allah, peace and blessings be upon him, had them take out the standards and banners and distributed them among the tribes. Each tribe had been organized under their own standards and flags and this is how they would enter the battle. There were more than thirty flags in the army. When they came to Juhfa they were faced with a surprise. The blessed Messenger's uncle Abbas had his bags on his shoulder and was coming to Medina. A smile appeared on the face of the Messenger of Allah. He first had Abbas's load sent to Medina and then said to him: "Just as my Prophethood is the last one, so is your migration the last one as well."

This compliment also signaled that Mecca was going to become Muslim and that there would be no more reason to migrate. When they came to the valley called Marr az-Zahran near Mecca, the sun had set and the army was given the order to relax. But the Messenger of Allah had another order; each believer was going to go and collect brushwood and light a fire where they were. At the head of the watch guards was once again Umar.

The Quraysh still did not know what was happening; they could guess that they were going to be held accountable for what they did but they did not know when or where this would happen. That is why they were worried when they had not been able to receive news from Medina for quite a long time. In the end they decided to send Abu Sufyan and Hakim ibn Hizam in the direction of Medina: "If you meet Muhammad, ask for surety for us," they were saying.

On the way the two friends would come across Budayl ibn Warqa. They wanted him to come with them, and so the three of them set out together in the direction of Medina. When they came to the location of Arak which was located in Marr az-Zahran, in the dark of the night they experienced a great shock for they saw an army as big as the sea, and army with tents and fires in front of tents. They were frightened by the neighing of the horses and the bellowing of the camels—they were at the end of the road.

On the other side the Messenger of Allah had called some of his Companions to his side and ordered them to catch Abu Sufyan who he told them was in the region of Arak. When they were approached from behind Abu Sufyan and his two travelling companions were busy watching the terrifying scene before them. At a moment they were not expecting they were surrounded and brought to Umar.

Umar was running to the blessed Messenger with happiness. Abbas who saw this state of his had also taken to the road and was making haste to come to the presence of the Messenger before Umar. His aim was, contrary to Umar's request of solving the issue through easy methods, was to give Abu Sufyan, his friends of many years, safe custody. And so it would be. When he saw the power of the Messenger of Allah, peace and blessings be upon him, and his Companions, the obedience they showed their leaders, and their practice of worship, the expected change would start to take place in Abu Sufyan, and he would become a different man. For him all roads had been blocked and there was no other alternative; Abu Sufyan, the mighty leader of Mecca, was entering a new phase of his life. After long conversations, the following words would finally be heard coming from his lips: "I bear witness that there is no deity but Allah, and I also bear witness that Muhammad is His Messenger!"

Meanwhile, Hakim ibn Hizam who had been on the road with him had become a Muslim as well, and with him they were asking the Messenger of Allah to give surety to the people. At this moment, the wisdom of Abbas would come into play and he would speak about the importance that a leader such as Abu Sufyan would receive. Upon that the Messenger of Allah, peace and blessings be upon him, said: "Those who enter Abu Sufyan's house are safe."

Upon request this concession would be widened and it was declared that those in the Ka'ba and those who had locked themselves in the house of Hakim ibn Hizam would be under protection.

Just then the Satan had come and was trying to dissuade Abu Sufyan from faith; for one moment he had the idea of going round the surrounding tribes and gathering an army to attack the Messenger of Allah. But at that very moment a hand was placed on his shoulder: "Then Allah will humiliate you and we will triumph once again," said the voice, as if hearing his inner most thoughts.

Abu Sufyan was startled; he turned around to see that the hand was none other than the blessed Messenger's! He was embarrassed: "I bear witness that you are the Messenger of Allah," he said at first.

It was something that only he knew about; he had not spoken it out loud! Only the Knower of the Unseen, Allah the Almighty could know of it and could tell it to His Messenger, and so he added: "I ask of Allah the acceptance of my repentance, I seek forgiveness from Him for the fault I have fallen into! I had certain doubts about you being the Messenger of Allah till now, I was debating it with myself—but now all those doubts are gone! I swear by Allah that what makes me think this way is nothing but whispers of the devil and my carnal soul!"

They had experienced such surprises one after another that they had so many things to tell the Meccans. They asked for permission to return to Mecca but Abbas had another offer for the Messenger of Allah: "O Messenger of Allah," he was saying. "I am not sure that Abu Sufyan will not turn back on his heels. It may be better if you keep him by your side for a while longer so that they may see you and the soldiers and get a better grip of the situation."

Abu Bakr was of the same opinion and so he asked his Companions to go after Abu Sufyan who was making his way towards Mecca. It was again Abbas who caught up with him; when he saw him he asked: "Is this a betrayal, O you sons of Hashim?" so voiced Abu Sufyan his worry.

Abbas was not late in answering him: "Know that those who stand in Prayer behind the Prophet never betray people. We will not persecute you. But we want you to wait till the morning and see for yourself the soldiers of Allah and what Allah is preparing for the polytheists!"

On the morning of that day the voice of the caller of the Messenger of Allah was echoing throughout Marr az-Zahran: "Each tribe should start with their preparations for the road—let them put their weapons on their mounts and let them come together under their standard with their leader."

With this command the Muslim army started to move and the tribes, with their leaders, gathered under their standards. Now was the time for the message that would have the greatest impact on the Quraysh in the person of Abu Sufyan: the people would pass in front of Abu Sufyan one by one! The sight was magnificent.

The first was Khalid ibn al-Walid with his force of one thousand; they were carrying two flags! When he came in front of Abu Sufyan, Khalid started to voice the *takbir* which was repeated by his one-thousand strong army, and they would do this three times. They were like the stars in the dark of the night—twelve thousand fires in Marr az-Zahran, and the place was echoing to the sound of *takbir*s. This was a scene that sent shivers down spines. As they passed in front of him, Abu Sufyan asked Abbas who they were and he told him. The answers he got surprised Abu Sufyan even more. He found it hard to understand the speed at which people had changed and was speechless at the maturity that these people had attained.

Now the whole army of conquest was passing in front of him one by one. Zubayr passed with his force of five hundred, Abu Dharr passed with three hundred, Aslam with four hundred, the Banu Ka'b with five hundred, Muzayna with one thousand, Juhayna with eight hundred, Kinana with two hundred and finally Ashja with three hundred. Each time Abu Sufyan asked when it was that the unit that the Messenger of Allah was in would pass by. Finally the thousand strong unit in which the Messenger of Allah was came, with Sa'd ibn Ubada carrying the standard—one could hear the deep voice of Umar who was keeping them in order echo through. The flags of the various branches of the Ansar and the Muhajirun were of various colors; they were completely equipped with weapons. When Abu Sufyan saw such a spectacular sight, he sighed: "Who can stand against this army?"

Shock in Mecca

Now everything was ready for the great conquest; they were going to set off from Marr az-Zahran and then enter Mecca. Meanwhile Abbas, the uncle of the blessed Messenger, approached the Messenger of Allah and said he wanted to go to Mecca before them and give them the news of assurance and invite them to Islam. At first our beloved Prophet regarded this offer favorably and lent him his mule, but then said: "I fear that the Quraysh will mistreat him like the tribe of Thaqif mistreated Urwa ibn Masud," and then changed his mind and asked his uncle to be called back.

It was Abu Sufyan who was unaware of the developments and brought the first news to the Meccans, but he was not entering Mecca the way he had left it. The minute he entered Mecca he started to shout out: "O people of Quraysh! Muhammad is here! He has come with a great army that you cannot defend against!"

What they had feared had thus come to pass. All hope had gone and Quraysh was finished! What could they do against an army that had already come so close to them? As they were wallowing in their despair, it was once again Abu Sufyan who spoke: "Best for you would be to become Muslims and thus protect yourselves. Whoever closes his door and seeks refuge in his own home, he too will be protected! The people who take refuge in the Ka'ba are also secure, and they will not be harmed."

Although the majority preferred to wait and act according to how the events would unfold that day, people like Ikrima ibn Abu Jahl, Suhayl ibn Amr and Safwan ibn Umayya started preparations for resistance. They were saying: "We cannot let Muhammad enter Mecca just like that!" and were encouraging people to resist. People who were convinced of this propaganda from the tribes of the Huzayl and the Aslam, and the Banu Bakr and the Quraysh had also joined them in the preparations.

They felt encouraged by the fact that the surrounding tribes had answered their call favorably. In a resistance such as this which held great risks, they were hoping to put the desert tribes at the frontline and then decide, according to how this would turn out in front of the Muslim army.

On the other hand, the Companions had left Marr az-Zahran and reached a place called Dhi Tuwa. They were going to gather there and take the first steps of the conquest here together. It was a Friday, the thirteenth day of Ramadan. Before the sunrise the Messenger of Allah, peace and blessings be upon him, mounted Qaswa, and with Usama behind him on the camel, he joined the unit. Everybody wanted to gather around him and wanted to be with him as he entered the city which he had been exiled from many years ago.

There was already an atmosphere of triumph among the Companions. The conquest of Mecca—as it pertained to worldly causes—was about to take place and Allah the Almighty was about to add another victory to his name! The blessed Messenger, on the other hand, was bent in two on top

The Luminous Life of Our Prophet

of his camel in modesty such that his blessed beard was about to touch Qaswa's saddle.

"Dear Lord!" he was saying, "What is important is the abode of afterlife!"

With this perhaps he meant, "Whatever success may be gained in this world, the real success is in the steps one takes as investment in the afterlife."

He had tied a long turban on his head, and the end of the cloth was hanging down from his shoulder.

He absolutely did not want any blood to be shed and was warning his Companions against it. They were given permission to fight only those who resisted them. And so, our beloved Prophet's entry to Mecca would be unexpected as well; he had divided his Companions into different groups and ordered them to enter Mecca from different entry points. He himself was entering from the upper part of Mecca; the women were throwing the shawls they had in their hands towards the necks of the horses, thereby showing their joy. When he saw this he turned to Abu Bakr and asked: "What had Hassan said?"

The man of perception had already understood, and started to read a poem that described the scene they were experiencing. This was a poem that Hassan ibn Thabit had composed and read even before the conquest of Mecca—it was describing the way that the women of Qada would hit the necks of the horses with their scarves as they entered Mecca.

The blessed Messenger said to the group he was with: "Enter Mecca from the place that Hassan had pointed to."

Meanwhile, he had called Zubayr next to him and asked him to erect the standard at Hajun and wait for him there. At a time when they were taking the great step of conquering

Mecca, our noble Prophet wanted to visit the grave and pray for our mother Khadija with whom he had shared his life for twenty five years.

Then the conquest started from all four corners; the Messenger of Allah, peace and blessings be upon him, who had left Mecca with eight people was returning to Mecca with twelve thousand!

When he saw the houses of Mecca as he passed Azahir, he stopped and thanked Allah in full gratitude. While he was making his way on the Qaswa, he was reading the *surah*s of al-Fath and an-Nasr, saying: "These are the things that Allah had promised me."

Now the conquest was complete; there was no other resistance other than in the direction that Khalid had entered. As a result of the strategy that had been followed, Mecca had been conquered easily. Just as he had declared in his *aman*, or assurance he had given to Meccans, most of the people decided to stay in their homes, while others sought refuge in the house of Abu Sufyan and Hakim ibn Hizam and also the Ka'ba. They were waiting anxiously to see how our noble Prophet was going to treat the Meccans? There were those who had led the enmity towards our noble Prophet, they had no doubt that they would be executed. These people were trying to find places to run to or hide.

Things had calmed down and the Meccans were completely silent. The Messenger of Allah took ablutions in his tent and as an expression of gratitude for the result that Allah had bestowed on them, he prayed eight cycles and then he asked them to bring his camel. Qaswa was brought to the door of his tent but our noble Prophet would return to his tent in order to put on his helmet and armor. Now he had also donned his weapon and was walking towards the Ka'ba already!

The Companions, meanwhile, were walking in between Handama and Hajun, trying to provide a safe passageway for the Messenger of Allah. The Ka'ba was getting ready for a celebration!

On the way, the children had lined up on both sides of the street and were welcoming our noble Prophet. Especially the female children had untied the scarves on their heads and were waving them at the horses that were passing by them.

Now, the Messenger of Allah's destination was the Ka'ba. He was heading towards the place that the followers of Allah believed to be his twin! Then, the *minbar* in Medina met the *mihrab* in Mecca and our noble Prophet came to the Ka'ba. As soon as the blessed Messenger saw the Ka'ba, he first saluted it with his body from afar and started to recite the *takbir*. Everyone who heard the *takbir* of the blessed Messenger was repeating the *takbir* as loud as they could, such that Mecca was shaking! The polytheists ran to the mountains and they were startled by these sounds of the *takbir* and were deeply intimidated by this scene that they saw. Each passing moment increased their curiosity and they wanted to follow the events more closely! Then the blessed Messenger lifted his finger to his lips and said: "Now be quiet!" for they were going to start the *tawaf*, the circumambulation of the Ka'ba. Muhammad ibn Maslama was holding the reins of Qaswa, and the Messenger of Allah started his circumambulation mounted on his camel! First our noble Prophet came close to the Black Stone. After saluting it with his hand, he started his *tawaf*.

That day there were three hundred idols in and around the Ka'ba, all lead-plaited. The polytheists would come and sacrifice their animals near them, and when they were in need they would come to these idols, kneel in front of them and tell them their requests. Now that the Ka'ba had become one with Islam, it had to be cleansed from all idols, starting with the biggest, Hubal, Isaf and Naila. Our noble Prophet pointed to each one of them with the bow in his hand, and the idol he pointed to fell to the ground. When doing that he read the verse with the meaning: *"The truth has come, and falsehood has vanished. Surely falsehood is ever bound to vanish by its very nature"* (al-Isra 17:81).

He was saluting the Black Stone in every turn and now he had completed his rotation of the Ka'ba seven times. He was going to dismount from his camel; he could not find a place that he could use as a stool to step down on, and so his Companions helped him come down. Descending from his mount he directed himself to the Station of Ibrahim, he still had his helmet and armor on, he shook his blessed head; the turban was hanging down from his shoulders. He performed two cycles of Prayer and then turned towards where the Zamzam was: "Were I to be sure that the sons of Abdul Muttalib would not overpower me, I would get a bucket of water from there."

Upon that Abbas pulled out a bucket of Zamzam water and offered it to the blessed Messenger. He drank from it and took ablution with it. The Companions, in the meanwhile, crowded around the blessed Messenger to be able to get a bit of his ablution water, to rub it on their faces and eyes. Then, the Messenger of Allah ordered that they should destroy Hubal. Now Hubal, in front of which the Meccan prostrated themselves as "god" was in pieces, in ruin.

Meanwhile, our noble Prophet called Bilal to his side. He told him to go to Uthman ibn Talha. Take the keys of the Ka'ba from him and bring them to him. After much effort Uthman was able to get the keys from his mother and he started to run towards the Ka'ba. When he came close to the blessed Messenger he slipped, and the keys he had got from his mother against her wishes was now flung on the ground. But there was some good in this as well—the family of the Banu Talha who kept the keys of the Ka'ba with them at all times and believed that no one else could open it except for them had attributed some kind of sacredness to themselves. Now, with one action of our noble Prophet, this false belief was going to be shattered! The blessed Messenger went to where the keys had fallen and picked them up with the skirt of his dress. Then he went and opened the door of the Ka'ba himself—the Ka'ba was opening up to its rightful owner for the first time.

The Ka'ba was full of pictures and the Messenger of Allah appointed Umar to get rid of all of them—he was not going to enter it before it had been cleared of the remnants of polytheism. Now there was sweet excitement among the Companions: some were carrying Zamzam, some were cleaning the Ka'ba with whatever cloth they could find.

Addressing the General Public

Meanwhile, people had formed a circle around the Ka'ba and were following the developments with interest. They were curious about the judgment our noble Prophet would pass about them. Now the time had come to address these people and the blessed Messenger climbed the steps of the door of the Ka'ba to address them. He began his address by thanking Allah: "I thank Allah who has kept His promise," he said, "He is Allah and He is One, and He has no peer or partner; He defeated the armies of the Ahzab on his own, and He has kept His promise of help to His subject."

Then he called out, "O Quraysh! What kind of judgment do you expect me to pass onto you today?"

There was a great silence in the Ka'ba. They knew that they had done all they could against him until that day. They thought they were at the end of the road! For they had stood in his way many times and they had tried all kinds of torture, they had set all kinds of unimaginable traps against him and his Companions! They were guilty and had it been up to them to give the verdict, they knew very well what the punishment would have been. They did not speak a word—they put their heads down and waited for the verdict.

An embracing smile appeared on his lips at once and with a voice that went deep down into their hearts he addressed to the faces that had turned pale in fear: "I will say to you today, like my brother Joseph said, *'No reproach this day shall be on you. May God forgive you; indeed, He is the Most Merciful of the merciful,'* (Yusuf 12:92) go all of you, you are all free!"

The Meccans who had been expecting an order of death were shocked to see this freedom that had been granted to them despite all odds. It was difficult to believe, the Messenger of Allah did not hold their negative behavior against them and did not experience rancor! Such nobility could exist only in a Prophet; they were astonished by the reception they were having at the hands of the blessed Messenger. To forgive at a moment when one is most powerful, could happen only in a system that had a Divine source, and they started to feel sharp pangs of regret. Maybe this was the true moment of conquest; hearts had been softened to a great degree in the affectionate arms of the Prophet and now they were entering Islam in masses.

He had left Mecca with a hundred and eighty families, and now thousands of people were embracing Islam in the same town; the Person of Light was full of peace, and he was thanking his Lord! That day he spoke to them at length about the faith that they had entered—he was preparing the new believers for the future. Some of them asked him questions and he was answering these queries.

Now the Ka'ba was the scene of the joy of the Meccans who came to pledge their allegiance to our noble Prophet. They said they were submitting in faith to Allah, they were speaking the *kalima tawhid (There is no deity but Allah)*, and swearing their loyalty to the Messenger of Allah against whom they had been drawing their swords not long ago. Just like the rivulets of rain that come from the mountains of Paran and meet in the Ka'ba, they were coming and meeting where the blessed Messenger was. They were racing to come and hold his blessed hands and this race would continue for many days.

The Battle of Hunayn

Nineteen days had passed since the conquest. In that period the blessed Messenger had prayed his Prayers short because he was not intending to stay in Mecca; he was going to establish authority there and then leave. But it did not happen that way; because the news that came from the direction of Hawazin was not good at all.

He sent one of his Companions, Abdullah ibn Abu Hadrad to Hawazin, instructing him: "Go and bring us their news!"

Abdullah ibn Abu Hadrad went close to where they were living. He was to stay there for a while and observe the situation and then come back.

He had set off on the road as soon as he received the instructions. When he came to Hawazin, he saw that they were in intense war preparations. In order to be able to gather more information he stayed with them for two days. The tribes of Hawazin and Thaqif thought that following the conquest of Mecca, the Messenger of Allah would now attack them.

They said: "Now it's our turn! There is no obstacle in front of him. There is no reason why he should not attack us now. It will be better if we get together and attack him first! We swear that Muhammad has always fought with people who do not know how to fight wars. Come, let us go around people and prepare the army, let us attack him before he comes to us."

They were ready for war. They had been waiting for this moment for a year and they had been trying to get help from other tribes. The conquest of Mecca showed that now they had to be quicker in their war preparations. In a very short while, the Hawazin had convinced the tribes of Thaqif, Nasr and Jusham. They had got all their support.

Abdullah who had fulfilled his mission of observation spoke of what he saw and heard to our noble Prophet. Unfortunately the news they had been receiving was true. An army was coming at them and the Messenger of Allah, who received this news regarding the Hawazin, said: "Tomorrow our camp will be at the home of the Banu Kinana where they had plotted against us," thus calling his Companions to arm and prepare.

For the Companions who had thought that now they could take a break and relax, a new and difficult war was approaching. However they had to respond before these tribes attacked Mecca, and this war had to take place outside Mecca!

The calendar was showing the sixth day of the month of Shawwal, it was a Saturday. An army of fourteen thousand men had been prepared in the homelands of the Banu Kinana, and they were waiting for the orders to come from our noble Prophet. The Messenger of Allah, peace and blessings be upon him, gave his order, now the army was progressing in the direction of Hawazin! On this journey our mothers Umm Salama and Maymuna were accompanying the blessed Messenger.

The blessed Messenger had left a man of twenty years of age, Attab ibn Asid, as deputy in Mecca. He had also appointed Muadh ibn Jabal to preach people Islam.

The evening of the tenth day of the month of Shaww-al, they reached Hunayn, and it was Tuesday. With the early light of the morning, the blessed Messenger, peace and blessings be upon him, had put his Companions in their positions and had given the instructions and flags to their bearers. He had two armors and one helmet, and a shield. He was addressing his Companions encouraging them for the battle. He said that if they forbore and stuck to it until morning, Allah would give them victory.

Now the army was ready to move and they started to flow towards the valley of Hunayn. Our Messenger, peace and blessings be upon him, rode among his Companions, and visited the ranks one by one.

Eventually they would face a trap they had not been expecting in their descent to the valley of Hunayn. At a moment when they thought they would come face to face with an army and start fighting as had been the case in previous wars, enemy soldiers had attacked them like locusts from the two sides of the valley, and they had surrounded the soldiers of Islam from all sides! There was no challenging or daring as was the custom. On that particular day, Hawazin had left the conventions of war aside, and rather they had decided to set up a trap and reach their goal easily. The army of Islam had not yet drawn their swords. Those in the front were young men from Mecca who believed that victory was inevitable. Many of them didn't even have weapons in their hands, and even if they should have something, it was not enough to fight with. Everyone who looked around realized that they were surrounded by enemy soldiers all around.

There was a frightening scene in Hunayn. The horsemen that had gone in front had been shaken and they had to turn back. They were followed by the Meccans who had joined the army with expectations of spoil! This scene had demoralized the others as well and there was expectation of dissolution in the ranks of the Muslims. This was no doubt the result of trusting in numbers!

Meanwhile, a voice rose from the right side: "O people! Come towards me! I am the servant and Messenger of Allah, and there is no lie to this! I am Muhammad, the son of Abdul Muttalib."

That day, the Companions advanced on the enemy once again, and they would not see anyone who attacked the enemy quite as courageously as the Messenger of Allah! Now that they had come to the line prescribed by our noble Prophet, they were experiencing a great peace. Just like at other critical moments before, a peace descended on them once again and they forgot all the difficulties of the battlefield!

Meanwhile, a great thunder had appeared in the sky and the fear caused by this thunder hit the enemy at the very core. There was some kind of flow from the heavens to the earth; Allah the Almighty had sent armies of five thousand angels to increase the moral of the believers. They were coming in legions, they had the ends of their turbans hanging from their shoulders and with this appearance they were causing much fear in the hearts of the enemies. There were those among the Hawazin who fled that day, fled with such haste that they had sought refuge in the castles of Ta'if.

The army of Hawazin had finished. Their leader Malik ibn Awe had to flee with some of his men to Ta'if to seek refuge, and those who had been left behind had become war prisoners. Now the valley of Hunayn was filled with red camels, herds of sheep and other animals. There were also precious things as well! Many Meccans who had doubts about the Muslims' success had now observed the help that Allah had given to the Messenger of Allah. So they came to the blessed Messenger and became Muslims as well! The horsemen who had acted in the Name of Allah had become victorious over those who had spent their life bowing in front of Lat and Uzza. They had defeated them in a way that the polytheists could not have imagined.

It seemed like the wrestler who had lost the match was looking for a new challenge. Those who had fled Hunayn had sought refuge in Ta'if, closing the castles from behind, trying to re-gather their forces in order to attack our noble Prophet once again. They knew that their attitude would not go undetected and so fearing that they would be sieged, they had stocked the castle with a year's worth of supplies. They had got into the castle all types of weapons that they could find. They had also asked for the help of other tribes to help them in this war and they had been successful to get help to some extent. The army laid siege to the city.

The time that passed between his departure from Medina in order to conquer Mecca and his return was around three months. In that time Mecca had been conquered, Hawazin had been fought and Hunayn victory gained, Ta'if had been laid siege to and then left alone until the day they would open their doors and come out of their own volition.

Most importantly though, thousands of people who the Muslims feared could attack the blessed Messenger and in-

vade Medina had become Muslims, chiefly the Meccans.
Those who had involved in the campaign with the Messenger
of Allah had returned with large spoils.

Our noble Prophet, who entered Medina after a long absence, made straight for the Masjid as usual and firstly thanked
his Lord as a servant.

The Platform of Tolerance
of an Enlightened World

Medina, the hub of activities, had become the center of peace, tranquility, security and trust. The age of chaos had come to an end, and a peaceful smile had started to appear on the face of a new civilization.

Certainly, this was not meant to be a temporary peace. The blessed Messenger assigned his Companions to various duties, such as teaching people the subtleties of religion and carrying his letters of invitation to Islam, thus further spreading the word. Some of the apostles were in charge of establishing peace and security, forming alliances with forces that accepted the political authority of Medina without becoming Muslim, and disbanding those who disturbed the general peace by causing harm to the people. While others were assigned to collect *jizya* and *zakah*, the former was collected from those who did not accept Islam as their religion but were under the protection of the Muslim community and the latter from those who accepted Islam. The quantity of the assigned depended on the nature of the duty. Some were sent alone, while others were formed into groups of hundreds. With these expansions and developments, no doubt was left on the people's minds that Hijaz was under the single authority of Islam.

For this very reason, starting with his return to Medina, the blessed Messenger, peace and blessings be upon him, at varying times sent envoys to different regions. He was thus going to confirm the authority of Islam at a vast geography.

As another aspect of this matter, when a merciless war launched against the blessed Messenger and Islam by the Quraysh ended with defeat, the people who initially thought "Let us leave him alone with his tribe, so if he is defeated by them, the problem would be solved, but if he defeats them, we would rethink our position" now had to make a decision. After some hard thinking, they chose to submit themselves to the Messenger of Allah.

Henceforward, Medina witnessed not only the outward-heading delegations, but also those groups of people who flocked into the city. Until recently suffering under wars, only within a short period of nine years, Medina left the days of chaos behind, and it became a center from where security and trust emanated to the world. People, like moths who have been craving for light, rushed and surged in crowds to Medina from all over the world, to be in the Prophet's presence, and to reach the honor of being one of his Companions. There, people took shelter in the Messenger's trusted city.

It was the season of observing the beauties of Islam in their simplicity and without hindrance. They were going to be absolved from their past and future. Some were filled with the joy of witnessing the beauties that they had not noticed until then, while others were eager to learn Islam in its totality that previously they came to know partially. Certainly, just as there were people who wanted to make a decision by learning more about Islam, there were those opportunists who wanted to shift their fortune's downturn by receiving concessions from the blessed Messenger. Nevertheless, all these people would melt down and become purified in the presence of the blessed Messenger, and will not return without submitting to this light that they witnessed close-by.

Of course, all these back and forth activities contained their own story. When they encountered such phenomena that they had not seen before, they inquired about their nature from the blessed Messenger and took action according to his response. Thus, they acquired a lot of the religious knowledge.

The Battle of Tabuk

While these developments were taking place in communicating the message, some news arrived from the region of Damascus. The Christian Arabs of the region had written a letter to Heraclius to persuade him to take action against the blessed Messenger: "The person who claims to be a Prophet died, and his supporters are also dying from hunger. Their possessions are vanished, they have lost everything. If you have a wish to convert them to your religion, it is just the right time." Meanwhile, the tribes of Lahm, Juzzam, Amila and Ghassanids revolted and announced that they would support the Byzantine forces if they were to attack the Muslims.

While on one side, there was the Ghassanid leader Shurahbil ibn Amr, who killed the envoy of the Messenger of Allah, fought his forces at Muta and planning to attack Medina with a full-fledged plan, there were the Jews of Medina on the other side, trying to persuade our noble Prophet to go to Damascus, by saying: "O Abu'l Qasim! If you really are a Prophet, you should go to Damascus, since that is the land of the Prophets."

If the timing of these is taken into consideration, all these have a specific meaning. Those who could not find the power to withstand this emergent power rallied to mobilize the strongest power of the era, the Byzantines, hoping that they would reach their goal from afar. They wanted to play their last card against the power that they could not over-

The Luminous Life of Our Prophet

come themselves. About the same time, the merchants who came to Medina from the Damascene lands brought the news that a Byzantine contingent was advancing, and that they had reached Balka.

This was discomforting news. It meant another interval for those who came running to the enlightened world of Islam. But it had to be taken care off—it would be unthinkable to do nothing while armies of thousands were marching toward Medina. Meanwhile, the messages brought by the Truthful Gabriel were stating that the line that was drawn between the polytheists and the believers had to be made clearer. These messages were declaring that they should not refrain from entering a war against those who had no faith.

From one perspective, these were expected developments: the Byzantine Empire at the time was one of the two powers that shaped the political face on earth, and eventually if not today, they were going to face each other tomorrow. Since Islamic community was experiencing a progress generated by its own forces, the important powers in the world who witnessed this independent progress were not going to digest it easily.

Soon the Messenger of Allah, peace and blessings be upon him, ordered his Companions to prepare for war. He was sending word to the tribes in his vicinity, asking them to be on his side at this critical juncture. He also sent word to Mecca, requesting them to show the same loyalty.

The day of the battle of Tabuk was the critical point when the true believers who strived on the path of Allah with sincere hearts were differentiated from those who did their tasks half-heartedly and were not able to throw away the seeds of discord from their hearts. On the one hand, there were those who whole-heartedly accepted the Messenger of Allah's call and came running, and on the other, there were those who collapsed on the ground presenting the most unimaginable excuses in order not to comply with this Prophetic invitation to go to Tabuk.

It's time for the army of Islam to be on its way again. The Messenger of Allah was telling all the tribes to prepare their standards and flags, encouraging them to war. Abu Bakr had been given the duty of leading the Prayers of those who had started to advance before the others, and he had also given him the bigger standard.

It was Thursday in the month of Rajab that the blessed Messenger left Ali in his place in Medina and gave marching orders to his army of thirty thousand men. But the hypocrites made the fact that Ali had been left behind in Medina a point of contention: "The Prophet left him behind because he underestimates him and thinks him incapable," trying to change the agenda.

They had achieved their aim and thus disconcerted Ali. Hearing this, he had run all the way to Jurf and spoke to the Messenger of Allah about what he had heard. He said that a man like him had to be on the battlefield. At a time when the Sultan of Messengers was running on the battlefield he did not want to be sitting in Medina with women and children! The blessed Messenger, peace and blessings be upon him, turned to him and said: "They are lying; I left you behind so that you may look after those left behind, my family and your family. Would you not want to be to me what Aaron was to Moses O Ali? It is true that there will not be another Prophet after me."

The Luminous Life of Our Prophet

Most probably our noble Prophet was leaving him in Medina so that he may stay alert to the dangers as the hypocrites who were fleeing the battle by lying to him were trying to build up a base in the town. Having received the blessed Messenger's order, Ali returned to Medina.

They waited at Tabuk for days but could not see an army or any movement that could point to the existence of an army. There were two possibilities; either the Byzantine army had decided not to fight and pulled back its soldiers, or maybe, a slight possibility, they had prepared a very cunning trap for the Muslim army. But the passing time diminished the possibility of this latter. The only way to find out was to get in touch with the other side and the noble Prophet sent Dihyah al-Kalbi to Heracles as he had done so many years ago. In the letter he gave him the noble Messenger listed three options for Heracles: embracing Islam, staying in their own lands by giving *jizya* tax, or to fight.

At the time, the Byzantine king Heracles was in Hims. As soon as he received the noble Messenger's letter, he held counsel with his viziers and clergymen. He was reminding them of the information they had at hand, and saying that a new religion that was developing now was going to reign supreme in his lands one day! But the viziers and the clergymen were not of the same opinion, and seeing that they opposed his views strongly he stepped back in order to keep his position. Heracles chose not to fight the noble Messenger or to ally himself to him. He kept away from speaking his opinion in front of the army that had come all the way to Tabuk and displayed a neutral position.

Meanwhile the Messenger of Allah had sent Khalid ibn al-Walid with a force of four hundred in the direction of

Dumatu'l-Jandal. His orders were to take the king of Banu Kinda Ukaydar ibn Abd al-Malik prisoner and then return.

The blessed Messenger communicated Islam to Ukaydar and his men when they came to Tabuk with Khalid, but they did not accept it. They rather accepted to be under the rule of Islam and pay yearly tax. Our noble Prophet made an agreement with the two brothers and set them free.

Meanwhile, fearing that the forces that went and captured Ukaydar would come to him as well, the king of Ayla, Yuhanna ibn Ruba, came to the blessed Messenger with presents and made a deal with him, accepted to pay tax.

The blessed Messenger gave special importance to forming platforms for dialogue with people, and he gave a written assurance to Yuhanna. He included the people in the regions of Damascus, Yemen and Bahr in it, taking on the protection of these people's lives and property.

Even though there had been no direct contact with the Byzantines in Tabuk, the purpose had been accomplished and people had an opportunity to meet the encompassing face of Islam. The Jewish tribes of Jarba and Azruh had also come and made an agreement with the Messenger of Allah. According to this agreement they too would pay a tax of a hundred dinars to be collected in the month of Rajab and with it they would have entered the protection of Islam. The blessed Messenger was declaring that as a result of their free choice, he was taking on the protection of their lives and property. The people of Jarba and Azruh would come and bring the tax of that year before our beloved Prophet.

Meanwhile, the people of Makna also came and made a deal with the blessed Messenger. According to the agreement, they were to give one fourth of their fruit produce and one fourth of the clothes they weave as *jizya* tax, thus in return, preferring to be within the peaceful climate of Islamic rule.

Tabuk had thus given its fruits and our noble Prophet started to speak with his Companions about not pushing forward towards Damascus demanding for more. Umar, may Allah be pleased with him, said: "O Messenger of Allah! If this has been ordered to you, then continue on your way."

But he did not want to continue without consulting with his Companions, because Allah the Almighty had told him not to proceed in his business without exchanging views with his Companions. He said: "Had I been ordered to continue to march forward, I would not be consulting with you."

Upon that Umar replied: "O Messenger of Allah! The Byzantine Romans are a large community and they have no Muslims among them! We are at very close quarters with them at the moment, and that you have come all the way here has given them a great fright! Let us, if you like, return, to see what the developments will be and to wait to see what Allah tells you to do on this matter."

Since this was the general view, the blessed Messenger, peace and blessings be upon him, decided to leave Tabuk; now the destination was Medina. Now the journey had ended; they were about to enter Medina. The women and children who had not seen our noble Prophet among them for two months were very happy to see him come into town— they were on the streets. They were rejoicing in the light of the full moon that had come upon them from the heights of the Veda hills. They were singing songs and praise and showing their happiness in welcoming him.

The Important Events of the
Ninth Year

Abdullah ibn Ubayy ibn Salul who was the leader of the hypocrites died after the return from Tabuk. His son Abdullah also knew what was said about him and he came to the blessed Messenger to ask him if he could lead his father's Funeral Prayer. He was a sincere believer despite his father, and the blessed Messenger would have responded favorably to his request. Although his father had done all types of destructive things behind doors, he had been a believer in his appearance, and therefore asked for forgiveness for him.

But before long, the Truthful Gabriel came and brought the message with the meaning: *"And never do the Funeral Prayer over any of them who dies, nor stand by his grave to pray for him. They surely disbelieved in God and His Messenger, and died as transgressors,"* (at-Tawbah 9:84) which explained that the blessed Messenger had to take a more definite attitude towards the hypocrite, that he should not ask for forgiveness for them, nor attend their Funeral Prayers to be performed.

Uthman, the son-in-law of the Prophet was sad because one of the blessed Messenger's daughters, our mother Umm Kulthum died within that year as well. As is known, the blessed Messenger, peace and blessings be upon him, had married her to Uthman after the death of our mother Ruqayyah. Now our mother Umm Kulthum had died as well. The

The Luminous Life of Our Prophet

noble Messenger's sadness was doubled with her death and he turned to Uthman, who was twice his son-in-law, to say: "Had I a third daughter, I would surely wed her to you," trying thus to console Uthman, who was a pillar of modesty.

The verse that was revealed in the month of Dhu al-Qadah of the ninth year declared: "It is Allah's due of the Ka'ba that all who have the means to visit it should visit the House of Allah," and thus made the Hajj an obligation.

Having received the Divine order and already wanting to visit the Ka'ba with his whole heart the blessed Messenger would remember the wrong things that the polytheists did there and said: "They will be there and will circumambulate the Ka'ba naked; I would not want to perform Hajj as long as this situation continues."

And so he called Abu Bakr to his side, and appointed him as emir of Hajj and sent him to Mecca. He told him to teach people how to perform the Hajj and what they had to be careful about. There was going to be an Islamic Hajj in the Ka'ba for the first time!

Abu Bakr, may Allah be pleased with him, set off on the road at once with three hundred of the Companions, however, the revelations kept coming. After his departure, the first verses of the Surah at-Tawbah revealed and there were now new rules regarding the polytheist in the Haram area. The blessed Messenger called Ali at once and sent him to Abu Bakr to let him know of these rules so that they may be communicated. Ali took the instructions and went after the Hajj caravan and caught up with them at the location called Arj, or Dajnan. Abu Bakr took the verses from him and then they continued their journey to Mecca.

They performed their circumambulation, and their walks between Safa and Marwa. They had stood *waqfa* in Arafat and stayed at Muzdalifa, and now they had reached Mina. That day Ali came to where the sacrifices were being slaughtered and standing next to the Jamra, he communicated to the people all the points that the Messenger of Allah had given him.

Thus, the wishes of our beloved Prophet were becoming true and this declaration meant that the ideology of idolatry was being dismissed from the Haram altogether.

Recently the Truthful Gabriel's visits to the Messenger of Allah had become more frequent. They read the Qur'an to each other from beginning to end twice in the month of Ramadan that year, and thus the exact places of which verse would be in which section of what surah, and what the sequence of the chapters would be was set for certain.

In that period, the Truthful Gabriel came to him in the form of a man and sat with him. He was asking him what Islam, faith and beneficence were, and when Judgment Day would come. And so the Messenger of Allah, peace and blessings be upon him, explained to him what Islam, faith and beneficence were; and said that no one could know when the end of the world would come, and yet spoke of its signs! To each answer he received, this stranger Companions said: "You spoke the truth."

The Companions were intrigued by this man. When the intention was accomplished and the man left, the blessed Messenger asked: "Do you know who this man is?"

It was clear that there was something they had not quite understood, and so they let him explain. He said: "He was Gabriel; he came to teach you your religion."

The Farewell Hajj

Now the Ka'ba had been cleansed from the polytheist and the House of Allah had been introduced to the form of worship that it deserved; those who circumambulate it did not clap, nor did they walk around naked! There were no obstacles to the blessed Messenger coming and performing his Hajj duty. When the Dhu al-Qadah month of the tenth year was reached, the Messenger of Allah, peace and blessings be upon him, declared to his Companions that he was setting off to go to Mecca in order to perform the Hajj duty. People were coming to Medina in groups and were getting prepared to do their Hajj duty with the noble Messenger!

He started the journey one Saturday when there were five days left till the end of the month of Dhu al-Qadah, right after the Noon Prayer. He took the Shajara route; he was to go as far as Dhu'l-Hulayfa and spend the night there. He did, and when the morning came, he addressed his Companions and said that a messenger from his Lord came to him and told him that they were to perform Prayer in this blessed valley. He also told them that his intention for the trip was both Hajj and *umrah*.

Before he entered the ihram, the blessed Messenger took *ghusl*, or full body ablutions, and put on nice scents as he was setting off for the Hajj in a spirit of celebration. Before he did, he turned to the people and informed them about the rituals, the *takbir*s and the *talbiya*s. He had brought with him around one hundred sheep as sacrifice, and had marked them all to make them known that they were sacrificial animals.

Then his Companions joined in his talbiya and said: "*Labbayk, Allahumma labbayk*, here we are O Lord, *Labbayk la sharika laka labbayk*, here we are O Lord, and You have no partner, *innal hamda, wa'n-ni'mata laka wa'l-mulk*," thanks and richness and property are all Yours, *la sharika lak*, "You have no partner," and these sounds were echoing the heavens and the earth!

He was following the route of the Hijra going through Bayda, Malal, Sharafu's-Sayyala, Rawha, Irqu'z-Zibya, Munsaraf, Asaya, Arj, Lahy al-Jamal, As-Suqya, Abwa, Juhfa, Humm, Arzaq, Kudayd, Mushallal, Usfan, Ghamim, Marr az-Zahran, Sarif and Dhi Tuwa.

The journey took a week and when he came to Dhi Tuwa, he took a break and spent the night there. It was the fourth day of the month of Dhu al-Hijjah and the Messenger of Allah, peace and blessings be upon him, performed the Morning Prayer and then took *ghusl* ablutions and then walked to Mecca. He entered Mecca at the time when the sun was at its zenith, and his entry was once again from the upper region.

He turned towards the Ka'ba as soon as he arrived; he saluted the Rukn and then started to circumambulate. In the first three circumambulations, his steps were very quick. In the remaining four, he was slower and thus he completed his circumambulations. Then he turned to the place of Abraham, "Rukn istilam," and read the verse with the meaning:

We made the House (the Ka'ba in Mecca) a resort for people,

and a refuge of safety (a sanctuary, that is, a sign of the truth). Stand in the Prayer (O believers, as you did in earlier times) in the Station of Abraham. And We imposed a duty on Abraham and Ishmael: "Purify My House for those who go around it as a rite of worship, and those who abide in devotion, and those who bow and prostrate." (al-Baqarah 2:125)

Having the place between himself and the Ka'ba, he prayed two cycles; he recited the chapters al-Kafirun and al-Ikhlas. Then he came back to Rukn, saluted it and then walked towards Safa. When he came close to Safa, he started to quote the verse with the meaning:

As-Safa and Marwa are among the emblems God has appointed (to represent Islam and the Muslim community). Hence, whoever does the Hajj (the Major Pilgrimage) to the House (of God, the Ka'ba) or the Umrah (the Minor Pilgrimage), there is no blame on him to run between them (and let them run after they go round the Ka'ba as an obligatory rite). And whoever does a good work voluntarily (such as additional going-round the Ka'ba and running between as-Safa and Marwa, and other kinds of good works), surely God is All-Responsive to thankfulness, All-Knowing. (al-Baqarah 2:158)

And heeding the sequence in which the Qur'an speaks of them, the Messenger of Allah, peace and blessings be upon him, first went to Safa and then started to walk between Safa and Marwa. When he went on top of Safa, he turned towards the Ka'ba and called out the *takbir*, and then raised his hands and prayed.

He then turned towards Hajun; this was the place he had spent three very difficult years with his Companions. His uncle, his greatest supporter had died there, his beloved wife, his life companion of 25 years, our mother Khadija had walked towards Allah from here. Her grave was also there; the person of loyalty was clearly showing his Companions what it was to be a real loyal person.

The Messenger of Allah stayed in Mecca for four days starting from Sunday; on Thursday he would turn towards Mina with his Companions at the time of the Duha (Forenoon) Prayer. A tent was set up for him in the place called Namira and there the blessed Messenger would pray his five times Daily Prayers. When they passed Batni'l-Wadi and came to Arafat, he turned towards them and gave a sermon. There were a hundred and twenty Companions around him; all were listening to him with great attention: "O people!" He started his sermon and the continued: "Listen well to my words! For I do not think I will be able to meet with you here after this year!"

No one even thought that one day the noble Messenger would leave this world; but it was himself who reminded people of this fact! The hearts were seared, and there was a great air of sadness now. The Messenger of Allah, peace and blessings be upon him, was giving these signals at the very time when the Muslims were enjoying success. He was saying: "Your life and property are sacred as of this day and month and land of yours is sacred and protected against injury! Take heed; I have abolished whatever is to do with Jahiliyya, the ignorance before Islam! The blood feuds of Jahiliyya have also been lifted; the first I lift is that of the son of Rabia bin Al-Harith bin Abdul Muttalib, who was nursed in the area of the tribe of Banu Sad, and whom the tribe of Huzayl killed. It is the first blood feud from the time of Jahiliyya that I annul. Verily, every transaction of interest is annulled, and the first that I annul is that Abbas ibn Abdul Muttalib was to have—it has certainly been abolished.

Take heed concerning women and fear Allah; for you have taken them as trusts from Allah, and made them your lawful Companions with the word of Allah. The right you have over them is that they should not let into your house people you do not approve; if they do that you can punish them without going too far. It is your duty to provide for their sustenance and provide them with good clothes! I leave you such a great value and as long as you hold on to it you will not be misguided after me; it is the book of Allah!"

These were the fundamental issues to be taken care of in order for the social structure to continue to work in the absence of our noble Prophet. Therefore the blessed Messenger was warning them to be careful about these matters before he left them, so that they may be able to walk towards the future with firm steps and that the cause of Allah stand on its feet till the end of time. People such as Rabia ibn Umayya were repeating these words of his so that they may reach people who were further away! After saying these, he turned to his Companions and asked: "They will ask you about me tomorrow; how will you speak of me?"

There was great surprise among the Companions. They lifted their heads and answered him: "We swear that You have completed the mission of communicating the word of Allah and have been a guide to us all; you have given your advice most effectively." This voice that spilled over from Arafat was hitting the mountains of Paran and come back!

Having had people bear witness, the Messenger of Allah raised his finger to the skies and said: "My Lord! You bear witness!" And then he repeated this three times.

Then the call for Prayer was called; and so they performed noon and the Afternoon Prayers together! After the Prayer, he would come to the skirts of the Mountain of Mercy (Jabal Rahma) and stand there in *waqfa*. He had turned towards the *qiblah* and he prayed to his Lord until the Night Prayer; the person of Light was now like a pillar of light, asking for mercy from his Lord!

And then the truthful Gabriel came again and the signs of revelation were upon the blessed Messenger. It was clear that there was a message from Allah once again: "*This day I have perfected for you your Religion (with all its rules, commandments and universality), completed My favor upon you, and have been pleased to assign for you Islam as religion*" (al-Maedah 5:3).

And so this was the last fruit of a long process that had started in Mount Nur, in the cave of Hira. There were those who had upon hearing this, had gone in a corner and cried! This had not escaped from the notice of our noble Prophet. He approached Umar and asked: "Why are you crying?"

The great Umar was in no state to answer, but then he pulled himself together and said: "I cry because we were always experiencing more in our religion, now we understand that since it has been completed, there will now be a process of getting less."

This was Umar's clear-sightedness and the Messenger of Allah, peace and blessings be upon him, said to him: "You speak the truth."

Then he took Usama with him and went to Muzdalifa. He prayed the Night and Evening Prayers there together
(what is called *jam*, "jamming") with a single call for Prayer,
and two iqamahs (*the second call, given more quickly, immediately before the Prayer*).

It was the tenth day of the month of Dhu al-Hijjah. When
it was time for the Morning Prayer, the blessed Messenger
prayed his Morning Prayer in Muzdalifa. He then came to the
Mashar al-Haram and turned towards the *qiblah* and directed
himself to his Lord in Prayer and supplication, speaking *takbir*s and *tahlil*s, in deep remembrance of his Lord.

Before the sun rose, he mounted Qaswa again and came
to Mina. This time he had Fadl ibn Abbas on his back. Meanwhile he had told ibn Abbas to collect the stones that he
would use for stoning the Satan. When he came to the valley
of Muhassir, he spurred on his camel; this was the location
that the people of the elephant had been decimated!

He then reached Mina. The sun had just risen, he then
came near the Jamra of Aqaba and started to stone the Satan
mounted on his camel. Then the blessed Messenger turned
back to his Companions once again and said the following
as an appendix to his sermon: "There is no doubt that today,
time has come to the position that it was on the day Allah first
created the heavens and the earth; a year is twelve months.
Four of these are months of prohibition; three of them are
consecutive: Dhu al-Qadah, Dhu al-Hijjah and Muharram.
The other is Rajab, between Shaban and Jumada al-awwal.

The devil has lost all hope of anyone following him in
this land of yours. But that you should follow him on what
you consider to be unimportant, small things will make him

happy. Take your guidance about the Hajj obligation today from me; for I believe I will not be able to perform the Hajj again after this year!"

In each of his sentences was a kiss of farewell. He was looking at his work and experience of twenty-three years with his glistening eyes, and he was trying to prepare his congregation for the days to come.

They now understood better why he had asked those questions; he was taking his farewell from his Companions and at the same time he was taking them on a journey of knowledge through his own method of teaching.

Then he drew their attention and asked them another question: "Did I fulfill my duty?"

He was asking his Companions whom he had educated by his side whether he had done the job given him. The desperate Companions shouted: "Yes," and upon that he turned to his Lord and said: "Dear Lord! You bear witness!"

Then he advised his Companions: "Let those who are here today take these to those who aren't here today; many people who are informed afterwards may be more perceptive than the one who has been listening!

The Army of Usama

Four days were left until the end of the month of Safar. It was a Monday and the Messenger of Allah ordered his Companions to get ready for a campaign. The voices of threat from the land of the Byzantine Romans were getting louder and they were subjecting the believers who lived there under terrifying pressures and tortures. The last drop was what had happened to Farwa ibn Amr, the governor of Mean, a province close to the land of the Byzantine Romans. The Byzantines who were hostile to any trace of Islam in their lands had found it in themselves to kill the governor of the blessed Messenger as well.

The place where the headquarters was going to be set up was Juruf. The excitement of jihad had already spread among the honorable Companions. They were impatient to go and pursue another goal! The next day, our noble Prophet pulled his freed slave Zayd ibn Haritha's eighteen year old son Usama and said to him: "I appoint you as commander of this army that has been prepared; be quick and advance on those who killed your father." He then told him which direction he should go and how he should act when he was there and what he should be careful about.

As he was moving with his army, he said that they should move quicker than the news, and drew attention to the fact that they could win the battle only if they could have control over enemy intelligence!

The Messenger of Allah, peace and blessings be upon him, gave the young Usama the standard of the army with his own hands. Having taken the standard, Usama gave it to the standard bearer of the Hijra, Burayda ibn Husayb, and then went to Juruf to prepare the army of our noble Prophet. And so whoever was prepared ran to Juruf.

The Illness of the
Blessed Messenger

It was on a Wednesday the noble Prophet has fallen ill the day after he had given the standard to Usama. He had high fever and a very heavy headache. But this illness of his did not prevent the formation of the army that he had taken great pains to organize. He wanted the army to reach its goal and was encouraging his Companions to do all they could to make it successful.

In this army that would be commanded by Usama, there were very important names such as Abu Bakr, Umar, Uthman and Ali, may Allah be pleased with them. It appeared that the blessed Messenger wanted his Companions to be young; he wanted to build his mission on the youth. This also meant the dismissal of certain old perceptions; Usama was the son of a freed slave and the Arabs would never want to see a slave as their commander! And thus the blessed Messenger was breaking all the 'idols' that were connected with the old ignorance, was routing them out from the society! But this was not something that everyone would be able to understand at first and some people considering how young Usama was and the greatness of the state they were challenging in battle were voicing different views about his commandership. Especially people like Ayyash ibn Abi Rabia were saying: "This young person has been appointed as commander while the first Muhajirun are still here," expressing his surprise at such a choice.

It was a Saturday, and the Messenger of Allah, who had been informed of the situation, wrapped his turban around his head and mounted the *minbar*. Turning to his Companions he said: "O people! I swear that just as you are objecting to Usama being the commander, you objected to the issue with his father, and you also gossiped about his commandership. By Allah, he is the one who is best suited to lead. It is also a fact that his father was the dearest of people to me, and after him, the dearest is Usama."

Meanwhile, the leading men from among the Companions who were going to war with Usama came and took their leave from our noble Prophet. This was the last farewell he would have with his Companions. The illness of the Messenger of Allah became worse and yet he advised them: "Do not leave the army of Usama behind at any cost, and see him off!"

And so the Companions had run to Juruf and they spent Sunday there. Usama came to our noble Prophet again on Sunday and he could not hold his tears, because the Messenger of Allah had a very high fever, and they were putting medication in his mouth in order to lessen his pains. He had come to take his leave but his heart was not content to leave him in that state and go! He bent down and kissed our noble Prophet. The blessed Messenger could not speak. He lifted his hands towards the sky for a while and then put them on Usama; it was clear that he was praying for the young commander!

Usama returned to Juruf that day, but he had left his heart by our noble Prophet; and so he came back again the next day. It was a Monday; it appeared as if the difficult phase for the Messenger of Allah was over and Usama returned to his army in order to fulfill the command of our beloved Prophet!

While this action continued on this side, our noble Prophet had already started to say his farewells to his Companions and he had turned towards the Exalted Friend, *Ar-Rafiq al-A'la*! He had been giving signs of this farewell for a year now; what he had said when he sent Muadh to Yemen, and the way he asked for their good commendation when during the Farewell Hajj. Differently from previous years, he had gone into twenty days of *itikaf* (retreat) that Ramadan. His custom had been ten days. With the Truthful Gabriel they had recited the Qur'an to each other not once but twice from beginning to end. He had visited Uhud, to which he had entrusted his Companions. He said farewell to those around him at the time, but also to those who were buried there. After these farewells he went up the *minbar* again and addressed his Companions in the following manner: "There is no doubt that I want to be united with you. I am your witness. I swear by Allah that now I see my abode. I can see the keys of the treasures of this world being handed to me. I swear not that you will be in *shirk* after I leave, but that you will fight each other surrounding *shirk* after I leave."

It was the last Monday of the month of Safar. He had come to the Al-Baqi cemetery again in order to perform his last duty for a Companion. He had not forgotten his Companions whom he had entrusted there; he visited them, and his manner suggested that he was speaking to them and asking good commendation from them as well.

On the way back, he suffered from a severe headache. He was also running a high fever. Such that the temperature of his blessed body could be felt from the outside of the turban they had wrapped around his blessed head. It was clear that this was not an illness that would go away easily, and during the eleven days that it lasted, he performed his Prayers with his Companions.

On Wednesday the illness got more severe still, and when his fever rose even more, he fainted. He did not want to leave his Companions even in that state, and so when he felt just a little bit better, he said: "Pour water collected from different wells over me seven times so that I may be able to go out and take covenant with the people."

What he asked for was carried out and when he came to his senses somewhat more he said: "This is enough! This is enough!" And then stood up and went to the Masjid. There he said: "O people! Come close to me," he was speaking to the Companions. It was clear that he had an important message and he wanted to draw attention to an important matter. He first spoke of the wrongs that previous *Ummah*s had fallen into and then said: "Do not turn my grave into an idol's house where people come to worship." One could see in him the excitement of being about to leave and so it appeared he was taking his leave from all, making sure that he would recognize the dues he owed to anyone present.

"Whomever I have hurt among you; here is my back, let him come and take his due by hitting on my back! Whomever I said a hurtful word and broke his heart, let him come and say to me what he feels inside, and take his due."

Yes, he was saying these but no one came to the front. But he was insistent; after they had prayed the Noon Prayer, he repeated his request.

　　　　The Luminous Life of Our Prophet

Then somebody stood up and said that he owed him three *dirhams*. He called out to his cousin and said: "Give it to him O Fadl!"

Then he said the following about the Ansar: "My parting wish and advice for you is that you should recognize the importance of the Ansar. They are the apple of my eye; they have done their duty in the best way possible and they will get their reward. Now the people are many and the Ansar are in the minority; they are like the salt in a dish! Whoever among you becomes a leader over them and is faced with good or harm from them, let him accept the good and forgive them the harm!"

He then said: "There is no doubt that Allah the Almighty had let His subject choose between getting the wealth of this world or attaining what is by His side, and the subject has chosen what is by Allah's side."

He had not yet finished his words when a cry was heard from where Abu Bakr was: "Let our mother and father perish for you O Messenger of Allah!"

They were looking at where the voice was coming from in surprise, for they did not understand what he had understood, for he had understood that the subject that had been given the choice was our noble Prophet himself and that was why he was reacting that way.

The noble Messenger who saw this sensitivity of his loyal friend who had not left him since the very first day would point to Abu Bakr and establish his place among his Companions. He held his hand and said: "For me Abu Bakr is the most trustworthy of people when it comes to material and spiritual sacrifice; were I to have any friends other than my Lord, I would certainly have Abu Bakr as my friend. From now on, one can only speak about the brotherhood of Islam, and love stemming from that brotherhood. Let all the doors that open to the Masjid be closed except for that of Abu Bakr!"

Now each day for our noble Prophet was a farewell. It was Thursday. Until that day, he had gone out to his Companions despite the strength of the pain and the level of his fever and thus led the Prayers. After the Prayer, his illness got worse again, and although it was already time for the Night Prayer he could not come to the Masjid. The last Prayer he had led was the Evening Prayer on Thursday and in that Prayer, he had read the chapter al-Mursalat.

For the Night Prayer, Bilal had called the call for Prayer; the congregation had run to the Masjid and started to wait for their leader. They were unaware of what was happening in his room of happiness; for his illness had gone quite severe and our noble Prophet had become unconscious. As soon as he woke up, he asked our mother Aisha: "Was the Prayer performed?"

"No, O Messenger of Allah! They are waiting for you," was the reply.

"Prepare water for me to take ablutions," he said. It was clear that his heart was at the Masjid. Then they did what he asked. He stood up and took ablution with difficulty. Just as he meant to go out for Prayer, he fainted again where he was. They ran to help him. He then regained consciousness and asked once again: "Have the people prayed?"

He wanted to go to Prayer but he did not have the energy to do so; he kept fainting. At last he asked Abu Bakr to lead the Prayer and he would go out to Prayer later with the help of two people.

When he came upon those who were expecting his arrival like the full moon, there was a wave of excitement that day in the Masjid. Abu Bakr, the man of perception, wanted to move back to leave the job to its rightful owner, but our noble Prophet pointed with his finger, meaning "Stay there!" He came near the imam among the rows of believers that opened up for him. He had no strength to stand and that day he was only able to finish his Prayer while sitting. The blessed Messenger, who had called the Daily Prayers "the light of my eye," was no longer able to lead the Prayer for his Companions. From then on Abu Bakr, may Allah be pleased with him, the imam that he had appointed, would lead the Prayers in his place.

Time to Part and the Last Day

S ince Thursday, the Messenger of Allah, peace and blessings be upon him, had not been able to go out for the
Prayers and had not been able to lead his Companions in
Prayer. But the hopeful wait of the Companions continued.
They were thinking he could come today just as he came that
day. It was a Monday again and the calendars showed the
twelfth day of the month of Rabi al-awwal. They had come
to the Morning Prayer of that day with the same hope; they
wanted to see him well again, leading them in Prayer at the
front. The Masjid gathered its usual crowd with the *adhan* of
Ibn Umm Maktum and with that of Bilal; it had been filled to
the brim and overflowed.

The blessed Messenger had not been able to come that
day either; the Morning Prayer of that day was being led by
the imam he appointed, Abu Bakr, may Allah be pleased with
him. At one point there was a commotion in one corner of
the Masjid; the curtain of our mother Aisha's room had been
pulled aside a little bit, and his radiant face rose into the Masjid. He had wrapped his head again and was standing like
that at the door, and that pure face, pure like the pages of the
Qur'an, was gazing at the imam at the *mihrab*. People could
see that smile on his face; he was at peace.

The Luminous Life of Our Prophet

This gaze was the last gaze that the Companions would be able to see in this world! They almost halted their Prayers due to their happiness! They had stood up for the second cycle. They had formed orderly rows, and they could sense his coming and gave him way! He came all the way behind Abu Bakr and put his hands on his shoulders. Abu Bakr wanted to step back. It was clear that he wanted the blessed Messenger to remain and continue with the Prayer.

Sitting, he started to pray behind the imam that he himself had appointed. When the imam finished and saluted both shoulders, the blessed Messenger prayed the cycle he had missed.

This was his last Prayer. Then, leaning on one of the pillars and raising his voice, he warned his Companions about the kinds of *fitna* and then turned his gaze once again to the Qur'an. He thought two religions were too much for the Arabian Peninsula, and he did not want any other understanding to have a home there. He said the following as he left: "A Prophet does not die until someone from his congregation has led him in Prayer!"

He seemed to be better. It was as if all the worries were now over. The congregation was very happy. He had returned to them once again and had stood with them in Prayer. It was as if everything was returning to normal.

At one point the young Usama, whom he had appointed as commander to the land of the Byzantine, came to him. He was about to start on the journey, he wanted to inform the blessed Messenger about the army and to take his leave. He had come a day before as well and had been given the order to move "even if this meant farewell." When Usama approached him and sat next to him, the blessed Messenger stroked his head with his blessed hands and he would pray for the young commander Usama, who was eighteen years of age, before he set off.

When the sun rose and noon time came, he called his daughter Fatima to his side and whispered something in her ear. His daughter whom he called "a part of me" let out a cry, and then sobbed: "Woe is me! My dear father!"

He turned to her once again and gave the good news: "From this day on your father will not face any difficulties again!"

But this was not enough to lessen the pain of separation; Fatima continued to cry.

The Messenger of mercy was not able to bear this scene and so he asked his daughter to come close to him again. He bent over to her daughter again and whispered something else in her ear. Fatima who was in complete mourning and crying her heart out a minute ago was now overjoyed, she was smiling. It was as if the Fatima of a little while ago had gone and another Fatima had come in her place!

He approached her again and gave her the good news that she was the mistress of all the women in the world. He then took his grandsons Hasan and Husayn in his arms, kissed them and advised them. He also addressed his wives who were present and advised them as well.

His uncle Abbas was already too anxious about this separation; he had pulled his nephew Ali to one side and told him that the Messenger of Allah was about to pass on to the realm of the eternal and he wanted him to tell them what he would want to have happen after his death. The Messenger of Allah, peace and blessings be upon him, however, were advising those near him and reminding them that they should try to work for the Hereafter in this world while they still had time; the opportunities one had must be used for the good and these good works should be dressed in clothes of eternity.

He had turned to his Companions before and advised them: "Take heed! Whoever feels the signs of death come upon him should die with the good hope and expectation that Allah will forgive them."

The Truthful Gabriel, who had come on Saturday and Sunday, was near him again but this time it was different; there were other angels by his side as well. There were seventy thousand angels, each of whom ruled over seventy thousand ones.

"O Muhammad!" He was saying once again. "Allah sends salutations and He sent me especially to exalt you. He the Almighty knows and yet He wants me to ask you, how are you feeling? How are you?"

"I am a little weak and I have pains, O Gabriel," the blessed Messenger said. He wanted him to approach him a little more.

"Your Lord says," said Gabriel, "I can cure him if he likes, or take Him to me and embrace Him with my compassion."

"This is something that belongs to my Lord; He the Almighty will do whatever he wishes for me," he responded.

Then the angel of death whom the Truthful Gabriel had introduced asked for permission: "May the peace and compassion of Allah be upon you, O Messenger of Allah," angel

Azrail said. "Allah sent me to you and told me to do whatever you tell me. O Ahmad! If you tell me to take away what has been entrusted to you now I will do it; if you ask me to leave it and go back, I will do that as well!"

There was no difference in his choice: "O angel of death," the blessed Messenger called to him. "Do whatever you need to do!" He stroked his face with his hands which he had sprinkled a little water on. While doing that he prayed: "Dear Lord! Help me against the difficulties of death."

The time had come and the signs of the voyage had appeared. Our noble Prophet was about to pass to the other side of the thin curtain between the world and the Hereafter. He had put his blessed head on the bosom of our mother Aisha and directed his shimmering coal-black eyes towards the ceiling.

At that moment Abu Bakr's son, Abdurrahman entered his presence; the *miswak* in his hand caught his attention. Aisha who had a great faculty of perception understood that he wanted the *miswak* and so asked: "Shall I take it for you?"

The Messenger of Allah, peace and blessings be upon him, was nodding his head as if to say "Yes."

Aisha took it from her brother and wanted to give it to the blessed Messenger. But the *miswak* was very hard, and so our mother Aisha asked: "Shall I wet it and make it softer for you?"

His blessed head moved again to say "Yes."

It was clear that the tongue had now gone silent and the eyes did the talking. What he meant was understood; she softened it in her mouth and gave it to the noble Messenger.

He took it and started to move it across his pearl-like teeth. Even when going to the eternal realm he was cleaning his teeth. And meanwhile he was saying: "There is no deity but Allah! There really is great unconsciousness for death."

At one point he looked at our mother Aisha who held his hand and wanted to pray so that he may be cured: "No," he said.

It appeared that it was not fitting to ask to stay here when he had already entered the pathway of going to the original home. And so he took his hand away, and then fainted again.

A little while later he came to his senses. Meanwhile he had lifted his finger upwards. His eyes turned towards the ceiling once again and it was as if his lips were moving. Our mother Aisha brought her ear to his blessed lips in order to hear what he was saying, and she heard him say: "Dear Lord! Forgive me and embrace me with Your compassion like those among the Prophets, martyrs, the loyal ones and the good that You have shown Your grace. Accept me to the *Rafiq al-A'la*, to Your Exalted Friendship and Company. Dear Lord! I want your exalted friendship."

He ended this journey that he started travelling on a Monday, again on a Monday. In the twenty three years in which revelations poured like rain he had led a full life that could answer to all kinds of questions that could possibly be faced till the end of time. He was leaving the mission of communication of the word of Allah to those who were left behind him.

There was a beautiful scent in the room. Then his hand fell on the water bowl that was sitting on the side and the *miswak* he was holding in his hand fell on the ground. The Messenger of Allah had left the path and those on it to those had hoped for and passed on to the realm of the eternal.

The standard that he had entrusted to his Companions would now flutter on the shoulders of those who represented heroism and chivalry.